The Loss and the Silence
Aspects of Modernism in the Works of
C.S. Lewis, J.R.R. Tolkien & Charles Williams

Margaret Hiley

The Loss and the Silence

Aspects of Modernism in the Works of C.S. Lewis, J.R.R. Tolkien, and Charles Williams

2011

Cormarë Series No. 22

Series Editors: Peter Buchs • Thomas Honegger • Andrew Moglestue • Johanna Schön

Editor responsible for this volume: Thomas Honegger

Library of Congress Cataloging-in-Publication Data

Hiley, Margaret:
The Loss and the Silence
Aspects of Modernism in the Works of C.S. Lewis, J.R.R. Tolkien, and Charles Williams
ISBN 978-3-905703-19-1

Subject headings:
Inklings
Literature, Comparative
Modernism
Jones, David, 1895-1974
Joyce, James Augustine Aloyisus, 1882-1941
Lewis, C.S. (Clive Staples), 1898-1963
Tolkien, J.R.R. (John Ronald Reuel), 1892-1973
Yeats, William Butler, 1865-1939
Williams, Charles (Walter Stansby), 1886-1945

Cormarë Series No. 22

First published 2011

© Walking Tree Publishers, Zurich and Jena, 2011

All rights reserved. No portion of this book may be reproduced, by any process or technique, without the express written consent of the publisher

Cover illustration (The Record Book of Mazarbul) and drawings by Catherine Anne Hiley
Copyright Catherine Anne Hiley

Set in Adobe Garamond Pro and Shannon by Walking Tree Publishers
Printed by Lightning Source in the United Kingdom and United States

Board of Advisors

Academic Advisors

Douglas A. Anderson (independent scholar)

Dieter Bachmann (Universität Zürich)

Patrick Curry (independent scholar)

Michael D.C. Drout (Wheaton College)

Vincent Ferré (Université de Paris 13)

Thomas Fornet-Ponse (Rheinische Friedrich-Wilhelms-Universität Bonn)

Verlyn Flieger (University of Maryland)

Christopher Garbowski (University of Lublin, Poland)

Mark T. Hooker (Indiana University)

Andrew James Johnston (Freie Universität Berlin)

Rainer Nagel (Johannes-Gutenberg-Universität Mainz)

Helmut W. Pesch (independent scholar)

Tom Shippey (University of Winchester)

Allan Turner (Friedrich-Schiller-Universität Jena)

Frank Weinreich (independent scholar)

General Readers

Johan Boots

Jean Chausse

Johan Vanhecke (Letterenhuis, Antwerp)

Patrick Van den hole

Friedhelm Schneidewind

To my parents

Ann and David Hiley

without whose support and
encouragement this book would never
have been written

Contents

Series editors preface
Acknowledgments
Note on translation
List of abbreviations

Introduction   1

Chapter One: Inklings and Modernists – Shared Contexts
    The Modernist Movement   7
    Inklings and Modernists: The Biographical Connections 11
    Shared Literary Concerns   20

Chapter Two: War
    Modern War, Modern Literature   33
    Fantasy and War   39
    The Inklings at War   45
    Charles Williams, David Jones and the Matter of Britain 51
    Celtic Literature of Defeat   58
    Waste Lands   67
    Bodies and Corpses   76
    Heroes   83
    War, Language and Liturgy   90

Chapter Three: History
    Modernist Histories: Yeats's Historical Models   97
    Fantastic Cycles: Tolkien's History of Middle-earth   103
    Myth and History   107
    Nationalist Histories   117
    Escapes from History and Time   133
    "Lateness"   142

Chapter Four: Language
    Fantasy, Modernism and Language   153
    Worlds of Words: Joyce and Lewis   163
    Mythic Language   178
    Language, Creation and Control   189
    Language and the Fall   198
    Language, Identity and Exile   208

Conclusion: Modernist Fantasy, Fantastic Modernism   221

List of Works Cited   229

Index   247

Series Editor's Preface

It was – once again – Tom Shippey who gave the first impulse towards a new productive approach in Tolkien studies. In his *Author of the Century* (2000) he suggested to consider Tolkien as a 'man of his time' (and thus to compare him to other authors of the first half of the 20th century) rather than as a medieval anachronism. This attempt to contextualise Tolkien in his own era received even greater importance with the publication of John Garth's *Tolkien and the Great War* (2003). Shippey's own selection of authors and works that he linked with or rather contrasted to Tolkien's texts shows a bias towards 'canonical literature', i.e. mostly works of modernists such as James Joyce and T.S. Eliot. What covered only a few pages in Shippey's book later became the focus of the two volumes *Tolkien and Modernity* (2006, edited by Frank Weinreich and myself), which united papers by more than a score of scholars from different fields of study, and to which Margaret Hiley contributed a paper on 'late style'.

Margaret Hiley's study, which grew out of her PhD thesis, broadens the approach outlined above by drawing in-depth comparisons not only between Tolkien and contemporary modernists, but also between his fellow Inklings Charles Williams and C.S. Lewis and writers such as T.S. Eliot, W.B. Yeats, James Joyce, and David Jones among others. As the reader will discover, it is not only the 'fantasists' whose works contain key-modernist elements; many of the writings of the modernists in turn include characteristics that can be called 'fantastic'.

Seeing this study from manuscript into print has been a rewarding experience – and has been made possible by Margaret's and Frank's untiring effort of striving for the best text possible, by the support of my co-series-editors, by the members of the Board of Advisors who evaluated the initial project submission, and the students who served part of their internship as proofreaders and layouters for WTP. I would like to thank all of them and mention only one of the latter by name, Christoph Keller, who proofread the entire manuscript with great care.

I wish, in the name of WTP, an enjoyable and stimulating reading!

Thomas Honegger
Jena, October 2011

Acknowledgements

The first seeds of the present study were sown many years ago when I was an M.A. student at the University of Regensburg. I was extremely lucky to be taught by Rainer Emig, who turned out to be not just a formidable modernism scholar, but also to have a keen interest in Tolkien and a willingness to indulge me in my somewhat strange desire to write about the connections between Tolkien and the modernists. His support as a supervisor, mentor and finally colleague has been invaluable, and it is fair to say that he is the real godfather of this book – thank you, Rainer!

Rob Maslen was a further supportive and helpful supervisor during my time as a PhD student at the University of Glasgow. Drafts of this book in its previous incarnation as a PhD thesis were also read and commented upon by Adam Piette, Willy Maley, John Coyle and Adam Roberts – many thanks to all of you.

Further support for this project has come from Thomas Honegger, who read a first draft and suggested it be published with Walking Tree, and last but not least Frank Weinreich, who read (yet another) draft and helped me with the editorial procedure at a point when I well-nigh despaired of ever getting this book finished!

Thanks are also due to the Bodleian Library and the Tolkien Estate for allowing me to consult and publish quotations from MS Tolkien 24.

Most of all thanks are due to my family – to Frens for coffee, jokes, and putting up with my hobbit obsession; to Cathy for the phone calls and the pictures; and to my parents Ann and David, for their love, help and unconditional support. This book could not have been written without them.

Exton, Rutland (the Shire), March 2010

Note on translation

I have made extensive use of German criticism, literature and philosophy in this study. In some cases, there is no extant translation of these works, and I have placed a translation of my own in the footnotes. For consistency's sake I have also chosen to cite other German texts in their original language, even where an English translation is already available in print. For citations from texts in other languages I have quoted only from extant English translations.

List of abbreviations

The following abbreviations and editions have been used:

OSP: C.S. LEWIS, *Out of the Silent Planet*. London: Pan, 1952.

THS: C.S. LEWIS, *That Hideous Strength*. London: Pan, 1955.

TWHF: C.S. LEWIS, *Till We Have Faces*. Glasgow: Collins, 1978.

LWW: C.S. LEWIS, *The Lion, the Witch and the Wardrobe*. London: Collins, 1998.

TMN: C.S. LEWIS, *The Magician's Nephew*. London: Collins, 1998.

VDT: C.S. LEWIS, *The Voyage of the Dawn Treader*. London: Collins, 1998.

TLB: C.S. LEWIS, *The Last Battle*. London: Collins, 1998.

FW: James Joyce, *Finnegans Wake*. London: Penguin, 1992.

LotR: J.R.R. TOLKIEN, *The Lord of the Rings*. London: HarperCollins, 1997.

TTL: Charles WILLIAMS, *Taliessin Through Logres*. Oxford: Oxford University Press, 1938.

RSS: Charles WILLIAMS, *The Region of the Summer Stars*. Oxford: Oxford University Press, 1950.

Introduction

This is a study built upon unlikely combinations. For a good half-century now (I begin my time reckoning with the publication of Tolkien's seminal *The Lord of the Rings*), fantasy has been established upon the literary scene, and has gradually (if perhaps grudgingly) won academic recognition. There is by now a mass of studies devoted to literature of the fantastic and its historical and theoretical contextualisations, most of their titles running along the lines of "fantasy and realism", "fantasy and children's literature", "fantasy and gender", "fantasy and religion", "fantasy and politics", following the changing emphases and fashions of academia. I have yet another, but perhaps less predictable pairing to add to this long list: fantasy and modernism.

Fantasy and modernism seems an unlikely combination for a number of reasons, and a number of very basic problems face the scholar who would compare the two. It is difficult to even determine a functioning terminology that will cover both: while literary modernism is generally seen as an artistic movement or, more broadly, as a literary-historical epoch, fantasy is regarded more as a genre, often without taking its historical context into consideration (although often even its status as a genre is contested). It is for this reason that, instead of attempting to make a fully comprehensive comparison, this study has chosen to focus on only three writers of fantasy that are, by and large, contemporary with modernism: the self-styled "Inklings" C.S. Lewis, J.R.R. Tolkien and Charles Williams. In the three main chapters of the present study each of the Inklings is specifically compared to a single modernist author: Williams to David Jones, Tolkien to W.B. Yeats, and Lewis to James Joyce. A comparison between the work of these three friends and that of the modernists is made meaningful through their shared historical context.

This study does not aim to give a monolithic picture of "The Inklings" and counter it with another of "The Modernists". Earlier studies of both the Inklings and modernism have tended to see both groups of writers as self-enclosed. More recently however, modernism has ceased to be read as one coherent movement centred around one specific group of writers; instead, the very different kinds of modernisms to be found throughout the literatures and art of the early twentieth century have been examined and contrasted.[1] The picture of modernism given in this study aims to take this diversity into account. For this reason, the close comparisons in each of the main chapters are preceded by more general overviews looking at a range of authors to give a more rounded picture, and canonical modernists as well as more marginal figures are taken into account. Furthermore, the modernist authors chosen for the close comparisons are purposely very different: both W.B. Yeats and James Joyce are giants of modernism, but write in vastly different ways; David Jones by contrast is less well known, but his work is no less idiosyncratic.

This same diversity can be seen among the Inklings. In spite of John Wain's claim that they were "a circle of instigators, almost of incendiaries, meeting to urge one another on in the task of redirecting the whole current of contemporary art and life" (cit. Carpenter, *Inklings* 160), the style of their works is very different and they cannot be seen as a closed-off group. This is borne out in Lewis's letter to Clyde Kilby, in which he states that the latter's proposal to write a study of the Inklings as a movement "may be chasing a fox that isn't there" (Lewis, *Letters* 287). It is more useful to see the Inklings as a group of writers and thinkers with shared concerns and thoughts on fiction, language, myth and fantasy rather than a closed circle where each artist was "influenced" by the others and by nothing else. This open view of both the Inklings' fantasy and the modernist movement is a necessary precondition for this study.

That a study such as the present one is not just meaningful but necessary is borne out by the direction studies of the Inklings have taken in the past years. One of the major criticisms always directed against these writers has been that they were uninterested in and cut off from contemporary literature. Therefore, the argument follows, their work must be unimportant, not to say irrelevant, in the broader context of twentieth-century writing. In recent years, many studies

---

1 Important studies here are Peter Nicholls's *Modernisms. A Literary Guide* (Los Angeles: University of California Press, 1995) or the *Cambridge Companion to Modernism*, edited by Michael Levenson (Cambridge: Cambridge University Press, 1999).

of Lewis, Tolkien and Williams have refuted this; yet what they have not done comprehensively (which this study aims at rectifying) is to provide a detailed picture of where these writers fit into the twentieth century, and to compare them to their contemporaries. Claims that Tolkien is "the author of the century" (as Shippey does in *Tolkien: Author of the Century*) and is just as important a novelist as Joyce (cf. 310-312), or, more strangely, that Lewis is the true heir to Jerome, Dante and Chaucer rather than "artists of the high culture such as Joyce or Woolf" (Myers, *Lewis in Context* 217) fall flat if no serious comparison between the authors named is made. Unfortunately, many scholars of fantasy and modernism alike seem to have been conditioned by their authors' (supposed) dislike of each other and shy away from this challenge. When a comparison is made, it is often superficial. For example, Shippey's *Author of the Century* draws a quick comparison between Tolkien's work and that of the modernists; however, the definitions of modernism Shippey relies on are brief ones given in *The Oxford Companion to English Literature* and the *Johns Hopkins Guide to Literary Theory and Criticism* (cf. *Author* 313). This leads to a misinterpretation of what is meant by terms such as Eliot's "mythical method", and the accusation that the modernists were interested in experiments with language and reality simply because these experiments were engaging intellectually, not because they took these experiments seriously (cf. 313-316). If the Inklings need "to be looked at and interpreted within [their] own time, as […] 'author[s] of the century', the twentieth century, responding to the issues and the anxieties of that century" (Shippey, *Author* xxvii), an evaluation of their work in the terms of the *literature* of the twentieth century, comparing them to their greatest contemporaries, is surely essential. If Lewis, Tolkien and Williams are to be taken seriously alongside Eliot, Pound, Joyce and Woolf, then they must first be situated next to them – as Brian Rosebury (*Cultural Phenomenon* 5) writes, "it is no use declaring an anathema on modern literature and then worshipping Tolkien[, Lewis and Williams] in a temple in which [they are] the solitary idol[s]."[2]

---

[2] Several recent books on Tolkien in particular contain brief evaluations of his work in relation to modernism; e.g. Brian Rosebury's *Tolkien: A Cultural Phenomenon* (Basingstoke: Palgrave, 2003), which notes that "it is easy to point to respects in which [*The Lord of the Rings*] participates in the shifts of taste and sensibility that characterise the twentieth century. Like many modernist texts, for example, it makes creative and adaptive use of myth" (149-150), and Martin Simonson's *The Lord of the Rings and Western Narrative Tradition* (Zurich: Walking Tree Publishers, 2008), which points out that Tolkien's masterpiece is "within a concrete literary context, much closer to modernism than to […] William Morris" (15).

This can seem problematic as Lewis and Tolkien, if not Williams, had a marked dislike of the work of most modernists, with attitudes ranging from incomprehension to dislike and, in some cases, utter condemnation. However, these opinions did change over the years and with personal acquaintance (something often not taken into account by scholars). The very fact that they read modernist literature at all, apart from the fact that they were acquainted with a surprising number of major modernists, should make a dismissal of possible interrelations impossible. Indeed, one might say that the idea of looking for interrelations between the modernists and Inklings rather than between the Inklings and other contemporary writers they liked more is necessary because of, not in spite of, the antagonism that some writers of the different groups felt for one another. I purposely choose the term "interrelations", rather than "influences": instead of searching for distinct points among the works of the Inklings or the modernists that can be directly attributed to contact with a member or members of the other group (although these do exist), this study aims to achieve a broader scope. For this reason, general themes common to both fantasy and modernism and typical of twentieth-century writing (war, history and language) are examined and the often surprisingly similar manner in which they are dealt with focused on. In this book's main chapters, I have attempted to include both close readings of particular work passages as well as more sweeping overviews, in order to combine the specific with the general.

I have taken for granted that the main readership of the present study will be familiar with the works of the Inklings and fantasy in general, but perhaps not as knowledgeable on modernism and its authors. Thus a brief description of literary modernism is given in Chapter One, followed by a general overview of the Inklings' and modernists' shared literary concerns. This overview is further elaborated on at the beginning of each of the main chapters, where each topic examined is briefly put in the context of modernism and where works by various authors (modernist and fantastic) both preceding, contemporary with and following the Inklings are mentioned. These broader overviews should give a picture of what concerns fantasy and modernism share in general, and not just in the specific cases of the authors focused upon more closely. It is hoped that this will provide the reader with a well-rounded picture of the shared traits of fantastic and modernist writing.

I have, as stated above, made unlikely combinations of authors for the main comparative chapters of this study and avoided obvious choices. Both Lewis's and Tolkien's works might, at a first glance, seem more suited to the topic of war than Williams's poetry; similarly, Tolkien would for many be the prime choice for the topic of language. It might have appeared more useful to compare Lewis to Yeats, whom he admired, rather than to Joyce whom he loathed, and to choose Eliot, a friend and admirer of Williams's, as the latter's modernist counterpart rather than Jones whom he never met. These choices have not been a matter of purposely avoiding the easy way out. Rather, they have been made so as to testify to the great range within the works of all these authors, a range so great that shared concerns can be detected between the most diverse of them. I have also tried to achieve a balance between works of different literary genres – I compare the poetry of Williams with the poetry of Jones, the fiction of Tolkien with the poetry and drama of Yeats, and the fiction and poetry of Lewis with the fiction of Joyce. I am the first to admit that there are many other authors I could have made reference to – Flann O'Brien and Mervyn Peake to name but two – but a line has to be drawn somewhere, and connections between Tolkien and Peake for example have already been explored elsewhere.[3]

It is not my aim to show that the Inklings were, in fact, secret modernists at heart, nor that the modernists were really writing fantasy; there is no need for claims of that magnitude. Instead, I hope to show that the works of both modernists and Inklings are intriguing and multi-faceted enough to profit from being read parallel to one another. Such a comparison may open up new dimensions of those works that have hitherto gone unnoticed, and should also help to change the conviction that the one group has nothing whatsoever to do with the other. All in all, this study is a testament to the extraordinary breadth and depth of the works of Lewis, Tolkien and Williams as well as the many modernist authors (and indeed other fantasy authors) that it focuses on. I have been constantly surprised, challenged, and thrilled by the works examined – works I thought I knew well before I started working on this book. In the course of writing it, I have been taken in directions I had never thought of by their sheer range and diversity. I hope the readers of this study will, besides being shown new ways of

---

3 Fairly recently the BBC ran a series called "The Worlds of Fantasy" that examined Tolkien and Peake as exemplifying "The Epic Imagination" (BBC Four, August 2008).

reading these works, simply be able to enjoy the diversity that both modernism and fantasy have to offer.

Chapter One

Inklings and Modernists – Shared Contexts

The Modernist Movement

Studies of literature and the arts of the early twentieth century are dominated by a comparatively small group of writers, artists and composers, exponents of the artistic movement known as modernism. In the Introduction the diversity of this movement, consisting of many "modernisms" rather than one monolithic "modernism", has been alluded to; and recent studies of modernism stress the fact that it "comprises numerous, diverse and contesting theories and practices which first flourished in a period that knew little of the term as it has now come to be understood" (Kolocotroni et al. xvii). Indeed, as Goldman states, "it is absurd and misleading to try and force an account of the rise of modernism and the avantgarde into neat, linear, chronological order. Many of the movements of this era sought so creatively to interrupt, abolish, conquer or transcend history and time" (xvi). Nonetheless a very brief outline of the main concerns and traits of the most influential modernist writing is necessary here before the relationships between this movement and the writing of the Inklings can be addressed in more detail. However, it must be borne in mind that although many modernist authors share these concerns and certain traits, the way in which these concerns and traits are expressed in their writing is often very different.

According to most literary histories,[1] the modernist movement is said to have begun around 1890 or 1900 and to have lasted until 1945. The crucial event bringing modernism to its prime was undoubtedly the First World War. The beginning of the Great War in 1914 ushers in that phase in modernism frequently called "High" or "Classical Modernism", which is said to have lasted until the end of World War II. Although these dates are the later constructions of literary historians, they do not simply represent an arbitrary dovetailing of historical events with literary developments in order to construct a neater nar-

---

1 Cf. for example Jane Goldman, *Modernism, 1910-1945. Image to Apocalypse* (Basingstoke: Palgrave, 2004), or Malcolm Bradbury and James MacFarlane's classic *Modernism: A Guide to European Literature 1890-1930* (London: Penguin, 1991).

rative of modernism. Rather, they stress the centrality of war to the modernist experience – a centrality that will be explored in detail later in this study. The First World War was generally perceived as a cultural catastrophe, proving beyond doubt what avant-garde artists had already proclaimed: the failure of the old Victorian value system and the need for a fresh start, not only in the arts, but in politics and society as well. Modernist literature, which both anticipated and responded to this catastrophe, is characterised by a sense of disillusionment and of the loss of values and meaning. This loss leads to a deep-rooted cultural pessimism: thus Ezra Pound's post-war poem *Hugh Selwyn Mauberley* dismisses Western culture as "a botched civilization […] two gross of broken statues, […] a few thousand battered books" (Pound, *Selected Poems* 101). On the other hand, this pessimism is matched by a search for new alternatives and joy in experiment. Gertrude Stein for example wrote of her famous line "a rose is a rose is a rose" (from the longer poem *Sacred Emily*) that "in that line the rose is red for the first time in English poetry for a hundred years" (cit. *The Norton Anthology of American Literature II* 1105). The rejection of tradition led not just to hopelessness, but also to a freedom that allowed for new intensity of expression.

Modernism expresses (both positively and negatively) the loss of certainties, the belief in one unifying truth and one linear history through fragmentation. That there is more than simply one way of viewing things is shown clearly in the work of painters like Picasso, who deliberately use a variety of perspectives in one picture, so the viewer can see – for example – the front and side of a figure simultaneously. In literature, this fragmented perception of the world is reflected in (and created through) literary techniques such as narrative discontinuity, ever-shifting points of view, montage and collage effects and stream of consciousness narration. These fragmented elements are then fused together to create a new whole. Frequently, this new whole is not created through traditional chronological and causal continuity; instead, this is discarded in favour of associative, illogical technique. For example, Virginia Woolf's *Mrs Dalloway* gives us the thoughts of Clarissa Dalloway as she walks through London, thinking both of her past and the party she is holding that evening, blending past and future; as she passes by certain landmarks, the narrative jumps to the thoughts of other people viewing the same landmarks, who have completely different concerns and whose lives do not, it would appear, touch that of Clarissa. Yet through her narrative Woolf creates a bond between these disparate characters, showing that they are parts that make up the whole of human consciousness.

Another important structural device used to give coherence is that of myth, recreating a complex unity in literature no longer to be found in external reality: works like Joyce's *Ulysses* use ancient myth as a pattern onto which to map their modernist narrative. This was seen as a way of "giving a shape and significance to the immense panorama of futility and anarchy which is contemporary history" (Eliot, "'Ulysses', Order, and Myth." *Selected Prose* 177). Often enough, modernist writers sought refuge from "contemporary history" in cultural renovation: not in something entirely new, but in things ancient – modernism "repudiated the present and the recent past in order to establish contact with a more authentic remote past" (Bergonzi, *The Myth of Modernism* xi). Eliot's *Waste Land*, for instance, quotes literary works from classical Greece and Dante and Shakespeare, aligning itself with a time in which literature was still seen to possess more creative power.

The role of language in the movement cannot be underestimated. This statement might seem a rather obvious one, but at the turn of the century and especially after the Great War there was a deep dissatisfaction with contemporary (literary) language and a deep-rooted desire for a "revolution of the word" (Ezra Pound, cit. Ackroyd 24). Late Victorian rhetoric had become so overblown and diffuse, literary imagery so predictable, that it seemed that all language's significance, its power to communicate something meaningful, had been lost. Modernism is characterised by the attempt to recapture the magic of words, by for example breaking up traditional conventions of syntax, by creating new relations of word and meaning, and indeed by defying the traditional view of words as vehicles of meaning, showing them to be tangible entities within themselves. Imagist poetry (a brief movement centred around Ezra Pound) vows "to use absolutely no word that [does] not contribute to presentation" (F.S. Flint in *Poetry*, March 1913; cit. Emig, *Modernism* 121), and in consequence produces such radical, concentrated works as Pound's famous "In a Station of the Metro":

> The apparition of these faces in the crowd:
> Petals on a wet, black bough.
> *(Selected Poems* 53)

Modernism was a truly international and cosmopolitan movement. Its most important literary figureheads writing in English include W.B. Yeats (from Ireland), James Joyce (originally from Ireland, but later living in Italy, France and Switzerland), Ezra Pound (originally from the United States, later living in England, France and Italy), T.S. Eliot (originally American, later becoming a British national), Gertrude Stein (American, emigrated to Paris), Virginia Woolf (English), and D.H. Lawrence (English, but travelled the world). A second generation of writers associated with modernism, whose figurehead was W.H. Auden, lived similarly cosmopolitan and migratory lives. The modern city with its crowds of inhabitants and roaring technology plays a central role in the development of modernism, both as the location in which artists produced their work and as a symbol of modernity itself. At the beginning of the movement, the modernists deliberately put themselves in radical opposition to the literature and literary establishment of the time. Because of their isolation (frequently as exiles from home in large cities) they formed small, clique-ish circles, which often attacked other, less adventurous contemporary writers (Virginia Woolf's harsh criticism of Arnold Bennett is one example – not that he did not retaliate in kind!). By the 1940s, however, the former avant-garde had itself become the establishment. Its aesthetic tenets, often formulated aggressively to shock their readers out of lethargy, appeared one-dimensional and élitist, leaving the modernists open to accusations of intellectual snobbery and extremism (not helped by the flirtations of some of the most prominent writers with fascism). Nonetheless, the literary criticism of writers such as Eliot and Woolf played a central role in the creation of the academic literary canon that still dominates the subject of English Literature at universities today.[2]

Much criticism of the past decades has been concerned with challenging both the academic canon approved by the modernists and the principles of modernism

---

[2] One good example of this is Eliot's rediscovery and championing of the Metaphysical Poets (who had fallen out of favour after a negative evaluation by Samuel Johnson), or Woolf's dismissal of writers such as Arnold Bennett and John Galsworthy.

itself, and to a certain extent rightly so. Indeed, the present study itself represents such a challenge. However, critics condemning the modernists outright often seem to shrug aside the circumstances that helped the movement evolve. Without wishing to reduce modernism to a mere artistic expression of the times, the undeniable dead-end of Victorian culture and art and the trauma of the First World War made anything other than a radical break nonsensical. Under these circumstances, Ezra Pound's demand to "make it new" seems not dogmatic, but deeply and urgently felt (cf. Pound, *Literary Essays*).

Inklings and Modernists: The Biographical Connections

At the same time that the modernists were "making it new", another group of writers was engaged in another literary project. The Oxford "Inklings" (as they called themselves) were a circle of friends of C.S. Lewis's, many of whom wrote (some seriously, some not so seriously) and who gathered in the "Eagle and Child" pub or in Lewis's Magdalen College rooms to read one another their work and discuss it. The most famous members of this group are Lewis himself, as well as J.R.R. Tolkien and Charles Williams, and among the products of these meetings were works such as Tolkien's *The Lord of the Rings* and Lewis's space romances. While the Inklings never set forth their ideals in any formal way (unlike the manifestos of some modernist groups), the works of Lewis, Tolkien and Williams for all their differences have one significant factor in common: they engage, in some form or other, with the fantastic. On account of their popularity and influence on later writers they are often seen as the fathers of modern fantasy. However, although they were by and large contemporary with the modernists and indeed acquainted with not a few of them, the Inklings and the modernists are generally seen as two groups of writers with nothing at all in common. The present study obviously does not subscribe to this view, and this chapter aims to give a brief overview of the contacts that existed between Lewis, Tolkien, Williams and modernist writers, as well as discussing the supposed mutual dislike between the authors of these two groups.[3]

---

[3] I am assuming a certain level of background knowledge on the Inklings and their works; readers who wish to find out more about the group and its activities are referred to Humphrey Carpenter's standard *The Inklings* (London: HarperCollins, 1997).

Of the three Inklings examined here, Charles Williams is the author whose style is most obviously modern, and it was he who had the most contact with modernist writers (mainly as a result of his work for Oxford University Press). His opinions on the modernists are more difficult to pin down. His attitude towards his own most prominent admirer, T.S. Eliot, was not so much one of dislike as one of bewilderment: "I feel a real apology is due to Mr Eliot, for whose work I profess a sincere and profound respect, though I fail to understand it" (*Poetry at Present* 7). Williams's mature poetry is similar not so much to Eliot's as to W.B. Yeats's, with whose work Williams shares an idiosyncratic symbolism indebted to a certain extent to the mysteries of the Order of the Golden Dawn, of which both men were members. Thus they both make use of a personal symbolic system strongly influenced by the occult, and they both use the image of Byzantium as a centre both spiritual and artistic. According to A.M. Hadfield, for Williams their first meeting was "enormously exciting" (31). However, as the Order swore its members to secrecy, practically nothing else is known of any interaction they may have had within the Order. They certainly were in contact when Yeats compiled the new *Oxford Book of Modern Verse* for Oxford University Press in 1936. Another poet that Williams's mature style has much in common with and to whom he was linked through his work at the Press is Gerard Manley Hopkins. Williams edited a second edition of Hopkins's poems in 1930, and his friend and fellow poet Anne Ridler believes that it was this experience that finally led to his finding his true poetic voice in the *Taliessin* poetry: "Hopkins gave him a key [...] something [that] was needed to break the too-facile cadence of his earlier verse" (Ridler, "Introduction" lxii).

T.S. Eliot and Williams were first introduced in 1934 by Ottoline Morrell. Eliot describes the meeting as follows:

> I remember a man in spectacles who appeared to combine a frail physique with exceptional vitality. He appeared completely at ease in surroundings with which he was not familiar, and which had intimidated many; and at the same time was modest and unassuming to the point of humility. One retained the impression that he was pleased and grateful for the opportunity of meeting the company, and yet that it was he who had conferred the favour – more than a favour, a kind of benediction, by coming. (Eliot, Introduction to *All Hallows' Eve* x)

Of Williams's novels Eliot wrote: "There are no novels anywhere quite like them [...] seeing all persons and all events in the light of the divine, he shows us a significance, in human beings, human emotions, human events, to which we had been blind" (cit. Carpenter, *Inklings* 97). It was Eliot who, besides C.S. Lewis, finally gave Williams the recognition he craved as a writer. This recognition Eliot was able to show by publishing Williams's last novel *Descent Into Hell* with Faber after Williams's usual publisher Gollancz had rejected it. Both men wrote religious plays for the Canterbury Festival: Williams's *Thomas Cranmer of Canterbury* was given in 1936, one year after Eliot's *Murder in the Cathedral*, and some critics are of the opinion that Williams's figure of the Skeleton owes something to the Tempters in *Murder in the Cathedral* (cf. Ridler, "Introduction" xxviii). The opinion has also been voiced that Eliot's use of Shelley's *doppelgänger* quote in *The Cocktail Party* can be traced back to Williams's use of the same passage in a similar situation in *Descent Into Hell* (Ridler, "Introduction" xxviii), and Eliot himself acknowledged that the image of the world as dance in "Burnt Norton" was taken from Williams (cf. Medcalf, "Athanasian Principle" 39). And while Williams had pronounced himself bewildered by Eliot's poetry, he still praised it (in typically idiosyncratic style) in a review of "East Coker" (1940): "Mr. Eliot has been admired, times without number, for describing the disease. What his poetry has always been calling is the note of strange and beautiful health" (cit. Ridler, "Introduction" xxviii). After Williams's death Eliot gave a touching memorial broadcast, in which he said of Williams: "He seemed to me to approximate, more nearly than any man I have ever known familiarly, to the saint" (Carpenter, *Inklings* 107).

Williams was perhaps most influential in the case of a slightly younger modern poet – W.H. Auden. The two met for the first time in 1933, when Oxford University Press were considering giving Auden the task of compiling the new *Oxford Book of Modern Verse* (which was eventually done by Yeats). Williams wrote of the meeting: "[Auden] is an extraordinarily pleasant creature, and we found ourselves in passionate agreement against the more conservative poets, such as Binyon, Richard Church, and even a doubtful Wilfred Gibson" (Carpenter, *Auden* 223). Auden was overwhelmed by Williams's presence, and later stated: "For the first time in my life [I] felt myself in the presence of personal sanctity" (224). Williams's book on the operation of the Holy Spirit, *The Descent of the Dove*, was greatly influential in Auden's turn towards Christianity. In 1940 Auden wrote to Williams, telling him "how moved he was by the *Dove*" (Williams to his wife; Carpenter, *Auden* 285). The book's influence can be seen directly in poems such as "New Year Letter", but Williams's thought was to colour Auden's philosophy and writing until the end of his life – in his late poem "A Thanksgiving" he names Williams as one of his major models. In 1949 Auden wrote the poem "Memorial for the City" in memory of Williams. He also admired Williams's novels and poetry.

By contrast, C.S. Lewis distrusted modernism from an early age, and often styled himself as fighting against the modernist "enemy" (Ricks 197). While he read much modernist work attentively, and also criticised it seriously, this is somewhat obscured by his polemical utterances against the modernists (always pounced upon with glee by critics). Already during his time as an undergraduate at Oxford he and some fellow students published an anthology of their poems "as a kind of counterblast to the ruling literary fashion [...], which consists in the tendencies called 'Vorticist'" (Lewis, *Letters* 52). Lewis condemned this kind of poetry as "arising from the 'sick of everything' mood" (*Letters* 52), and his tastes did not change in later years:

> For twenty years I've stared my level best
> To see if evening – any evening – would suggest
> A patient etherized upon a table;
> In vain. I simply wasn't able.
> (Lewis, "A Confession" *Poems* 1)

In 1942 Lewis praised E.R. Eddison and his fantasy *The Worm Ouroboros* in Eddison's own mock-mediaeval style as being better than "all the clam jamfrey and whymperinges of the raskellie auctours in these latter daies, as the Eliots, Poundes, Lawrences, Audens, and the like" (Carpenter, *Inklings* 190). Yet it must be repeated that in all fairness Lewis never condemned writers without reading them carefully first; thus he disliked Henry James and Lawrence but apparently "could quote [their works] or refer to [them] knowledgeably on occasion" (Green and Hooper, *C.S. Lewis* 151). And in spite of his talent for catchy dismissals such as "*steam* of consciousness" (Lewis, *The Dark Tower* 11) he gave serious reasons for his criticism of modernist literary techniques. Thus he wrote that stream of consciousness was, instead of a true portrayal of what goes on in a person's head, blatantly unrealistic:

> the disorganised consciousness [of Ulysses] is discovered by introspection – that is, by artificially suspending all the normal and outgoing activities of the mind and then attending to what is left. In that residuum it discovers no concentrated will, no logical thought, no morals, no stable sentiments, and (in a word) no mental hierarchy. Of course not; for we have deliberately stopped all these things in order to introspect. (*Preface to 'Paradise Lost'* 153)

In spite of this, Lewis was intrigued enough by the concept as such to write a kind of "stream of consciousness" story of his own – "The Shoddy Lands", where the narrator becomes trapped in the mind of a superficial and vain young woman.

The young Lewis loved the works of William Morris and George Macdonald, but one of his particular literary heroes was Yeats. Lewis was particularly enchanted by Yeats's use of Celtic myth and mystic symbolism; thus he wrote to his friend Arthur Greeves in 1916: "We have had a book of Yeats' prose out of the library, and this has revived my taste for things Gaelic and mystic" (*They Stand Together* 157). Upon his move to Oxford, Lewis admitted that "[Johnson] and all the other literary people I have met since I left home for Oxford, have made me feel how deep is my ignorance of modern, that is to say, *contemporary* literature, especially poetry" (*Letters* 202), but stated "[a]t the same time I am often surprised to find how utterly ignored Yeats is among the men I have met: perhaps his appeal is purely Irish – if so, then thank the gods that I am Irish" (*Letters* 202). A couple of years afterwards, Lewis finally had the opportunity to meet his eminent countryman. Yeats had taken a house in Broad Street, Oxford, where he spent the winter of 1919 and to which he returned for various shorter visits. Lewis voiced the intention of "bearding the lion in his den" (*Letters* 263) in 1919, adding: "I think his vanity is sufficient to secure us a good reception if we come with the obvious purpose of worshipping devoutly" (*Letters* 263). But it was 1921 before he was introduced to Yeats by his friend William Force Stead (who is perhaps best known as the minister who baptised T.S. Eliot into the Church of England in 1927). Lewis was overawed by the poet's presence:

> Yeats himself is a very big man – very tall, very fat and very broad: his face also gives one the impression of vast size. There would have been no mistaking which was THE man we had come to see, however many people had been

in the room. [...] I have seldom felt less at my ease before anyone than I did before him: I understand the Dr Johnson atmosphere for the first time.
(*They Stand Together* 286)

After this first visit, during which Yeats talked nearly all the time about "magic and apparitions" (287), Lewis concluded that Yeats must be mad, stating: "I could never have believed that he was so much like his own poetry" (*Letters* 57). A second visit a week later impressed him more favourably, as he wrote to his brother: "And would you believe it, he [Yeats] was almost sane, and talked about books and things, still eloquently but quite intelligently?" (*Letters* 57). To Arthur Greeves he wrote of the same visit: "he is an enthusiastic admirer of Morris's prose romances: which shd. give us confidence" (*They Stand Together* 287). Whether Lewis, who was recommended to Yeats by Stead as having "a double claim to distinction as an Irishman and a poet" (*Letters* 56), made any impression at all on the great man is not recorded. Unsurprisingly, Yeats's later style did not appeal to Lewis: he said in 1944 "the early Yeats [is] worth twenty of the reconditioned 1920 model" (*Letters* 205).

Charles Williams introduced Eliot and Lewis to one another in 1945. This was quite a brave move on his part, for Lewis had for many years vociferously expressed his dislike of Eliot. While he never questioned Eliot's talent as a poet, he condemned his works above all for their consciously highbrow approach to literature, and from that deduced that their author suffered from "arrogance" (Letter to Paul Elmer More, Ricks 198). In his eyes, Eliot's poetry was downright harmful: "most men are by [*The Waste Land*] infected by chaos" (Ricks 197), his criticism uninformed: "His constant profession of humanism and his claim to be a 'classicist' [...] are erroneous" (Ricks 197), his conversion to Christianity suspicious. Thus the allegorical "Mr. Neo-Angular" in *The Pilgrim's Regress* is modelled on Eliot: "What I am attacking in Neo-Angular is a set of people who seem to me [...] to be trying to make of Christianity itself one more highbrow, Chelsea, bourgeois-baiting fad. [...] T.S. Eliot is the single man who sums up the thing I am fighting against" (Green and Hooper 130). In fact, Lewis went even further than this in the letter to More cited above, and in his intense dislike he reveals more of his own prejudices than any serious criticism of Eliot:

> Eliot stole upon us, a foreigner and neutral, when we were at war – obtained, I have my wonders how, a job in the Bank of England [sic] – and became (am

I wrong) the advance guard of the invasion since carried out by his natural friends and allies, the Steins and Pounds and *hoc genus omne*, the Parisian riff-raff of denationalized Irishmen and Americans who have perhaps given Western Europe her death-wound. (Ricks 198)

As Ricks points out, Lewis has unwittingly condemned himself along with the modernists: "what was Lewis but that doubly denationalized Irishman, the Ulsterman who lives in England?" (198). He had more in common with Eliot than he himself was willing to admit, and Ricks may be right when he states that Eliot's art and Lewis's rhetoric "both begin in pain at foreignness and at denationalized disintegration" (198).

On a more objective level, Lewis had attacked Eliot's literary criticism openly in 1930, actually sending him an essay for the *Criterion* titled "The Personal Heresy in Poetics" in which he attacked Eliot's interpretation of Dante. The essay was (unsurprisingly) never published. Lewis further took Eliot to task in *Preface to 'Paradise Lost'* (1942), in particular for his claim that only a poet has the right to criticise poetry, and only a poet can decide who is truly a poet. This position of Eliot's is expressed in the essay "The Function of Criticism", which also contains his view of Classicism which so aggravated the Classics scholar Lewis. Lewis points out: "Poets become in [Eliot's] view an unrecognizable society (an Invisible Church) […]. The republic of letters resolves itself into an aggregate of uncommunicating and unwindowed monads; each has unawares crowned and mitred himself Pope and King of Pointland" (*Preface* 10).

After all this, it can hardly have come as a surprise that Lewis's and Eliot's first meeting in 1945 was a complete failure. Eliot – uncharacteristically rude on his part – opened the conversation with the remark "Mr Lewis, you are a much *older* man than you appear in photographs." According to Green and Hooper's biography, Lewis responded with a "poker-face" (223), and Eliot went on to state: "I must tell you, Mr Lewis, that I consider your *Preface to Paradise Lost* your best book." As it was in this work that he had criticised Eliot so strongly, Lewis was immediately filled with suspicion and altogether "a very bad time was had by all except Charles Williams, who is said to have enjoyed himself hugely" (Green and Hooper 224). Lewis recorded of the meeting in his notebook: "Mr Eliot has asked me not to write about his literary criticism. Very well. I obey" (Green and Hooper 224). It took a long while for both men to finally come to terms with one another. Yet ten years later, they were both on a committee to revise the new translation of the Psalms and soon became quite reconciled to one another – "which the pre-war Lewis would have declared to be in every respect impossible" (Carpenter, *Inklings* 246). Eliot and Lewis corresponded and met occasionally until Lewis's death in 1963.

J.R.R. Tolkien is the most difficult of the three writers focused on here to relate to his contemporaries because of his overwhelming passion for pre-modern literature and language, which played a fundamental role in his own literary creation but also pushed aside any deeper interest in contemporary writing. His specialization in philology did not require him to have much knowledge of literature after Chaucer either as a student or a teacher. As an undergraduate, "he did make a few sketchy notes on Johnson, Dryden, and Restoration drama, but there is no indication that he had more than a passing interest in them" (Carpenter, *J.R.R. Tolkien* 77). That he had some knowledge of Romantic poetry and literary theory is evident from his own essays – "On Fairy-stories" draws on Coleridge – but as for contemporary poetry and fiction, while he was surely exposed to them to a certain extent through his position as a university professor and through the Inklings' discussions, he had little genuine interest in them. Even his involvement with the Inklings had no marked influence on his work, as Lewis states quite plainly in a letter:

> No one ever influenced Tolkien – you might as well try to influence a bandersnatch. We listened to his work, but could affect it only by encouragement. He has only two reactions to criticism: either he begins the whole work over again from the beginning or else takes no notice at all. (Lewis, *Letters* 287)

Only when the works of contemporary modernist authors dovetailed with his own interests did Tolkien engage with them closely: for example, the language games of Joyce in *Finnegans Wake* intrigued him sufficiently that he took down notes upon Joyce's novel.[4]

The only contemporary writer with whom Tolkien had much to do apart from Lewis and Williams was W.H. Auden, and Auden's Anglo-Saxon poetry can be attributed to Tolkien's influence. Auden heard Tolkien's lectures as an

---

[4] These notes are preserved among Tolkien's papers in the Bodleian Library as MS. Tolkien 24, fols 44-45; I am very grateful to Dimitra Fimi for alerting me to the presence of these notes – irrefutable proof that Tolkien *did* read modernist literature!

undergraduate at Oxford, and said of them: "I do not remember a single word he said but at a certain point he recited, and magnificently, a long passage of *Beowulf*. I was spellbound. This poetry, I knew, was going to be my dish" (cit. Carpenter, *Auden* 55). Auden was also, as mentioned earlier, one of the first admirers of Tolkien's literary work and always defended him against hostile criticism. The relationship between the two was not always easy, unsurprisingly enough for two men so completely different in character and lifestyle, and Auden offended Tolkien on several occasions, for example by calling Tolkien's home "hideous" at a talk given at the New York Tolkien Society in 1965 (cf. Carpenter, *Auden*, note to 379). Tolkien nevertheless was always deeply grateful for Auden's friendship, as he wrote in 1971:

> I am [...] very deeply in Auden's debt in the recent years. His support of me and interest in my work has been one of my chief encouragements. He gave me very good reviews, notices and letters from the beginning when it was by no means a popular thing to do. He was, in fact, sneered at for it. (*Letters* 411)

When Tolkien turned seventy he was honoured with a "Festschrift", to which Auden wrote a brilliant prefatory ode; Tolkien returned the compliment with an Anglo-Saxon poem for Auden's "Festschrift" (an edition of *Shenandoah* celebrating his work) in 1967. According to Carpenter's biography, "Auden was delighted. 'Wasn't it nice of Tolkien to write something in Anglo Saxon?' he wrote to E.R. Dodds. 'I was terribly flattered.'" (Carpenter, *Auden*, note to 379). The two remained in contact until their deaths in 1973. The impact Tolkien's work had on Auden is evident in the essays he wrote on fantasy and myth in the collection *Secondary Worlds* – which was, incidentally, *in memoriam* T.S. Eliot. Though Auden's own work had no discernible influence whatsoever on Tolkien, and they never discussed it in their correspondence, it is nonetheless interesting that so much of their work displays parallels.

The so-called world of letters was a much smaller place at the beginning of the twentieth century than it is now, and it should not come as a surprise that these very different writers knew each other's work and were acquainted personally. "[T]he density of the particular social space that bound together the [modernist] authors" (Rainey, "Cultural Economy of Modernism" 35) has often been remarked on; it is however equally often forgotten that the modernists increasingly turned to the universities for support after 1922 and the onset of the Great Depression which deprived them of their private patrons. Thus it was natural that they should come in contact with writer-academics such as Lewis, Tolkien and Williams. Modernist authors such as Eliot gave lectures at university, and publishing institutions such as Oxford University Press published work by academics and creative writers alike (among them Lewis, Williams, Tolkien, and Auden). Cambridge University Press published works by Lewis and Eliot; Faber, Eliot's publishing house, published Williams and Auden. Thus the writers focused on in this study crossed each other's paths mainly in two cities, Oxford and London – two very different yet closely associated places (not least because OUP had offices in both). The literary world of London and the academic world of Oxford were not so far apart, and to a certain extent complemented each other; writers such as Yeats, Eliot, Lewis and Williams moved between the two. To portray the Inklings as enclosed in Oxford and the modernists as of London and the rest of the world but *not* of Oxford is to give a false picture of both groups of writers.

Shared Literary Concerns

The Inklings themselves did not acknowledge any influence of modernist authors upon their works. Rather, they cited nineteenth-century writers such as George Macdonald and William Morris as their models.[5] However, while it is possible to trace these influences, the situation in the twentieth century during which the Inklings were writing was markedly different from that in the nineteenth. During the Victorian era, there was a proliferation of "a variety of non-realistic techniques that included nonsense, dreams, visions, and the creation of other worlds" (Prickett xv). In his attempt to give an overview of what he calls Victorian fantasy, Stephen Prickett considers writers as diverse as Mary Shelley, Charles Dickens, and Edith Nesbit alongside Edward Lear, Carroll and Macdonald. In another study, *Victorian Fantasy Literature*, Karen Michalson also includes Rider Haggard and Rudyard Kipling in her list of fantasy authors along with the usual suspects. These writers all make use of what could be termed fantastic elements, but there is a remarkable lack of con-

---

5   On Morris's influence, cf. Lewis, *Joy* 132; Carpenter, *Tolkien* 77-78; Hadfield, *Exploration* 156. On Macdonald, cf. Lewis, Introduction to *George Macdonald: An Anthology* xi.

sistency in their various expressions of the fantastic, which include the gothic, dream-like, and nonsensical. What unites them are their attempts to justify using the fantastic, in contrast to the (supposedly) predominant realism which was regarded as more truthful and hence as morally superior.

In the twentieth century, however, we find a number of writers whose creative work is remarkably similar to each others', in that it makes use of consistent secondary worlds, whether purely imaginary or set on a distant planet, such as Lord Dunsany, David Lindsay, David Eddings and, of course, the Inklings. Their work often harks back to mediaeval influence both in language style and setting; this pre-scientific setting often brings with it the use of magic and the supernatural. The change from the Victorian to the modern era left its mark on fantastic literature, and the writings of Lewis, Tolkien and Williams are distinctly twentieth-century. They all suffered through the First World War, were familiar with the changes in thought that the works of Nietzsche, Darwin and Frazer had brought about, and along with their modernist contemporaries sought for new ways of writing and expressing their changed perception of reality. Instead of trying to justify the use of fantastic elements to a dominant realist mainstream, they have to try and justify literary creation in general as consensus realities (and realisms) break apart; art becomes a way of giving the world meaning and making it cohere. This distinctly modern note in their work brings out parallels to the works of their modernist contemporaries.

I want to begin my summary of these parallels with the comments of W.H. Auden. In one of his reviews of *The Lord of the Rings*, titled "At the End of the Quest, Victory", Auden differentiates between so-called subjective reality, that is "a man's experience of his own existence" (44), and objective reality, which he defines as the "experience of the lives of others and the world about him" (44). Thus, a difference is made between inner consciousness and self-experience on the one hand, and the perception of the outer world and other individuals on the other. One of the great problems of literature that tries to give a complete picture of reality – especially narrative fiction – lies therefore in the bridging of this "gulf between the subjectively real [...] and the objectively real" (44).

This problem is crucial to the period both modernists and Inklings were writing. External reality appeared overwhelming and incoherent; it no longer seemed possible for an individual to understand the world around him or her, or to form valid and objective opinions on fellow human beings. The synthesis of objective reality and subjective reality broke down; only the subjectively real could be fully known. In reaction to this, classic modernist fiction no longer attempted to bridge the gulf between the two realities. The development of new narrative techniques – the disappearance of the omniscient narrator behind reflector figures, impersonal narration, and, above all, stream of consciousness or interior monologue – bear out this divorce of subjective from objective reality in favour of the subjective perspective.

One way of coping with this separation is the way of Joyce, Woolf, Faulkner: to acknowledge it and plunge into subjectivity, expressed through literary techniques such as interior monologue or stream of consciousness. A different way of circumventing the divide is to negate it and to seek refuge from the incoherent outside world in the creation of a secondary world, an imagined reality coherent in itself, more or less independent of outside reality. In the works of the Inklings, this is often a fantastic secondary world. In the secondary world, the gap between subjective and objective reality no longer exists, as there is only one reality: that of the sub-creator.

> An imaginary world can be so constructed as to make credible any landscape, inhabitants, and events which its maker wishes to introduce, and since he himself has invented its history, there is only one correct interpretation of events, his own. What takes place and why is, necessarily, what he says it is. (Auden, "Quest Hero" 50)

This kind of negation is also to be found in the cosmic models of much of Eliot's poetry and of Pound's *Cantos* (a body of works called by their author "a poem including history", which attempts to include all of culture and civilisation). These works, in trying to incorporate the entire outside world in their creation, similarly negate any rift between subjective and objective reality in "declar[ing] the text to be reality" (Emig, *Modernism* 117). Thus the alienation central to the modern experience of reality and the concern with what actually constitutes reality is addressed in the works of both Inklings and modernists, and is often dealt with in similar ways.

The dominance of the sub-creator and the problem of power is a central issue in fantasy. Auden states that secondary worlds are created out of a desire for omniscience and omnipotence, the position of God: "In the secondary worlds we make, we are omnipotent, with absolute freedom to say what they shall contain and what shall happen in them. [Furthermore], we are omniscient, aware of everything which exists and happens in it, and understanding exactly why" (*Secondary Worlds* 52). Even Tolkien himself, who wrote that he disliked intensely any "purposed domination of the author" (*LotR* xv), admitted that as the sub-creator of a secondary world, "as you are the master your whim is law" (*Sauron Defeated* 240). One result of this desire for omnipotence is the overextension of secondary worlds to incorporate the primary world in order to preserve the authority of the secondary world. Tolkien's Middle-earth is an example of this, as will be explored in detail in later chapters. The question of power and authority is also one that lies at the heart of much modernist writing. The modernists, in an attempt to rescue art from its (supposed) commercialisation during the Victorian era, were quick to reclaim the romantic position of the artist as "unacknowledged legislator of the world" (Shelley, "A Defence of Poetry" 36): if no longer of the world in its entirety, then of the world of culture and art. This has consequences for the power structures within texts, which seek to preserve their authority and identity as part of high literature in their cosmic models. There is no room for alternatives: modernism "present[s] itself as all-inclusive" (Emig, *Modernism* 130), and thus as all-powerful. This again parallels textual structures that can be found in fantasy texts.[6]

One form that modernism's will to power takes is intertextuality. It is this feature that is most often criticised as being deliberately obscure and pretentious – many readers feel threatened by the sheer size of the cultural heritage invoked by this method. Many modernists use quotes from other works in their texts, playing with notions of tradition and textual wholeness, and often incorporating fragments of other texts without any reference to where the fragment is actually from. Some texts, like Eliot's *The Waste Land*, can almost appear like a guessing game, where only the most educated person (the author himself?) recognises all the quotes. That it is a game perhaps not to be taken entirely seriously is borne out by Eliot's tongue-in-cheek "Notes" which supposedly "explain" the poem. This is a form of open intertextuality, where the fact that there are quotes

---

6 For a discussion of modernism and Tolkien's *The Lord of the Rings* as all-inclusive, "encyclopaedic literature", cf. Simonson Chapter 3.

and fragments remains evident, even if the fragments are used to form a new whole. Fragmentation as a literary technique effectively symbolizes the lack of coherence felt in modern life. It is, however, also a method of placing the modernist work within a literary tradition: the modernist text uses other, older texts to create its identity. This is no different in the works of Lewis, Tolkien and Williams, which are also extremely intertextual – a fact the full import of which has perhaps not yet been realised. Tolkien's Middle-earth, as has been admirably demonstrated by Tom Shippey, is in fact a great amalgamation of Old English and Norse sources (cf. Shippey, *Road*), which Tolkien fused together in his attempt to create a "mythology for England" (cf. Tolkien, *Letters* 144-145). Williams's Arthurian poetry is by nature of its theme intertextual, though it quotes and refers to religious and spiritual texts – particularly Dante, a taste he shared with both Lewis and Eliot – more than to other Arthurian poetry. In all of Lewis's novels we come across obvious borrowings and reworkings of texts from classical antiquity through the Renaissance up to H.G. Wells. In fact, intertextuality becomes especially interesting in Lewis as it becomes a means of survival for the characters in his novels – they recognise situations familiar to them from books, and act accordingly in the unfamiliar worlds they are thrust into. Intertextuality is more obvious, and the reader's attention drawn to it more, in Lewis and Williams than in Tolkien; however all three authors try to incorporate their quotes and references organically into their original work. This is the main difference between the intertextuality of these three and that of the modernists; for the modernists the fragmentation of the quotes is the whole point of the exercise. However, both versions of intertextuality, both open and closed forms, betray a concern with notions of originality and reclaiming the culture of the past in order to construct the present.

For both, Inklings and modernists, the way of reclaiming the past and constructing the present lay in language. The aestheticist and decadent movements in the later nineteenth century saw a turn towards the surface of language, which culminated in an overblown rhetoric that by 1900 had exhausted itself completely. At the same time, as modern existence became increasingly bewildering, it seemed that language in general had lost its capability to grasp reality, its power and its meaning. The turn of the century thus saw a collapse of faith in and an intense frustration with language. This crisis lay at the heart of the modernist endeavour to find new artistic modes of expression. Modernism not only broke up traditional forms and conventions, but traditional syntax too; it attempted to create new relations of word and meaning, indeed sometimes defying the view of words as vehicles of meaning, showing them to be tangible entities within themselves. Nevertheless, in spite of the emphasis laid on language through these techniques, the fundamental doubt of its material is never far from the surface in modernism, and the failure of language is a recurrent theme: for example, in his *Four Quartets* Eliot described writing poetry as "a raid on the inarticulate / With shabby material always deteriorating" ("East Coker" *Collected Poems* 203), and elsewhere he writes of having "to force, to dislocate if necessary, language into his meaning" ("The Metaphysical Poets" *Selected Prose* 65). Similarly, fantasy is a genre that places great emphasis on its medium, language. Its secondary worlds exist only as linguistic constructions,[7] and this fact is often subtly emphasised in the texts themselves. Various languages are spoken in the secondary worlds, animals have the power of speech, and language is invested with magical powers. However, it is seldom left at that, and at least in the texts of the three authors under study here, language's power is often questioned and shown to be in crisis. In Tolkien's Middle-earth, languages die out and lose their creative power; in Lewis's space trilogy, it is made clear that language on Earth (the "Silent Planet") is twisted as a result of the Fall, and at the end of his *Chronicles of Narnia*, the beloved talking beasts' gift of speech is taken away again; in Williams's Arthurian poems, the realm of Arthur dissolves in chaos and there are "mutes or rhetoricians instead of the sacred poets" ("The Prayers of the Pope" *RSS* 51). The fantasy of Lewis, Tolkien and Williams thus shares with modernism a paradoxical emphasis on language that at the same time questions its power. It is perhaps also this fundamental doubting of language that creates the need for an all-powerful sub-creator.

Modernism questioned traditional artistic forms as well as language. Kathryn Hume has observed that "[m]odern literature is in its way a literature of quest, a

---

7 Tolkien, in fact, sees language itself as inherently fantastic: "The human mind, endowed with the powers of generalisation and abstraction, sees not only green-grass, discriminating it from other objects (and finding it fair to look upon), but sees that it is green as well as being grass. [...] The mind that thought of light, heavy, grey, yellow, still, swift, also conceived of magic that would make heavy things light and able to fly, turn grey lead into yellow gold, and the still rock into swift water. If it could do the one, it could do the other; it inevitably did both. When we can take green from grass, blue from heaven, and red from blood, we already have an enchanter's power" ("On Fairy-stories" 122).

literature [...] in search of its proper form rather than already possessed of that form" (43). Its refusal of tradition led to art both ambitious and adventurous, that seemed to contemporaries to defy categorisation: were *Ulysses* and *The Waves* really novels? Was *The Waste Land* a poem, a cycle of poems, or something else entirely? And what were Pound's *Cantos*, that simply kept growing and growing? Modernism emancipated the work of art from its position as exponent of a certain genre, and demanded that each work be studied under its own terms – but those terms were often difficult to establish. While new subject-matter demanded new forms, the form was notoriously elusive: the extensive work and revision on *The Waste Land*, which Eliot himself acknowledged would never have been possible without Pound, is symptomatic of this, as are Pound's various schools of poetry such as Imagism and Vorticism, whose strict forms he was driven to define only to cast them aside again. Hume's picture of the movement as in quest of a form is particularly apt when it is taken into consideration that much modernist literature is indeed concerned with the quest motif, whether it be ironic as in *Ulysses*, ultimately frustrated as in *The Waste Land*, or never-ending as in *The Cantos*. The quest story is, of course, also the form *par excellence* of fantasy and that of nearly all the works of Lewis, Tolkien and Williams. By now, the fantasy trilogy is so firmly established as a genre form that it is easy to forget the confusion that greeted the first publication of *The Lord of the Rings*, when doubts were expressed as to whether this thousand-page story, with its introductions and massive appendices, could be classed as a novel at all.[8] Even more problematic was Tolkien's *The Silmarillion* (or, to be precise, earlier drafts thereof), which was refused by publishers even after the phenomenal success of *The Lord of the Rings*. Williams's novels were also met with bewilderment: were they thrillers, or religious works? One critic's confusion is evident in his coinage "spiritual shockers" (R.W. Chambers, cit. Carpenter, *Inklings* 98).

This rejection of traditional form, though felt to be necessary, was not simply liberating. T.S. Eliot speaks of this in his discussion of Joyce's *Ulysses*:

> If it is not a novel, that is simply because the novel is a form which will no longer serve; it is because the novel, instead of being a form, was simply the

---

[8] Martin Simonson's *The Lord of the Rings and Western Narrative Tradition* discusses the problems of genre classification in Tolkien's text.

expression of an age which had not sufficiently lost all form to feel the need of something stricter. ("Ulysses", *Selected Prose* 177)

If the novel as form was to be rejected, then something else was needed to give shape to its subject-matter. This makes clear another modernist paradox: while old forms were broken and discarded and liberation from them proclaimed, the necessity was felt for new, "stricter" ones. The reductionism of the Imagist movement in poetry is an extreme example of the strict rules modernism laid upon itself. Art was believed impossible without order – and sometimes that order had to be imposed from above. This again brings the question of authority to the fore. That fantasy is also in search of order is borne out in what Lewis called the "longing for a Form" ("Sometimes Fairy Stories May Say Best What's to be Said" *Other Worlds* 71). While working on his Narnia stories, he also rejected the novel in favour of the form of the fairy story, which he found attractive because of its strictness:

> I fell in love with the Form itself: its brevity, its severe restraints on description, its flexible traditionalism, its inflexible hostility to all analysis, digression, reflections and 'gas'. […] its very limitations of vocabulary became an attraction. ("Sometimes Fairy Stories" 73)

Like the modernists, Lewis is drawn to a form (albeit an ancient one) which imposed strict rules on its subject-matter. Charles Williams's Arthurian poems are prime examples of artificial order: in them a complicated interrelation of political, spiritual, mathematical and physical levels produces the "body of the Empire", represented in the map accompanying *Taliessin through Logres* as a reclining woman whose head is Logres, breasts are Gaul, and buttocks are Caucasia. This subsequently structures the poetry. Thus a concern with order similar to that of modernism can be found in much of the Inklings' work.

One form of order that was espoused by both modernists and Inklings was that of myth. Many famous modernist writers (such as Eliot, Joyce, O'Neill, Yeats) used myth in their work, either drawing on pre-existing myths or creating their own systematic mythology (Yeats being the prime example of the latter). In the essay on *Ulysses* already quoted above, Eliot speaks of the "mythical method", which enables writers to impose an artificial order on their subject-matter: "It is simply a way of controlling, of ordering, of giving a shape and significance to the immense panorama of futility and anarchy which is contemporary history"

("Ulysses", *Selected Prose* 177). Myth also becomes a way of asserting authority, as its nature as a world-formula in story excludes competing narratives. Thus by using it writers could reassert authority in their works and their interpretation of reality. Myth has been an equally important term in the study of fantasy. Most fantasies either use pre-existing myths (such as the Arthurian myths in Williams's poetry, or classical myth in Lewis's space trilogy) or create their own mythology (such as Tolkien's tales of Middle-earth). What is often overlooked is the fact that these works, too, use myth as structure. Lewis states that "the Fantastic or Mythical [has] the power [...] to generalise while remaining concrete, to present in palpable form not concepts or even experiences but whole classes of experience, and to throw off irrelevancies" ("Sometimes Fairy Stories" 73).

In his late novel *Till We Have Faces* Lewis uses the myth of Cupid and Psyche as a frame for a very different kind of story – a tale of conversion. By means of the mythic background, the story of Psyche's sister Orual is presented as a "whole class of experience", as something universal. Myth, in its function as explaining "why the world is as it is and things happen as they do" (Abrams 170), is also used as a way of establishing authority within works – but it must exclude other viewpoints in order to do so. This is typical of the mythic cosmic models of secondary worlds. Classical and British mythology "comes true" in Lewis's space trilogy, establishing its relevance to and importance for contemporary life, and in doing so ultimately justifying the author's rather orthodox Christian convictions. This comes at the cost of marginalising or silencing those who do not conform to its ideals. In the trilogy's most blatant example of this, Jane Studdock, a married woman who is considering an academic career, is told by the main protagonist Ransom (revealed as an incarnation of Arthur, and thus bearing the legendary king's authority): "Go in obedience and you will find love. You will have no more dreams. Have children instead" (*THS* 250).

Each novel of the space trilogy ends with a climactic struggle between good and evil powers, and *That Hideous Strength* takes that struggle to an apocalyptic level. It ends happily – the gods descend to earth, the wicked scientists are destroyed and all is love and forgiveness. *The Chronicles of Narnia* end somewhat more ambiguously. The world of Narnia is rent by the "last battle" of the final volume's title, and ends with a terrifying day of judgement. The protagonists however rediscover themselves in another, more wonderful version of Narnia – to be told that actually they are dead and gone to heaven. This supposedly happy solution and the horror vision of Narnia's end hang uneasily in balance, making an ending that is ambiguously happy at the most. These doomsday visions of worlds ending in warfare can be found both in the works of the other Inklings – the War of Wrath or War of the Ring in Tolkien's *Silmarillion* and *The Lord of the Rings*, or the civil war that destroys not only Arthur's kingdom, but the entire Empire in Williams's poetry – and in modernist works. As stated above, the Great War of 1914 to 1918 was a cataclysmic event that greatly aggravated the traumata of modern existence and affected an entire generation of artists. Virtually all of modernist literature contains some reaction to the War, that killed some of the most promising young writers of the early twentieth century and haunted both those who survived and those who did not see active service. Works such as Pound's *Hugh Selwyn Mauberley* or David Jones's *In Parenthesis* (which, like Williams's poetry, uses the Arthurian myth) are responses to the Great War's mass mechanical slaughter. Both Lewis and Tolkien served in France and lost some of their dearest friends in what Tolkien called the "animal horror" (Carpenter, *Tolkien* 91) of the trenches. Charles Williams was not enlisted due to physical disability, but also lost close friends. The writings of all three were deeply influenced and to a certain extent triggered by their experience of the war. The "war to end all wars", as the First World War was called, was followed by the Second World War, and this conflict brought Williams to Oxford, and into regular contact with Lewis and Tolkien. Thus it is not surprising that visions of war should repeatedly appear in these writers' work. That these struggles are nearly always on an apocalyptic scale is to some extent a legacy of the Norse legend of Ragnarok, where the entire world perishes in flames, but far more so one of the immediate experience of the World Wars. Indeed, in the *Blitzkrieg* of the Forties, Ragnarok seemed to have come true, as entire cities were devastated by fire-bombs. Also, the biblical Apocalypse is naturally never far away for these Christian writers. This shared traumatic experience of war marks both modernism and the Inklings' fantasy.

Modern warfare, which reduced the amount of face-to-face combat with the enemy, also overturned traditional notions of prowess in battle and heroism. In David Jones's *In Parenthesis*, one of the central modernist works dealing with war, a mythic superimposition of the Arthurian knight Lancelot and the main protagonist John Ball is established, which questions Lancelot's role as the first knight of the Round Table: the chivalric heroic model so beloved of the Victorians is no longer valid. Other works which reject a traditional hero while referring back to him are Eliot's "The Love Song of J. Alfred Prufrock", who exclaims "No! I am not Prince Hamlet, nor was meant to be" (Eliot, *Collected Poems* 17), or Joyce's *Ulysses*, whose main protagonists are a failed artist and a Jewish outsider; this list could be continued *ad libitum*. The writer or poet as hero has been current since the *Künstlerroman* of the late eighteenth century. In modernism, with its preoccupation with the role of art and language, this figure is both taken up and reworked through the modernist doubt of the validity of that art and language. Stephen Dedalus, in spite of the title *Stephen Hero* that Joyce originally wanted to give *A Portrait of the Artist as a Young Man*, is an ironic figure who never accomplishes the great ambitions he has for his art. Thus a tension is developed in modernist art between the old heroic ideals and their failure in the modern world; the old heroes are invoked only to be rejected, yet the presence of the old ideal simultaneously paralyses the modern protagonist. The protagonists in the works of the Inklings also differ from the heroes of the epics and myths they loved and were influenced by. Tolkien's *The Lord of the Rings* sees victory accomplished not by the mighty warrior Aragorn, but by the hobbit Frodo, who symbolically casts away his armour and gives away his sword – and who afterwards cannot survive, leaving Middle-earth. Williams's novels see a very strange assortment of "heroes", which include an Anglican archdeacon (*War In Heaven*), a poet and playwright (*Descent Into Hell*), and a gentleman gipsy (*The Greater Trumps*). The central figure of his Arthurian poetry is not the king or one of his knights, but Arthur's minstrel Taliessin – the artist becomes the central figure in this modern version of the myth. But in the work of the Inklings, we move beyond the writer as hero – we get the *academic* as hero: the protagonist of Lewis's space romances is a philologist; the hobbits are historians. But in these works, too, the old heroic ideals are still present. The figures in the novels, poems and plays of Lewis, Tolkien and Williams all have to come to terms with them – and they often fall short: Frodo refuses to destroy the Ring, Taliessin ends as an old man, his "tongue tired of song, [...] the brain fey" ("The Prayers of the Pope" *RSS* 56), and Ransom, while seen as a reincarnation of Arthur, is simultaneously the wounded and impotent Fisher

King. Thus we can see that the reworkings of traditional hero figures and their strange alternatives are central to the works of modernists and Inklings.

One last overlapping concern of both modernism and fantasy which informs many of the points mentioned above is that of loss – loss both personal, cultural and artistic. The alienation of the modern condition, brought on by extreme cultural changes such as the disappearance of the certainties of religion, social hierarchies, and scientific progress, led to a deep-seated feeling of loss, the loss of values and roots. It is the loss of the heroic ideal that provokes many protagonists' sense of failure; and the loss suffered by the characters in fiction and poetry, the breakings of fellowships and companies, reflects the losses their authors sustained during the wars. While joy in experiment is central to both modernism and fantasy, there is often an underlying note of despair that the worth of the new can never be that of the old that is lost. This pervading atmosphere of cultural loss is behind the concern with "making it new" out of the fragments of the old, thus establishing a link with an older tradition. But it is only fragments that can be recovered, and thus this link can never be completely established. Cultural decline and loss reappears repeatedly in fantasy: Middle-earth's elves are diminished and men forget their heritage; Narnia is invaded and destroyed by the country of Calormen; Arthur's kingdom and the sacred Empire collapse in ruin. The fragments of earlier and usually superior cultures play an important role – Tolkien's works for example are veritably obsessed with ruins and relics, and the forgotten heirlooms of the Golden Age of Narnia reappear at strategic points in Lewis's narratives – but again it is only fragments that remain. Writing proves a central strategy in both fantasy and modernism to try and combat this loss: for example, one central role of the hobbits that is often overlooked is that they are historians, preserving a record of the War of the Ring in their Red Book. Yet ultimately the failure of language – "the loss and the silence", as it is called in Tolkien's *The Lord of the Rings* (1038) renders these attempts futile; similarly, the old Irish myths and legends enshrined in the poetry of Yeats turn out to be nothing more than "circus animals" ("The Circus Animals' Desertion" *Yeats's Poems* 471). It is the loss of the power of language that provokes the tension inherent in both modernist and fantastic writing.

Alongside alienation and loss, it is perhaps tension that can be seen as the central common term in the study of both modernism and fantasy. In his study *Modernism in Poetry*, Rainer Emig states that "the essential character of the modernist work [is] tension" (241). Likewise, Lucie Armitt speaks of the "inherent tension" (33) and "presiding note of tension" (81) present in fantasy. The term recurs in discussing the various points of comparison enumerated above; thus the tension between subjective and objective reality is crucial to cosmic models and secondary worlds. The breaking of traditional rules is countered by the laying down of new ones, and the rejection of old forms results only in the longing for novel, stricter ones. A concern with artistic originality is coupled with the need to situate the work of art in a pre-existing tradition through intertextuality. An emphasis on language, the chosen medium of artistic creation, is undercut by the constant doubts cast on its power. Old heroic models are both rejected and constantly called to mind. Both modernism and fantasy are literatures full of tension and full of paradoxes; they are literatures born of the same historical situation and reflecting similar concerns.

The broadening of the canon, making academic study of the Inklings acceptable, and the questioning of traditional concepts and definitions of modernism has enabled new aspects of both fields to be explored. It is to be hoped that their juxtaposition and comparison will throw further new light on modernism and fantasy: not only is the fantasy written by Lewis, Tolkien and Williams to a certain extent modernist, but perhaps the work of the modernists is also to a certain extent fantastic.

Chapter Two

War

Modern War, Modern Literature

The twentieth century can with some justification be called the century of war, its "premier legacy the combined will and technology that made it the *bloodiest* in the history of the world" (Norris 505). In its first half Europe was ravaged and millions of lives destroyed twice over in the two World Wars, while the second half was dominated by the Cold War, its ever-present threat of total nuclear annihilation and numerous related proxy conflicts. "War", writes Alfred Kazin, can be seen "as the continued experience of twentieth-century man" (81). Thus it is not surprising that war forms a major topic of the literature of the twentieth century, and that this literature's language is coloured by war rhetoric, for, as Paul Fussell reminds us, "the diction of war resides everywhere just below the surface of modern experience" (189).

Generally, the Great War is seen as the turning-point that finally shattered what was left of the Victorian world-view and way of life, fundamentally questioning its myth of progress, and, in the words of Henry James, "plung[ing] civilisation into [an] abyss of blood and darkness" (James 384). The unprecedented literary response to the Great War has earned it the name of the "literary war" (cf. Fussell 155). The War Poets, such as Sassoon, Owen and Blunden, wrote from the trenches themselves, but the First World War also played a major role in the writing of their contemporaries not actively engaged in military combat. Indeed, the breadth of this response (and subsequent criticism) has endowed the First World War with the "mythopoeic stature" of a "cultural monument" (Lassner 793), and the "view of modernism as a reaction to the primal trauma of the war" (Kibble 545) is one still current in criticism today.

It is easy to link the Great War to the modernist movement in literature, for although few of its greatest figureheads actually saw active combat, representative works such as Pound's *Hugh Selwyn Mauberley*, Eliot's *The Waste Land* or Woolf's *Mrs Dalloway* all deal with the horror of the War and the (futile) attempt to come to terms with it afterwards. While many modernist experimental techniques such as fragmentation, temporal discontinuity and the use of disjunct subjectivities were used before the War, the First World War both confirmed and aggravated the distress of the modern condition addressed by the writers. The War was also central in the development of what has come to be seen as the modernist canon, "the more conservative formulation of modernism that developed during and after the war, the authoritarian aesthetic associated with T.S. Eliot's doctrines of 'impersonality' and 'orthodoxy'" (Kibble 542).[1] This resulted in the sidelining of feminine versions of modernism that have only recently started to be reclaimed.[2]

For some avant-garde artists, the War was welcomed as the catalyst that would once and for all do away with all traces of Victorian and Edwardian reaction. Particularly the Futurists were "very excited by the dynamism manifested in modern war" (Bergonzi, *Heroes' Twilight* 27), and their Manifesto published the year before the Great War conceives of literature "as a violent attack" (7th article, reproduced in: Kolocotroni 251). The Vorticist sculptor Gaudier-Brzeska, writing from the trenches, famously stated that the war "SERVES AS A PURGE TO OVER-NUMEROUS HUMANITY. THIS WAR IS A GREAT REMEDY" (*Blast 2*, 1915; cit. Bergonzi, *Heroes' Twilight* 30). However, after the war was over, it became clear very quickly that the avant-garde's hope for a new civilization had been disappointed,[3] and many of the modernists felt that the war and loss of lives had all been for nothing:

---

[1] Maud Ellmann reads these theories of Eliot's, as expressed in "Tradition and the Individual Talent", as a direct response to the war: "Since 'Tradition and the Individual Talent' was published in 1919, its attitude to death may be seen as a reaction to the war just ended: as an attempt to come to terms with the immolation of the West by disavowing its finality" (M. Ellmann, *The Poetics of Impersonality*, 40).
[2] The reinforcing of gender stereotypes during the war left its traces on literary history and criticism. The voice of the male (combatant) is seen as central, the female (civilian) response marginalized. Similarly the male modernist responses to war are often cited, while the war literature of female writers such as H.D. or Gertrude Stein has been left aside. Recent studies such as, for example, Suzanne Raitt and Trudi Tate's *Women's Fiction and the Great War* (Oxford: Clarendon, 1997) or Gill Plain's *Women's Fiction of the Second World War* (New York: St. Martin's, 1996) have attempted to set the record straight and address the imbalance caused by studies of war literature that focus almost exclusively on male authors (such as, for example, Bergonzi's *Heroes' Twilight* and Fussell's *The Great War and Modern Memory*). Elaine Showalter's *Sexual Anarchy* (London: Bloomsbury, 1991) also contains a chapter on war, gender and shell shock.
[3] The Soviet Union can possibly be seen as an exception. The Great War provoked the 1917 Revolution that did away with the Tsarist regime and established a completely new form of society based on claims that many before had dismissed as utopian. However, the ensuing civil war and establishment of a Communist dictatorship of course question the progress possible under that system.

> Died some, pro patria,
> non "dulce" non "et decor"...
> walked eye-deep in hell
> believing old men's lies, then unbelieving
> came home, home to a lie,
> home to many deceits,
> home to old lies and new infamy[.]
> (Pound, *Hugh Selwyn Mauberley*, *Selected Poems* 100)

And indeed the outbreak of the Second World War a mere thirty years after the armistice confirmed that the Great War had not been the war to end all wars people had hopefully assumed it to be.

It is generally agreed that the Second World War further exacerbated the literary tendencies attributed to the first conflict – fragmentation of style, personalities, and time. But the systematic cruelty of Nazi genocide revealed new depths of human brutality and, with the relocation of war through the aeroplane and V2 from the front to the civilian city, the lived experience of the war was markedly different, giving rise to a different kind of literature as well.[4] However, as many of the writers who had addressed the First World War lived through and wrote about the Second (for example, T.S. Eliot's *Four Quartets* were written during the Second World War, and use the imagery of sky warfare and the bombed city), it is easy and to a certain extent useful to group the two wars together in literary-historical terms. Thus the present study will use texts dealing with both wars without trying to distinguish too closely between them; indeed, in the case of the Inklings, it is difficult to know which of the two wars was more influential on their works, as the writers experienced the First World War as active combatants, but many of their most important texts were written during the Second.

The relationship between modernism and war goes beyond mere thematisation of war in modernist writing, for, as Alyson Booth states, "the dislocations of war often figure centrally in modernist form, even when the war itself seems peripheral to modernist content" (4). Both modern war literature and (perhaps in consequence) modernism have in common the central constitutive paradox

---

[4] Adam Piette's study of Second World War writing, *Imagination at War*, claims that the "Second World War, in literary terms, has too often been dismissed as a dry rerun of the first", while actually "this fear of repeating oneself [...] ineluctably alter[ed] the ways the war stories were told" (Piette 2).

that language is seen as incapable of expressing their realities, yet they are driven to utterance by a simultaneous need to express.[5] Paul Fussell states that "the presumed inadequacy of language itself to convey the facts about trench warfare is one of the motifs of all who wrote about the war" (Fussell 170), yet this does not result in silence (which Fussell fails to point out): if all else fails, the inability to speak is thematised, as in the Dadaist Ernst Jandl's poem "Schtzngrmmm", where the word *Schützengraben* (trench) is deprived of its vowels, representing the failure of the word to convey the material reality of the trenches (Jandl, *Gesammelte Werke* 125). The mutilated word, however, gains new symbolic meaning: in its new form it points towards the destructive nature of war itself, thus representing war as a whole and not, as in its complete state, just one standard prop of the war experience (the trench). Jandl also plays with the remaining consonants, reproducing the noises of gunfire and explosions: "t-t-t-t", "grrrmmmmm" (Jandl 125). Rainer Emig states:

> Wenn der zentrale Satz der Kriegsdarstellung "words cannot express" ist, beweist die Paradoxie des Satzes selbst, dass ein Ausbrechen aus der Darstellung nicht möglich ist. […] der Verzicht auf Sprache, das Verstummen und Schweigen, [wird] häufig als einzig adäquate Reaktion auf die gemachten Erlebnisse gesehen […]. Geschwiegen wird aber in den Texten nie. Immer wird selbst das Schweigen noch narrativ vermittelt. Sprache kann sich nicht ungesprochen und ungeschrieben machen. Genauso wenig kann Sinn sich selbst auflösen. Es ist lediglich möglich, die inadäquaten Sprachzeichen mit neuen zu überschreiben und damit ein sprachliches Palimpsest zu erzeugen, das in seinen Schichten selbst quasi mimetisch den Kampf darstellt, der Auslöser dieser Sinnoperation ist. (Emig, *Krieg* 46)[6]

Modernism is thus dependent on war for creating the inability to speak that it paradoxically needs to constitute its own fragmented language.

Similarly, modernism's obsession with history and new beginnings needs war as the destructive force generating the *tabula rasa* upon which it can create itself,

---

[5] Margot Norris writes of "literature's participation in the deadly combination of the inability to speak and the necessity to speak that lies at the heart of the cruel therapeutic paradox that makes resistance to healing one of war's most painful legacies" (Norris 507).
[6] Translation: 'If the central statement of war representation is "words cannot express", the paradox of the sentence itself demonstrates that there is no escape from expression. Giving up language, falling silent, is often seen as the only adequate reaction to the experience. But the texts themselves are never silent. They still always *narrate* silence. Language cannot un-speak and un-write itself. Similarly, meaning cannot dissolve itself. It is only possible to write new linguistic signs over the inadequate old ones, creating a palimpsest in language that in its various layers mimetically represents the battle that set off this operation of meaning in the first place.' (emphasis added)

and it depends on war's shattering of constructs of meaning and reality so it can replace them with its own constructs. The texts of modernism attempt to close war off – to place it "In Parenthesis" (to quote the title of David Jones's war epic) – through mythic containment and to rewrite it as part of the modernist historical project.[7] Yet the omnipresence of war in the texts of modernism reflects not only the conditions under which they were produced, but also the nature of war itself as "uncontrollable and uncontainable" (Norris 506). Modernism's central concern with form and closure is, among other things, a reflection of war's "problematic of closure" (Norris 506). Modernism resorts to war as a way of resolving its central problems of unifying plot, narrative, and form – for war offers the possibility of finally resolving all these problems of unity and closure through the apocalypse (cf. Emig, *Krieg* 315). However, war cannot be appropriated and closed so easily, and modernism's appropriation of war as an aesthetic tool means it is ultimately dependent on it for its existence:

> Krieg als Klammer der Moderne repräsentiert deshalb die widersprüchliche Ästhetik der Moderne. Er steht für die Ästhetik der Absenz und des Verlusts. Gleichzeitig ermöglicht er aber auch dieser Ästhetik des Verschwindens die Erschaffung von paradoxer Kontinuität und Präsenz. Er schafft Geschlossenheit durch Apokalypse, Form durch Zerstörung und Kunstwerke aus Fragmenten. Man kann dies als Triumph der Moderne über den Krieg lesen. Man kann es auch als Bankrotterklärung der Moderne vor dem Krieg verstehen, einer Moderne, die sich selbst beständig in den Krieg investieren muss, um bestehen zu können. (Emig, *Krieg* 316)[8]

If war is, as cited above, "the continued experience of twentieth-century man", then it is never really over; this applies both to the perceived endlessness and close proximity of two World Wars, and the trauma that continues to affect those who have lived through war even after fighting has come to an end. Modernist texts' fragmented form and their references back to mythic wars suggest that war cannot be closed off; it is omnipresent, and the texts' vexed

---

7 Various modernists appropriate the Great War as abolishing history, thus becoming the starting-point of a new culture without history (e.g. Wyndham Lewis), as a catastrophe that has finally ruined Western culture and that can only be transcended by art (e.g. Pound), and as the fulfilment of a cyclical history of violence (e.g. Yeats).
8 Translation: 'War as modernism's parenthesis represents modernism's paradoxical aesthetics. It represents an aesthetic of absence and loss. Simultaneously it makes possible the creation of paradoxical continuity and presence for this aesthetic of disappearance. It creates closure through the apocalypse, form through destruction and art from fragments. One can read this as modernism's triumph over war. But one can also read it as modernism's declaration of bankruptcy in the face of war, a modernism that itself must constantly invest in war in order to exist at all.'

relationship to historical reality becomes especially clear in their relationship to the modern wars they seek to appropriate and contain.

Modernism's strategies of appropriation and containment – which will be addressed in greater detail in the example of Jones's *In Parenthesis* – raise the question of ethics and responsibility in the relationship between modernism and its wars. Modernism's use of war to create a *tabula rasa* or to create artistic closure reveals its potential nihilism, as Emig points out:

> Indem sie Krieg zu ihrem Geburtshelfer wie zu ihrem Totengräber macht, läuft die Moderne Gefahr, eine Ästhetik des Todes und der Zerstörung zu produzieren. Anstatt ihr Material (Krieg eingeschlossen) zu kontrollieren, was die Moderne anstrebt, wird sie selbst fatal von diesem Material bestimmt. "Die Rache des Objekts" nennt Jean Baudrillard die Attacke der Dingwelt auf das sich allmächtig glaubende Subjekt, das so schmerzhaft an seinen eigenen Objektstatus, seine Konstruiertheit und Historizität erinnert wird [cf. Baudrillard, *Fatal Strategies* 99]. Im Falle der offensichtlich konstruierten und synthetischen Subjektivität der Moderne stößt diese Rache das moderne Kunstwerk von seinem Sockel. Es zeigt es als potentiell nihilistisch und gefährlich. (Emig, *Krieg* 316)[9]

Ultimately, modernism's utilisation of war – to whatever end – involves complicity in its atrocities; seeking to transcend this complicity through myth, symbolism and the cosmic models of the self-contained artwork implies a denial of responsibility. Margot Norris comments on this ethical dimension of war literature when she claims that "literary modernism could maintain no innocence in the face of its ensuing wars" (Norris 509).

One central feature of (modernist) literature dealing with war is that it thematises disappearance and absence. Language breaks down and disappears into silence; the human body is destroyed – literally fragmented – and becomes the

---

9 Translation: 'Modernism, in making war both its midwife and its gravedigger, is in danger of producing an aesthetic of death and destruction. Instead of controlling its material (including war), which is what modernism aims at doing, it is itself fatally controlled by this material. "The revenge of the object" is what Jean Baudrillard calls this assault of the world of things on the supposedly all-powerful subject, which is thus painfully reminded of its own object status, its constructedness and historicity. In the case of the obviously constructed and synthetic subjectivity of modernism this revenge topples the modern work of art from its pedestal. It is revealed to be nihilistic and dangerous.'

corpse;[10] countries and the borders between them shift and vanish; meaning itself is questioned and destroyed in the horror of the war experience. However, as Rainer Emig claims as one of his central theses in *Krieg als Metapher*, the apparent disappearance in war of signs, meaning and language is not really a disappearance, but a transformation (cf. Emig, *Krieg* 47, 324). The literary work may thematise silence and the breakdown of language, as we have seen earlier, but through this it gains new forms and modes of expression – fragmented ones, it may be, but still valid. The meaning of words can fail, but through that very failure they are charged with new, symbolic meaning. This idea of war's transformations is of particular interest when we turn to fantastic literary texts. For while Tolkien, Lewis and Williams do not address their war experiences realistically in their fiction, Lewis even repeatedly stressing the "unreality" of it all, war dominates their literary output. If the experience of war is central in the shattering of a consistent primary reality, if war cannot be contained and given meaning through realism, that reality can be transformed into that of a secondary world – a secondary world in which wars feature but can (supposedly) be controlled. The historical war as a historical event has disappeared from the Inklings' texts, but is transformed into the fantastic conflicts of Tolkien's War of the Ring, Lewis's Last Battle, and Williams's War in Heaven. Thus fantastic texts repeat the modernist strategy of attempting to contain war by appropriating it for their own versions of history and ideology.

Fantasy and War

In *The Great War and Modern Memory*, Paul Fussell claims that "the drift of modern history domesticates the fantastic and normalizes the unspeakable. And the catastrophe that begins it is the First World War" (Fussell 74). This statement once again cites the centrality of the War in changing perceptions of reality in the modern age, and confirms the War as a significant factor in modernism's turning away from the conventions of realism towards ironic, subjective and

---

10 Alyson Booth's *Postcards from the Trenches* devotes an entire section to the problem of the corpse in the First World War: corpses that symbolise both presence and absence, the horrible presence of the dead at the Front and their absence at home (the Government forbade both photographs of dead soldiers and the return of their bodies for home burial). This problem will be returned to at a later point in the chapter.

fragmented modes of writing. However, it also introduces another term: that of the fantastic. The First World War was so far removed from the previous lives and experiences of those fighting that it appeared unreal. If one way of describing the war was through conventional literary models (if only to ironise and debunk them), and another was to thematise the very inexpressibility of the war experience, another was to utilise its unreality and reconstruct the war as a fantastic and supernatural experience. Thus Paul Goetsch states that to "articulate [the war's] incredibility, some English poets [...] tapped the tradition of fantastic literature. The fantastic mode enabled them to deal with the monstrous and absurd dimension of their experience" (Goetsch 125). In spite of many flaws in Goetsch's argument,[11] the claim that coherent reality breaks down in the face of war is undisputed, and that the one way of making sense of its fragments is to ascribe supernatural, magical properties to them is borne out in many texts (one example which will be examined below is David Jones's *In Parenthesis*). What then of war and fantasy texts that inhabit a fully-fledged secondary world?

G.K. Chesterton, writing before the First World War, states that "fairyland [is] at once a world of wonder and of war" (Chesterton 258). This implies that the war is a constitutive factor of fantastic worlds. In her study of Tolkien, *A Question of Time*, Verlyn Flieger draws some convincing parallels between these worlds and war:

> In the way that extremes can sometimes meet, War and Faërie have a certain resemblance to one another. Both are set beyond the reach of ordinary human experience. Both are equally indifferent to the needs of ordinary humanity. Both can change those who return [...] Perhaps worst of all, both War and

---

11 Goetsch's argument remains unsatisfactory not the least because he himself leads it ad absurdum with his final statements that the poets "made sparing use of the fantastic" and their "'compassionate realism' [...] set limits to the fantastic" (139). He uses Rosemary Jackson's theory of the fantastic and its dissolution of time, space and character, but seems unaware of Todorov's theories (on which Jackson bases her claims) that see poetry as by its very nature opposed to the fantastic (cf. Todorov, *The Fantastic* 60). For poetry – especially the shorter poems Goetsch uses – is itself not a realistic genre; thus applying essentially narrative concepts of time, space and character to it must be of limited use and certainly cannot be used to declare a poem fantastic in the Jackson and Todorov sense of the term. The fantastic depends on hesitation between the natural and supernatural: in many of the examples Goetsch cites, the supernatural elements are metaphors and poetic images (thus tanks are described as monsters), and the reader does not stop to wonder whether Flanders fields are really being invaded by supernatural monsters. Thus Goetsch's argument should really have been that the poets make use of fantastic imagery, not that they actually write in the fantastic mode.

> Faërie can change out of all recognition the wanderer's perception of the world to which he returns, so that never again can it be what it once was. (224)

The fact that war features so prominently in the fantasy of the Inklings and that of other writers of their time has been remarked on by several critics. For example, Tom Shippey in *Tolkien: Author of the Century* comments on the problem of evil that is thematised by "authors of the mid-twentieth century" (119) and concludes that this is due to "the distinctively twentieth-century experience of industrial war and impersonal, industrialised massacre; and it is probably no coincidence that most of the authors [...] were combat veterans of one war or other" (120). Shippey mentions Tolkien, Lewis, T.H. White, Vonnegut and Orwell, a group he elsewhere calls "post-war [World War II] writers" (cf. Shippey, "Tolkien as a Post-War Writer"); however, war is also central in earlier fantasy such as E.R. Eddison's *The Worm Ouroboros*, published four years after the First World War in modernism's *annus mirabilis* 1922. In this work, set on the planet Mercury, the kingdom of Witchland launches a war for total domination against the rest of the planet; they are chiefly opposed by the valiant Demons of Demonland, who achieve the final victory. Yet the Worm Ouroboros, a serpent with its tail in its mouth, the symbol of infinity and of Witchland, shows that war will never be over and the last paragraph of the book sees an ambassador from Witchland returning to the Demons who had thought that kingdom ended for ever.[12] This perception of war as neverending is one typical of the First World War experience, as described by Fussell: "the idea of endless war as an inevitable condition of modern life would seem to have become seriously available to the imagination around 1916" (Fussell 74). Another early fantasy classic that emphasises this even more strongly is Lord Dunsany's *Don Rodriguez: Chronicles of Shadow Valley*, published in the same year 1922. Don Rodriguez, travelling through a fantastic version of "the later years of the Golden Years of Spain" (11), comes to a castle where he looks through a magic window, and there sees the history of the world pass in war after war, from antiquity up to modern mechanical warfare:

---

12 Ironically, the Demons, after vanquishing Witchland, become so bored of life without conflict that they wish their old enemy would return: "Would [the Gods] might give us our good gift, that should be youth for ever, and war; and unwaning strength and skill in arms. Would they might but give us our great enemies alive and whole again" (Eddison 504). This can be read as reinforcing ancient heroic models, or, of course, as man's natural lust for death and destruction.

> Rodriguez saw man make a new ally, an ally who was only cruel and strong and had no purpose but killing, who had no pretences or pose, no mask and no manner, but was only the slave of Death and had no care but for his business. He saw it grow bigger and stronger. Heart it had none, but he saw its cold steel core scheming methodical plans and dreaming always destruction. Before it faded men and their fields and their houses. [...] In all the wars beyond that twinkling window he saw the machine spare nothing. [...] Rodriguez lifted his eyes and glanced from city to city, to Albert, Bapaume, and Arras, his gaze moved over a plain with its harvest of desolation lying forlorn and ungathered, lit by the flashing clouds and the moon and peering rockets. He turned from the window and wept. (59-60)

We can see that fantasy responds to the potential for total annihilation in modern warfare as much as more realistic literature does.[13]

The centrality of war – especially of total, apocalyptic war – in fantasy can thus be linked historically to the experience of modern warfare. Indeed, it can be claimed that it is war that generates fantasy in the first place, just as it generates (or at least reinforces) modernism. The fragmentation of reality caused by war necessitates the retreat into the coherent reality of a secondary world. Perhaps fantasy represents one of war's greatest transformations – that of primary reality, through its fragmentation and disappearance – into a secondary one.

In this secondary world, war can – supposedly at least – be contained and used for the subcreator's purposes. The return in much fantasy to older, heroic forms of battle – face-to-face combat, duelling, weapons such as arrows, swords and protective gear such as body armour and shields – represents an escape from the horrors of modern warfare to a form of conflict to which meaning and value could still be applied.[14] The fact that most fantasy also deals with an overtly black-and-white view of war, with one side definitely evil and the other more or less good, also shows the longing for a clear-cut separation between friend and

---

13 Dunsany remained concerned with the problems of war throughout his life. In 1945 he published a collection of essays commenting among other things on the dropping of the atomic bomb: "I think that a new era started yesterday ... henceforth we are all people with a mission, a strange mission, not to destroy the world" (cit. Bloom 57).
14 The term "escape" is defined (positively) by Tolkien in his essay "On Fairy-stories", and used in reference to war in several letters; for example: "I took to 'escapism': or really transforming experience into another form and symbol with Morgoth and the Orcs and the Eldalie" (*Letters* 85). This move towards mediaevalism also echoes the fantasies of William Morris.

foe.[15] However, in ways similar to modernist works, war in fantasy also figures as a means of structure, as central to historical cycles, and – in its apocalyptic shape – as making all things new, erasing the past and enabling a fresh start. Tolkien's mythology of Middle-earth, for example, structures Middle-earth's history entirely around great wars and battles. In *The Silmarillion*, the five great battles of elves and men against Morgoth culminate in the War of Wrath that ends the First Age. The Second Age is marked by the fall of Númenor in an attempted war against the Valar, and ends in the first war against Sauron, the Last Alliance. The Third Age ends with the War of the Ring. War is central to these historical cycles of conflict and is used by Tolkien to structure Middle-earth's history and mythology. Yet this means that at the same time, Middle-earth needs war to function as a coherent secondary world and is thus dependent on it – Middle-earth without war is (literally) unimaginable. War is, besides structure, also the driving dynamic force behind the plots of the *Silmarillion* myths and *The Lord of the Rings*: without conflict Middle-earth would be static, so that conflict must be introduced from the start. This is also the case in Lewis's *Chronicles of Narnia*. Here we can perceive the incontainability of war noted above: it cannot be restricted, and used to structure a world and create a plot it ultimately determines the material of that world. Here an interesting paradox becomes apparent: fantasy texts fear (war's) fragmentation and the modern acceleration of reality, retreating into a secondary world in order to preserve coherence, but they obviously also fear stagnation, and thus resort to the dynamics unleashed by war.

Another work where the incontainability of war becomes abundantly clear, and where the relation to the "real" wars of this earth is more problematic, is Lewis's space trilogy, written and set during the Second World War. In these novels the Second World War is put in relation to a greater cosmic struggle of good against evil, and this conflict becomes but "our own little war here on earth" (*Perelandra* 19), apparently easily subsumed under the greater war in heaven. Yet the trilogy's protagonist Ransom, a veteran of the trenches, can only make sense of all this and give the cosmic struggle meaning for himself (and thus, of course, Lewis's

---

15 Of course, this is an over-simplified statement; *The Lord of the Rings*, for example, makes it very clear that enemies are to be found everywhere, even within the heroic Fellowship of the Ring. Similarly, Lewis's *The Lion, the Witch and the Wardrobe* sees the Pevensie children betrayed by their own brother.

readers) by using the terminology of terrestrial warfare and relating it to the wars he has himself experienced, for example calling the earth "a kind of Ypres Salient in the universe" (*Silent Planet* 184). The language of the World Wars has invaded outer space. Thus we can see that, while war is used as a strategy by these writers to structure their works, it simultaneously creates a state of dependence on itself, in a way very similar to the way war functions in modernist works. This fact has hitherto remained unnoted by critics of fantasy and the Inklings. The name "Ransom" (which is also used by W.H. Auden in his *Ascent of F6* of 1936) shows an awareness that humanity is entrapped by war; both in the space trilogy, in Lewis's Narnia stories and Tolkien's *The Lord of the Rings* the protagonists feel tragically bound to war. Tolkien's Faramir probably expresses this most succinctly when he states: "War must be, while we defend our lives against a destroyer that would devour all; but I do not love the bright sword for its sharpness, nor the arrow for its swiftness, nor the warior for his glory. I love only that which they defend: the city of the Men of Númenor" (*LotR* 656). Thus we can perceive that even texts that appear to use war nostalgically are aware of war's problematics.

There is some scholarship dedicated to the Inklings and war. Much of this criticism links the writings of the Inklings to war biographically, tracing the writers' experience of the two World Wars and seeking to find parallels to that experience in their work. While the importance of these war experiences is undeniable and the traces of it are plainly to be found, the fact remains that the wars in the literary works (with the exception of Lewis's space trilogy, as seen above) are *not* either of the World Wars; thus comparing them to those wars, while inevitable, must form a somewhat one-sided approach. It is surprising that most criticism, while frequently citing Tolkien's injunction that his *The Lord of the Rings* should not be read primarily as a comment on the World Wars (and World War II in particular), proceeds to do precisely that, asking how aspects of the wars reappear in altered form in his works. A recent example of this approach is Janet Brennan Croft's *War and the Works of J.R.R. Tolkien*. Croft carefully and convincingly traces World War I and World War II themes in Tolkien's work, examines examples of military leadership in it and measures the texts against Tolkien's own views on war. However, she entirely neglects to ask what textual function war itself plays in Tolkien's novels and his mythology as a whole when the works are taken for themselves, without relation to their concrete historical background. That war ultimately is used as a way of ordering history and achieving textual closure is not perceived.[16]

The present study approaches war in the works of the Inklings from a different angle, and will, it is to be hoped, go some way towards redressing the lack of study of war's function in their texts. Before embarking on a close examination of a particular body of texts – Williams's Arthurian poetry cycles – and a comparison of these to the central modernist "war epic", David Jones's *In Parenthesis* – a short return to the biographies of the writers is necessary, and the centrality of the personal war experience in all three authors' turn towards fantasy as a form of expression will be addressed.

The Inklings at War

"[The Great War] is too cut off from the rest of my experience and often seems to have happened to someone else. It is even in a way unimportant" (*Joy* 157) wrote C.S. Lewis of the unreality, in retrospect, of his year in the trenches. He chooses to write little of it, stating that everything has already been said and described before by others, and what little he does write rehearses the standard tales of trench experience: the cameraderie in his "very nice battalion" (*Joy* 155), the weariness and wet, the "horribly smashed men still moving like half-crushed beetles" (*Joy* 157). The detachment he feels from the experience is emphasised by the fact he chooses to narrate it in the impersonal mode: "One walked in the trenches in thigh gum boots with water above the knee; one remembers the icy stream welling up inside the boot when you punctured it on concealed barb wire" (*Joy* 157). Only one moment is singled out by him as significant:

> It was the first bullet I heard – so far from me that it "whined" like a journalist's or a peacetime poet's bullet. At that moment there was something not exactly like fear, much less like indifference: a little quavering signal that said, "This is War. This is what Homer wrote about." (*Joy* 158)

---

16 Croft's study also suffers from the fact that she takes her themes entirely from Paul Fussell's *The Great War and Modern Memory* and its follow-up *Wartime: Understanding and Behaviour in the Second World War*. It has already been mentioned above that Fussell's studies are biased in that they privilege male, combatant viewpoints and analyse war purely in binary terms of oppositional forces. More recent studies of war literature, while they acknowledge the importance of Fussell's work, are critical of these aspects of it. Croft uncritically lifts Fussell's themes without explaining why she privileges his approach over that of other critics or taking account of the criticism that has been directed at it.

Using literary models to make sense of war's confusion was of course a stock response during the Great War; writing about it was another. Lewis's first publication, a collection of poems called *Spirits in Bondage*, came out just one year after the end of the War. Writing to his father he states that some of these poems were actually written in the trenches and in field hospital: "You are aware that for some years now I have amused myself by writing verses, and that a pocket-book of these followed me through France" (*Letters* 45). However, only a few of the poems make direct reference to the War;[17] this paucity has led biographers to ask "Why did he write almost nothing about the war?" (Sayer 86), and although Chad Walsh claims with surprising confidence that Lewis "was, of course, literally a war poet" (Walsh 37) he is forced to admit that "the wonder is not that he writes about war, but that he writes about it so rarely" (37). One of the reasons for this may be, as Sayer suggests, "that he felt it too strongly, so strongly he could not bear to recall it" (Sayer 86). However the emphasis Lewis puts on the unreality of his war experience might point in another direction. The significance he gives to that "one *imaginative* moment" of hearing the bullet whine, that "seems [...] to matter more than the *realities* that followed" (157-158; my emphases), seems almost to deny the importance of the war's reality altogether – in fact war becomes, as noted above, an imaginative, fantastic experience. The central theme of *Spirits in Bondage* is that of escape from the real world to "lands unknown, [...] the Hidden country fresh and full of quiet green" – a pastoral image typical of many war poems, with the exception that this is no Home County scene, it can only be reached by "Sailing over seas uncharted to a port that none has seen" ("Prologue" *Spirits in Bondage*, cit. Walsh 36). The fantastic reality of the trenches gives rise to fantastic modes of writing; hence the lack of realistic war poems in Lewis's work. However, the central position of war in Lewis's space romances and the Narnia stories would suggest that the war experience was, after all, one that left a significant mark on Lewis. It was only that he chose to narrate it through fantasy rather than realism.[18]

---

17 One of these poems, "Death in Battle", was published on the recommendation of John Drinkwater in Galsworthy's war periodical *Reveille* (1919), and has been called "deserving of inclusion in any anthology of Great War poems" (Sayer 81).
18 One wonders whether passages like the following from *Out of the Silent Planet* are autobiographical: "the gap between boyhood's dreams and [Ransom's] actual experience of the War had been startling, and his subsequent view of his own unheroic qualities had perhaps swung too far in the opposite direction" (40-41).

What certainly left a lasting mark on Lewis was his experience of his partner Janie Moore's brother and his mental illness caused by the war. Lewis wrote to his friend Arthur Greeves:

> We have been through very deep waters. Mrs Moore's brother – the Doc – came here and had a sudden attack of war neurasthenia. [...] Anyone who didn't know would have mistaken it for lunacy – we did at first: he had horrible maniacal fits – had to be held down. We were up two whole nights at the beginning and two, three or four times a night afterwards, all the time. You have no idea what it is like. He had the delusion that he was going to Hell. Can you imagine what he went through and what we went through? [...] We hold our mental health by a thread: & nothing is worth risking it for. [...] Isn't it a damned world – and we thought we could once be happy with books and music! (Lewis, *They Stand Together* 292-293)

Lewis deals with this topic of war neurosis in his unfinished "Belfast" novel, but hints of it are also to be found in the space trilogy.

That the Great War was a catalyst not just for literary modernism, but for fantasy as well, is borne out further by J.R.R. Tolkien. Tolkien fought on the Somme, in what he called the "animal horror" (Tolkien, *Letters* 72) of the trenches. Miraculously, Tolkien was not wounded, but at the end of October 1916 he was taken severely ill with trench fever – so ill, in fact, that he was sent back to England to recover in military hospital. He hints at the unforgotten horror of his war experiences in the Foreword to *The Lord of the Rings*:

> One has indeed personally to come under the shadow of war to feel fully its oppression; but as the years go by it seems now often forgotten that to be caught in youth by 1914 was no less hideous an experience than to be involved in 1939 and the following years. By 1918 all but one of my close friends were dead. (Tolkien, *LotR* xv)[19]

These experiences certainly influenced the invention of his fantastic secondary world. He first began inventing the "nonsense fairy language" (Tolkien, *Letters* 8) that was to become Quenya, or High Elvish, as early as 1912, but it was during his time in the army that his serious work on it took place:

---

19 It is the wish expressed by one of these fallen friends, "may you say the things I have tried to say long after I am not there to say them, if such be my lot", that Humphrey Carpenter sees as the decisive motivation behind Tolkien's starting to write his mythology (cf. Carpenter, *Tolkien* 94-97). For a more detailed study of his friends' influence on Tolkien's mythology, the significance of the War and their deaths, cf. John Garth's *Tolkien and the Great War*.

> Lots of the early part of [the mythology] (and the languages) – discarded or absorbed – were done in grimy canteens, at lectures in cold fogs, in huts full of blasphemy and smut, or by candle light in bell tents, even some down in dugouts under shell fire. (78)[20]

That this creative work was triggered by the war and the desire "to rationalize it, and prevent it just festering" (78) is admitted by Tolkien in the same letter. Yet, as in the case of Lewis, the War cannot be addressed realistically: it is the fantastic mode that Tolkien needs to express himself: "A real taste for fairy-stories was wakened by philology on the threshold of manhood, and quickened to full life by war" (Tolkien, "On Fairy-stories" 135). Another interesting fact that may be linked to the War is that Tolkien, who was an excellent artist as well as a writer, gave up sketches and paintings from real scenes and of real people almost completely after his return from France:

> In fact since 1918, almost all of Tolkien's art was related to the fantasy writings that increasingly occupied his thoughts. Only rarely in later years did he draw from nature. He seems largely to have lost interest in doing so, preferring his invented landscapes. (Hammond and Scull 31)

In this, Tolkien shows an interesting biographical parallel to David Jones, whose drawings also become surreal palimpsests after his war experiences.

Some of Tolkien's fantasy is unmistakably the product of his service in the trenches. "The Dead Marshes and the Morannon owe something to Northern France after the Battle of the Somme" (Tolkien, *Letters* 303), he stated, and C.S. Lewis declared that

> His war has the very quality of war my generation knew. It is all here: the endless, unintelligible movement, the sinister quiet of the front when 'everything is now ready', the flying civilians, the lively, vivid friendships, the background of something like despair and the merry foreground, and such heaven-sent windfalls as a cache of tobacco 'salvaged' from ruin.
> (Lewis, "Dethronement of Power" in Isaacs and Zimbardo, *Tolkien and the Critics* 14)

It is features such as these that lead critics to state that "the Great War played an essential role in shaping Middle-earth" (Garth xv) and indeed to see *The*

---

20 Rather confusingly, Tolkien actually denied this in a 1967 interview: "That's all spoof. You might scribble something on the back of an envelope and shove it in your back pocket, but that's all. You couldn't write" (Croft 15).

Lord of the Rings "in certain respects as the last work of First World War literature, published almost forty years after the war ended" (Rosebury, *Critical Assessment* 126).

Charles Williams did not fight in the First World War, having been declared unfit; instead he became involved in civilian war work. The War completely disrupted his personal life, and he lost – as did most civilians – some of his closest friends. At first, the experience was crippling: "I have wanted so much and so long to write a poem: but one can't, somehow" (letter to Alice Meynell; cit. Hadfield 23). The death of his friends was especially terrible as Williams's unconventional ideas of the simultaneity of time and the ubiquity of space made it impossible for him to "feel that their deaths were something which had happened elsewhere and in the past, and were now over. To him the whole thing was constantly happening" (Carpenter, *Inklings* 85). Strange people passing on the street echoed their marching footsteps; the clink of cups at breakfast was underlaid with their "Crying for drink in No Man's Land" (Williams, "In Absence" *Divorce* 16). This feeling of the omnipresence, at all times, of the horrors of the War and the intense guilt he felt that others should have fought and died in order to keep him safe, deeply influenced his thought and his writings, if only to bring to the fore concerns and interests that he had had before. The incredible nature of the War reinforced Williams's belief that there is only a thin barrier between the natural and supernatural worlds, and that the incredible and fantastic can at any moment break through into our everyday lives. Thus in his writings from the war and postwar years, the fantastic takes on an increasingly prominent role. It is also in the 1917 collection *Poems of Conformity*, that contains some war poems, that the first poems dealing with the Arthurian legends and the Grail are printed. The later collection *Divorce* contains a set of six poems called "In Time of War", dealing with aspects of the war experience. As in the cases of Lewis and Tolkien, the Great War is related to fantastic, almost mythical warfare. For example, the third poem, "On the Way to Somerset", relates the War in France to "Wantage [...], with her battles all of faery, / Kings half-divine who dammed the sea-swept hordes" (*Divorce* 15).

The Second World War was greeted with disbelief and despair by the writers. Lewis wrote to his brother:

> I quite agree that one of the worst features of this war is the spectral feeling of all having happened before. As Dyson [another of the Inklings] said, 'When you read the headlines (French advance – British steamship sunk) you feel as if you'd had a delightful dream during the last war and woken up to find it still going on. (Lewis, *Letters* 169)

The war was even worse for Tolkien, whose three sons were all called up.[21] "One War is enough for any man", he wrote, "[e]ither the bitterness of youth or of middle-age is enough for a life-time: both is too much" (*Letters* 54). For Williams, having to leave London – his Heavenly City – was bitter; its destruction through the German air raids was deeply painful to him. "When I had your letter this morning *and* was thinking of A.H. [Amen House, the seat of Oxford University Press in London] being no more, I very nearly broke down altogether. It wasn't only A.H.; it was all my poor loved City!" he wrote to his wife (Carpenter, *Inklings* 178). But for all this sorrow over London burning, it was because of the London air raids that Oxford University Press relocated, bringing Charles Williams to Oxford and into the weekly meetings of the Inklings circle. And in spite of all the personal sadness and inconvenience caused by the War, it was through it that Lewis, Tolkien and Williams were thrown together and it was during the war years, inspired by their mutual encouragement, that some of their most important work was written. Lewis spoke truer than he knew (at that point) when he wrote to his brother in 1939, "along with [the] not very pleasant indirect results of the war, there is *one pure gift* – the London branch of the Oxford University Press has moved to Oxford, so that Charles Williams is living here" (Lewis, *Letters* 168; my emphasis). The cross-influences of the writers upon each other are well documented in Humphrey Carpenter's study *The Inklings*, and there is no need to elaborate further on them here; it should however be kept in mind that all their discussions on fantasy and their works written at the time – Tolkien's *The Lord of the Rings*, Williams's *The Region of the Summer Stars*, *Arthurian Torso* and *All Hallow's Eve*, Lewis's *The Great Divorce* and the space trilogy – were written under the shadow of war. If it was the First World War that drove them to fantasy in the first place, the Second confirmed the importance of war for their theories and practice.

---

21 Janet Brennan Croft relates this personal experience of fatherhood during wartime to *The Lord of the Rings* characters Théoden and Denethor, who both lose a son (and heir) during the War of the Ring. Thankfully all of Tolkien's sons survived.

Charles Williams, David Jones and the Matter of Britain

David Jones's *In Parenthesis*, long on the margins of the modernist canon, is now regarded as one of the central texts of modernism dealing with the First World War. Jones, described by T.S. Eliot as "a Londoner of Welsh and English descent [and] decidedly a Briton" (Eliot, Introduction to *In Parenthesis* vii), served in France from 1915 to 1918, and his experiences in the trenches are addressed in *In Parenthesis*, written after the War and published in 1937. Jones writes in his Preface to the work:

> This writing has to do with some things I saw, felt & was part of. The period covered begins early in December 1915 and ends early in July 1916. The first date corresponds to my going to France. The latter roughly marks a change in the character of our lives in the Infantry on the West Front. From then onward things hardened into a more relentless, mechanical affair, took on a more sinister aspect. (*In Parenthesis* ix)

The form of Jones's work is controversial: neither wholly poetry nor wholly prose, it is sometimes called an epic or a book, but its author preferred to call it and his other main work, *The Anathemata*, simply a "writing" (cf. Jones, *Epoch and Artist* 30). It is essentially modernist in style, and Eliot accordingly noted that the "work of David Jones has some affinity with that of James Joyce (both men seem to have the Celtic ear for the music of words) and with the later work of Ezra Pound, and with my own" (Eliot, Introduction to *In Parenthesis* viii). Jones works, as these writers do, with fragments rather than a coherent, linear structure, with changing centres of consciousness rather than a traditional narrator, with myths, and with a non-linear concept of time stressing contemporaneity of different ages and flashes of experience and epiphany. In typically modernist fashion, *In Parenthesis* layers the First World War up against the tales of King Arthur and his Round Table, against old Welsh epic and the Song of Roland, to name some of the most common points of reference. Myth and epic are used to structure the work, give meaning to the events described, and through their intertextuality give a frame within which those events are to be interpreted. For example, the writing is divided into seven parts, each of which is preceded by a quote from the Welsh epic poem *Y Gododdin*, whose tale of tragic slaughter forms one of the several background layers of *In Parenthesis*. Like Eliot's *The Waste Land*, *In Parenthesis* uses a system of footnotes to (supposedly) elucidate the mass of its quotes and allusions; as W.H. Auden notes, "fully to appreciate his epic calls for a fairly thorough knowledge of Malory, *The Mabinogion*, *Y Gododdin* and the Offices of the Catholic Church" (Auden, "On *In Parenthesis*, On *The Anathemata*" 45). Auden here mentions the two central background areas that will be of interest to the present study: the Arthurian myth, particularly in its Malorian version, and old Celtic – particularly Welsh – epic.

Charles Williams first started writing poetry on the Arthurian theme during the First World War. He developed his own highly idiosyncratic take on the myth of Arthur in two cycles of poems, *Taliessin through Logres* (published in 1938) and *The Region of the Summer Stars* (1944). He also began writing a history of the development of the Arthurian myth which was left incomplete at his death, and was later published together with a study of Williams's poetry by C.S. Lewis as *Arthurian Torso*[22] in 1948. As in the case of Jones, Williams works with a large number of source texts to which he alludes or (more seldom) which he quotes directly; Lewis notes that Williams "assumes you know the Bible, Malory, and Wordsworth pretty well, and that you have at least some knowledge of Milton, Dante, Gibbon, the *Mabinogion*, and Church history" (Lewis, *Arthurian Torso* 189). The influence of Malory and of Celtic literature is again central. The poems are, in form, unmistakeably modern; Gisbert Kranz mentions the influence of Gerard Manley Hopkins's sprung rhythms, alongside other characteristics such as a highly idiosyncratic metaphoric and symbolic system, dialectic structures, irony, and a high degree of self-reflexivity (Kranz, *Arthur-Gedichte* 13). In addition to this, Williams's two cycles are not arranged as a linear narrative, neither within each cycle nor in relation to each other; Williams assumes the reader can him- or herself fill in the gaps in the story between them.[23] It was not the poet's aim to provide yet another retelling of the legend, as he himself wrote in the original blurb: "The poems do not so much tell a story or describe a process as express states or principles of experience" (cit. Ridler lxiv). Williams uses the Arthurian myth as an expression of his own personal philosophy and theology: thus Arthur's Logres becomes the "head" of

---

22 When citing this work, quotes from Williams's section will be referred to as "Williams, *Arthurian Torso*" and Lewis's sections as "Lewis, *Arthurian Torso*".
23 There has been some controversy as to how far this lack of narrative cohesion was actually intended by Williams, or whether it was due to the exigencies of publishing. The opinions of C.S. Lewis, Cavaliero, Moorman, and Hadfield are summarized by David Llewellyn Dodds in his "Introduction to Charles Williams." *Arthurian Studies* XXIV (3). Recent scholarship tends to read the two cycles as "distinct, deliberately-arranged wholes" (Dodds 3).

the symbolic order of the body of the Byzantine Empire, the figures of Taliessin and Lancelot exemplify the Areopagite's Way of Affirmation and Dindrane the Way of Rejection, and Arthur himself shows the failure of worldly power that comes about through excessive self-love (symbolically represented by his incest with Morgause). The two cycles' central character, the Welsh bard Taliessin, expresses Williams's ideals of poetry and the poet.[24] While Williams's cycles do not focus exclusively on war, some poems such as "Mount Badon" (*TTL*) thematise Arthur's battles and debate the various ideals of heroism represented by the king and his knights. The final poems of each cycle, "The Last Voyage", "Taliessin at Lancelot's Mass" (*TTL*) and "The Prayers of the Pope" (*RSS*) deal with the disintegration of Arthur's kingdom of Logres and his final defeat at Camlaan, with particular reference to the War going on at their time of writing: "'The Prayers of the Pope' is a long poem on the world of Charles's time [and] on the 1939-45 war" (Hadfield 219).

Modernist literature makes extensive use of myth, through which it can give its own fragmented narratives meaning and coherence, and the Arthurian myth was one of its favourites, used most famously (apart from Jones) by Eliot in *The Waste Land*. The Arthurian myth differs from other mythologies (particularly Classical ones) in that it is actually a myth of failure.[25] In it, a threatened culture establishes order and peace for a limited time, but finally falls into ruin through corruption at its own core, leaving it vulnerable and open to its enemies, and ending in total war. Perhaps it is this aspect, rather than the chivalry so beloved of the Victorians, that makes it relevant to twentieth-century writers: it is, as David Jones writes, a myth in which ultimately "the *status quo* is not restored, the wrongs go unrighted, the aggressed are aggressed to extinction, the 'noble fellowship' is dissolved for ever, no recovery at all" (Jones, "The Myth of Arthur" *Epoch and Artist* 258). It is this failure that is taken up by modernist writers, and its contemporary relevance is again pointed out by Jones: "that losing battle, in various forms, continues" ("The Myth of Arthur" 219) – a typically modernist

---

24 For extensive explanations of Williams's personal symbolism and theology, cf. Glen Cavaliero, *Charles Williams: Poet of Theology* (Grand Rapids, Michigan: Eerdmans, 1983), A.M. Hadfield, *Charles Williams: An Exploration of his Life and Work* (New York: Oxford University Press, 1983) and Gavin Ashenden, *Charles Williams: Alchemy and Integration* (Kent, Ohio: Kent State University Press, 2008).
25 Of course, other mythologies, even the Classical ones, can be seen as pessimistic. Norse myth ends in Ragnarök, and one form of Classical myth sees the world as in an eternal decline, from the Golden Age to the Silver etc.

move linking contemporary history and myth. Malory's version of the Arthurian legend must have carried especial resonance for those engaged in the World Wars, for the time of the War of the Roses during which he wrote

> was, as ours threatens to become, one of encampments and distressed and uprooted urban populations thrown back among tribal and enduring rustic communities; the whole unhappy mass being subject to what Mr. Churchill would call the 'swoop and scoop' of military manoeuvre. (Jones, "The Myth of Arthur" 257)

This is one of the reasons why Malory seemed so relevant to both David Jones and Charles Williams, and both refer to him so frequently.

It is not known whether Charles Williams read David Jones's work. Yet some affinities between the two have been noted: in his 1970 M.Litt. thesis *Medievalism in the Works of David Jones and Charles Williams*, Atholl C.C. Murray compares the two,[26] and John Heath-Stubbs writes that "[a]mong Williams's contemporaries, perhaps only David Jones was working a similar seam" (Foreword to *The Rhetoric of Vision* 8). Jones himself was familiar with Williams's Arthurian poetry, and wrote a review of Williams's and Lewis's *Arthurian Torso*, published in *Epoch and Artist* as "The Arthurian Legend". He commends Williams's specifically Christian approach to the myth, stating that he "writes with the understanding of a poet who understands also the Christian religion and its historic ability to absorb, integrate, develop, fulfil" (Jones, "Arthurian Legend" *Epoch and Artist* 203). But matters become more complicated when Jones turns to the subject of myth and history. He prefers Williams's take on the legend to Tennyson's: "one certainly feels that the 'tension' [between original myth and the intentions of the later author] in the case of Williams is, in actual fact, a great deal less" but states that the latter's historical awareness is due to the modern condition: "we have been forced to live history as Tennyson's generation was not" (205). Of course Jones is here referring to the catastrophes of the World Wars. Jones does however state some doubt as to the relevance of Williams's poetry to the present age: "I do not often feel this 'now-ness' in the words and images, or rather, I feel it does not inform and pervade the poems as a whole" (209), though he later admits that "some readers of Charles Williams's poetry

---

26 Murray still sees both writers as very different; his thesis does not really draw any satisfactory conclusions on shared traits, which suggests that his chosen aspect of mediaevalism is not the most fruitful one under which to examine the two.

may nevertheless feel that it is not a quality which that poetry lacks; some may even feel that it excels in this respect" (210). He concludes this paragraph with the interesting statement: "However that may be, it ['now-ness'] is certainly a quality which the Arthurian material particularly requires if we are to escape from something in the nature of fantasy, however intriguing the fantasy" (Jones, "Arthurian Legend" 210).

This statement is one of the keys to understanding the differences between Jones's and Williams's poetry, their different approaches to myth and their different uses of war. Myth is, of course, by its very nature ahistorical. This fact appears to trouble Jones, who demands that "[w]hat the artist lifts up must have some kind of transubstantiated actual-ness. Our images, not only our ideas, must be valid *now*" (Jones, "Arthurian Legend" 210), and that "concept and universality [be] married to the local and the particular" (210). This is what he himself sets out to achieve in *In Parenthesis* by linking the Arthurian myth with the events of the First World War. In a double manoeuver, the use of Arthurian material endows the events of the Great War portrayed in *In Parenthesis* with mythic "universality", and provides the author with a way of (in Eliot's phrasing) "controlling, of ordering, of giving a shape and a significance to the immense panorama of futility and anarchy which is contemporary history" (Eliot, "'Ulysses', Order and Myth", *Selected Prose of T.S. Eliot* 177), the chaos and boundlessness of war. At the same time, the foreground of the Great War justifies the use of myth with its "now-ness", giving the otherwise ahistorical legend of Arthur a "transubstantiated actual-ness". By contrast, the use of the myth without this contemporary slant to it results in fantasy. Jones appears to see fantasy[27] as essentially escapist, unrelated to the issues of its times that the true artist must confront.

Williams's poems, in marked contrast to *In Parenthesis*, work without a concrete historical point of reference and are more difficult to relate to events of the twentieth century. They are set in a mythical and fantastic "Logres", a world that (as is mentioned repeatedly in the poems) is different from historical Britain. It is the disaster at Camlaan that destroys Logres, and creates Britain

---

27 Jones is certainly not using "fantasy" in the way it is defined in the first chapter of the present thesis. However, it is obvious that it is the secondary world status of Logres and its ahistoricity that trouble him, and this ties in with the general definition given.

in the first place: "Logres was withdrawn into Carbonek; it became Britain" ("The Last Voyage", *TTL* 88). In the "Prelude" to *Taliessin through Logres* it is stated explicitly that Logres is outside history and that it is its fall that begins historical time:

> Galahad quickened in the Mercy;
> but history began; the Moslem stormed Byzantium;
> lost was the glory, lost the power and the kingdom.
> (*TTL* 1)

Williams thus uses the Arthurian myth to create a self-sufficient secondary world, which has much in common with the primary one but is nonetheless not identical with it.[28] Logres and the Empire act as a kind of pre-history to our own world much in the way Tolkien's Middle-earth does, offering a mythical explanation of our condition, a kind of parallel to the Fall: because of the failings and sins of Arthur, the Grail could not be brought to Camelot, and the land became spiritually waste – it became historical Britain. It is Williams's use of Logres as a secondary world that marks his poetry as fantasy, and thus Jones's statement about its lack of "now-ness" rings true (though, as Jones himself admits, Williams's poems are not necessarily without contemporary relevance because of this). In contrast to Jones, Williams uses the Arthurian myth not to "order" the primary, but to create a fantastic world distinct from the primary. War appears in his myth as the demarcator between Logres and Britain in the separation of a "before" and "after" Camlaan, as a structuring agent. This again sets his poetry apart from Jones's, who in his mythical superimposition of the figures of Arthurian legend onto the soldiers of the First World War tries to create an identity, through the condition of war, of legend and contemporary history. To a certain extent, their efforts can be read as opposites: Jones uses myth to (try to) contain his war, and Williams uses war to (try to) contain his myth.

However, as stated above, war is not to be contained or used so easily, and the ensuing problems are shared by both Jones's and Williams's works. Williams's use of war to achieve closure is clearly an example of the modernist attempt

---

28 This was also done, more famously, by T.H. White in his tetralogy *The Once and Future King*, published between 1939 and 1958. C.S. Lewis uses Williams's ideas of distinguishing between Britain and Logres in the concluding novel of his space trilogy, *That Hideous Strength*: "something we may call Britain is always haunted by something we may call Logres. Haven't you noticed we are two countries? [...] There has been a secret Logres in the heart of Britain all these years" (Lewis, *That Hideous Strength* 241).

to achieve closure through apocalypse (cf. Emig, *Krieg* 316); the structure of the secondary world Logres is thus dependent on war, and the poetry cycles themselves, with their lack of narrative coherence, depend on Camlaan to bring them to conclusion. And the notion that our history is begun through war and violence implies that war is the normal condition of mankind – a typically modern view, and one that is to be found in modernist writers such as Yeats,[29] as well as in David Jones. In *In Parenthesis*, the destruction of Private Ball's company in Mametz Wood that concludes the writing is also clearly apocalyptic, a way of bringing the soldiers' chaotic journey to the front to a final end. The use of myth by Jones has been the matter of some controversy; while Bergonzi states that *In Parenthesis* "blends myth and realism in a way that makes it one of the great achievements of the Modern Movement" (Bergonzi, *Heroes' Twilight* 212), Fussell is more critical:

> The poem is a deeply conservative work which uses the past not, as it often pretends to do, to shame the present, but to ennoble it. The effect of the poem, for all its horrors, is to rationalize and even to validate the war by implying that it somehow recovers many of the motifs and values of the medieval chivalric romance. (Fussell 147)

Although I believe Fussell misinterprets Jones's references – it is not the heroism or chivalry, but the inevitability of failure and defeat central to both the Arthurian myth, the *Geste de Roland*, and the Celtic epics (as will be pointed out later) that attracts Jones – he is right in pointing out that *In Parenthesis* depends on these works to create its own meaning. And through its emphasis on the eternal recurrence of war, from times mythical and mediaeval to the twentieth century, the writing seems to establish war as the natural condition of man: it is precisely through its attempt to contain war through myth that *In Parenthesis* gives war mythic, universal status. As Jones states in his Introduction: "We [humankind] find ourselves privates in foot regiments" (Introduction to *In Parenthesis* xiii). Also, the notion expressed in his essay that myth needs (in his particular case) war in order to achieve "now-ness" betrays a dangerous dependence on war. The use of the Arthurian myth of defeat, with all its modern resonance of total war and cultural catastrophe,

---

29 I find Yeats's concept of modern history as a cycle of violence (as expressed for example in "Leda and the Swan" or "The Second Coming") remarkably similar to Williams's ideas.

turns in the cases of both Jones and Williams into a capitulation before the nature of war as incontainable and uncontrollable.

Celtic Literature of Defeat

Both David Jones and Charles Williams have a more markedly Celtic take on the Arthurian myth than most of their Victorian predecessors. Jones stresses the essentially Welsh or British (as opposed to Saxon or English) character of Arthurian legend in his essay "The Myth of Arthur" (cf. esp. 216-218), and *In Parenthesis* uses Arthurian elements in a distinctively Welsh way. One figure exemplifying this is Lance-Corporal Aneirin Merddyn Lewis, who significantly shares his name with both the poet of the *Gododdin* and the Welsh bard later associated with the magician of Arthurian legend. Lewis is killed in the assault on Mametz Wood in Part 7 of the writing, and after his death is described in a mixture of images from Arthurian myth, the *Mabinogion* and the *Gododdin*; the disasters of Catraeth and Camlaan (referred to here as "by Salisbury") are juxtaposed to the First World War, comparing the dead of those battles to those fallen in the Great War, and making it clear that the destructive forces of modern mechanised war surpass even those of mythical creatures such as the boar Twrch Trwyth:

> No one to care there for Aneirin Lewis spilled there
> who worshipped his ancestors like a Chink
> who sleeps in Arthur's lap
> who saw Olwen-trefoils some moonlighted night
> on precarious slat at Festibert,
> on narrow foothold on le Plantin marsh –
> more shaved is he to the bare bone than
> Yspaddadan Penkawr.
> Properly organised chemists can let more riving
> power than ever Twrch Trwyth;
> more blistered is he than painted Troy Towers
> and unwholer, limb from limb, than any of them fallen at
> Catraeth
> or on the seaboard-down, by Salisbury,
> and no maker to contrive his funerary song.
> (*In Parenthesis* 155)

Williams is the first (and only) Arthurian poet to choose Taliessin as the central figure of his poems (although he is mentioned in Tennyson's *Idylls*). The historical Taliesin was a sixth-century Welsh bard, some of whose poetry is still preserved, and is mentioned in Nennius's ninth-century history of Britain which is one of the founding texts of the Arthurian legend. However, there is also a *Book of Taliesin* included in the thirteenth-century *Red Book of Hergest*, and fragments of a *Romance of Taliesin* was included by Lady Charlotte Guest in her 1848 edition of the *Mabinogion*, in which a mythical Taliesin's magical childhood and his many transformations are recounted.[30] Thus the figure of Taliessin (Williams adopts Tennyson's spelling of the name) combines a historical and a mythical person very much in the same way that the figures of Arthur and Merlin do. Williams draws explicitly on the Welsh fragments from the *Romance of Taliesin* included in the *Mabinogion* in the first poem of *The Region of the Summer Stars*, "The Calling of Taliessin", where Taliessin answers King Maelgwyn's question about who he is (in Williams's poem he is answering Elphin):

> My heritage is all men's; only my age is my own.
> I am a wonder whose origin is not known.
> I carried a banner before Lleon of Lochlin,
> and held in the sleeping-chamber a mirror for his queen.
> I am more than the visions of all men and my own vision,
> and my true region is the summer stars.
> [...] I was thrall to Ceridwen and free in the manger of an ass.
> Before speech came to pass, I was in danger of loquacity.
> It is a doubt if my body is flesh or fish,
> therefore no woman will ever wish to bed me
> and no man make true love without me.
> All doctors come to stand about me,
> yet I shall never have any near me to need me.
> Every king shall call me Taliessin,
> and till the doom I am handfast with all the dead.
> (*RSS* 6-7)

And Taliessin in the end returns to his Welsh homeland: "that which was once Taliessin rides to the barrows of Wales / up the vales of the Wye" ("Taliessin at Lancelot's Mass", *TTL* 91). The answer to Maelgwyn also forms the background to one of the central passages of *In Parenthesis*, Dai Greatcoat's boast in Part 4.

---

30 Robert Graves includes a history of these fragments, an account of the legend and an interesting interpretation of his own in his famous if controversial study of mythology, *The White Goddess* (cf. Chapter Two, "The Battle of the Trees" 27-48).

Here, Dai (who is often interpreted as an autobiographical portrait of Jones)[31] describes himself as a kind of changeling present at central points in history and myth: he was the spear that struck the dolorous blow, the adder that started the battle of Camlaan, he was at the murder of Abel and at the crucifixion, and takes part in war in heaven, which is described in the terminology of the First World War: "I was in Michael's trench when bright Lucifer bulged his primal salient out" (*In Parenthesis* 84). This verse is somewhat similar to C.S. Lewis's describing the earth in his apocalyptic cosmic struggle as "a kind of Ypres Salient in the universe" (*Out of the Silent Planet* 184).

Thus both Jones and Williams emphasise the essential "Britishness" (rather than "Englishness"), the Celtic sources of the Arthurian legend. As Jones says, "all things connected with this tangle should be of interest to people of this island, because it is an affair of our own soil and blood and tradition, our own 'inscape', as Hopkins might say – it is the *matière de Bretagne*" ("Myth of Arthur", *Epoch and Artist* 243). The Celtic spirit, according to Jones, "lies, a subterranean influence as deep water troubling, under every tump of this Island, like Merlin complaining under his big rock" (Preface to *In Parenthesis* xi). In *In Parenthesis*, the sleeping soldiers are described as "long-barrow sleepers", and one of them is actually related to the figure of Taliessin (Taliessin means "bright brow"): "And this one's bright brow turned against your boot leather, tranquil as a fer sídhe sleeper, under fairy tumuli, fair as Mac Og sleeping" (*In Parenthesis* 51). In the note to this passage, Jones states:

> In this passage I had in mind the persistent Celtic theme of armed sleepers under the mounds, whether they be the fer sídhe or the great Mac Og of Ireland, or Arthur sleeping in Craig-y-Ddinas or in Avalon or among the Eildons in Roxburghshire; or Owen of the Red Hand, or the Sleepers in Cumberland […] this abiding myth of our people. (*In Parenthesis* 198-199)

Jones thus envisions a Celtic underlayer to Britain (and Ireland), symbolised by Merlin or indeed Arthur, sleeping under some hill till his return. The final lines from Williams's "Taliessin at Lancelot's Mass" quoted above also suggest the notion of Taliessin returning to Wales to become such a "long-barrow sleeper",

---

31 Cf. for example René Hague, *Dai Greatcoat* (London: Faber, 1980).

as "that which was once Taliessin rides to the barrows of Wales" (*TTL* 91).³² In general, though, Williams's idea is slightly different: for him, as mentioned above, Logres is a kind of mythical superstructure to historical Britain.³³ These ideas of an underlayer and a superstructure complement each other to a certain extent, and both of them are clearly related to the idea of the palimpsest.³⁴ That the palimpsest is typically used in modernist war literature is claimed by Rainer Emig, who argues that the palimpsest's mechanism of over- and underwriting, which simultaneously hides and reveals, destroying identity and meaning and creating new meaning through the superimposition of fragments, mirrors the extreme experiences of war and represents war's transformations of meaning.³⁵ So in *In Parenthesis* and the Arthurian poems, their fundamental structure of the palimpsest is one determined by war. This is not immediately obvious as it is a mechanism based on transformation.

In his essay "Art in Relation to War", Jones posits a special connection between the Celtic culture and poetry used by both himself and Williams, and war:

> It is worth remembering that while it is customary to think of the "Celts" as the "poets" and the "seers", they were in fact proto-typic of, and pre-eminent as, warrior-aristocracies [...]. All our tradition is of war [...]. We have thought very much in terms of war, and the arts have in various ways reflected that thought. ("Art in Relation to War" *The Dying Gaul* 126-127)

---

32 Such long-barrow sleepers also occur, interestingly, in Tolkien's *The Lord of the Rings* in the form of the Barrow-wights, the evil spirits of warriors long dead that trap the hobbits underground, transforming them into long-barrow sleepers themselves. The hobbits in their enchanted sleep re-enact past battles: "The men of Carn Dûm came upon us at night, and we were worsted. Ah! The spear in my heart!" (*LotR* 140).

33 The notion that Arthur's Britain becomes separated into "modern" Britain and a "Celtic" Logres is also apparent in Marion Zimmer Bradley's *The Mists of Avalon*. In Bradley's retelling, Avalon (the seat of the Celtic religion) is lost in the mists after Camlaan and becomes a timeless fairy country cut off from the real world.

34 Jones plays with these ideas of different layers repeatedly in his work. The idea of the palimpsest is central to *The Anathemata*, and in *The Roman Quarry* (which through its very title carries notions of uncovering differents layers) speaks of layers of myth: "under-myth and over-myth, like the leaf-layered forest floor" (*Roman Quarry* 18). For further exploration of these ideas, cf. Simon Lewty, "The Palimpsest" *David Jones: Artist and Poet* 54-64.

35 "Gleichzeitig ermöglicht diese interne Doppelung oder das doppelte Verschwinden (der Referenz hinter dem Signifikanten, des Signifikanten hinter dem Signifikanten) im Palimpsest die ästhetische Spiegelung des Sinnbruchs in der Extremerfahrung. Nur in diesem gespiegelten Bruch, so steht zu vermuten, ist eine *Darstellung* von Extremen möglich. Die Darstellung wird so aber gleichzeitig zur Entstellung wie Verstellung: sie entstellt die Referenz und sie verstellt den Zugang zu ihr." Translation: 'At the same time this internal doubling or double disappearance (of the referent behind the signifier, the signifier behind the signifier) in the palimpsest allows the aesthetic mirroring of the collapse of meaning in extreme experiences. Only in this mirrored collapse, it is to be surmised, can these extremes be *portrayed*. But the portrayal thus becomes both a distortion and a blocking off: it distorts the referent and blocks the access to it).' (Emig, *Krieg* 70).

The attraction of this Celtic tradition and more specifically the Welsh sources for Jones and Williams and their connection to the Arthurian myth of defeat espoused by the twentieth century could lie in their representing a similar "literature of defeat", as it is termed by Charles W. Moorman. Moorman examines several mediaeval Celtic texts, including the *Mabinogion*, that were produced at a time when the producing culture was under threat or in the process of being destroyed. They are the texts that define

> the values, myths, mores, traditions, the aggregate cultural identity, of a people under duress, who *in extremis* are attempting collectively to bring together and preserve the elements of their common past and so produce what might be called a literature of defeat, of displacement and dispossession and disinheritance. (Moorman 47)

Moorman compares these Celtic sources and Malory's *Morte*,[36] and concludes by turning to modern "Celtic" literature. He claims that the twentieth century has seen a revival in the literature of defeat, particularly in Ireland with the works of Yeats, Joyce, Beckett and Kavanagh. Thus he links the Celtic literature of defeat with the modernist movement in twentieth-century literature,[37] which was indeed concerned – if not obsessed – with notions of cultural decline, often displaying a deep-rooted cultural pessimism which on the one hand welcomed the opportunity to make it new, on the other desperately tried to enshrine certain works of (not only) Western culture by shoring their fragments against their ruins. David Jones makes a connection similar to Moorman's, when in "The Myth of Arthur" he relates defeat in arms to the extinction of a culture as a whole. The British culture of Arthur was threatened by Germanic Saxon invaders, who drove Celtic Britain back into the hills to become a "highland" phenomenon opposed to the Saxon "lowlanders". Jones compares the situation of Arthurian Celtic Britain to that of the early twentieth century: "Whitehall, Wall Street, the cinema, the wireless, are inevitably the allies of the lowland thing, as surely as were the Court of Rome, and the rising civilisation of Europe, in the early Middle Ages" ("The Myth of Arthur" *Epoch and Artist* 219). The Saxon invasion of Celtic Britain is here linked to the destruction of a "high culture" by the "low" (*low*-land) popular

---

36 Surprisingly, Moorman sees Malory as "a closed system, complete in itself, unapproachable and unalterable, written [...] for a closed society in a closed age" (86). That Malory's *Morte* can however be read equally as the product of a culture under threat is demonstrated by the quotes from Jones above.
37 Of course this revival can be linked not just to modernism, but to the Irish (post)colonial situation.

culture in the modern day and age – a concern shared by many modernists, who lamented that "The pianola 'replaces' / Sappho's barbitos" (Pound, *Hugh Selwyn Mauberley* 99). Williams's version of the myth is more problematic for us today in its racism (this is not to say that Jones's espousal of the Celtic/Saxon binary is not racist, but this binary is not used as obviously in *In Parenthesis*). In the Taliessin cycles, Celtic (and Christian) Logres is threatened by the advance of Islam and the antithesis of the Byzantine Empire, the antipodean P'o-lu which seems distinctly Eastern Asian in character.

However this may be, it is the sense of a culture under threat, particularly under threat through military disaster, that links mediaeval Celtic writers and the modernists, and causes writers like Jones and Williams to turn to these texts for inspiration. Thus David Jones, in one of the most significantly laden passages of *In Parenthesis*, illustrates the pity of modern war with a phrase from the *Gododdin* ("Princes falling like green barley on the ground") and an allusion to the Battle of Arderydd that in its violence supposedly drove Merlin mad:

> Come with Merlin in his madness, for the pity of it; for
> the young men reaped like green barley,
> for the folly of it.
> (*In Parenthesis* 66)

Jones was not the only modernist poet to be inspired by the *Gododdin*: another modernist text thematising war that makes use of the Welsh epic is the Scottish poet Hugh MacDiarmid's poem "On Reading Professor Ifor Williams's 'Canu Aneirin' in Difficult Days". Writing immediately before the outbreak of the Second World War, MacDiarmid turns to Aneirin for guidance and links the Welsh poet's situation with his own:

> Note how (great topical lesson for us today)
> It is not the glory, but the pity and waste, of war
> That inspires its highest passages, but realise
> That the profoundest cause in these Islands today,
> The Invisible War on which Earth's greatest issues depend,
> Is still the same war the Britons fought at Catraeth
> And Aneirin sings. The Britons were massacred then. Only one
> Escaped alive. His blood flows in my veins today

> Stronger than ever, inspires me with his unchanged purpose,
> And moves me alike in Poetry and Politics.
> ("On Reading Professor Ifor Williams's Canu Aneirin" *Complete Poems* 690)[38]

But it is not just the theme of war and defeat that the modernists adopt from their Celtic sources. Moorman also notes formal and structural characteristics of literature of defeat:

> I have attempted so far to define a kind of literature, typified best perhaps by the Celtic literature of the Middle Ages, which would seem not to be based on the familiar structural qualities of mainstream Western literature – unity, order, coherence – but instead to present a more instinctively, intuitively conceived image of the world. And I would go on to say that this kind of exuberantly imaginative and Romantic literature, indeed this kind of art, having its own distinctive, though non-intellectual, procedures and value-structures, seems most often to arise from a particular kind of historical environment, the threatened extinction of the cultural identity of a defeated people. (Moorman 47)

This type of literature thus possesses a shape that, "however amorphous by classical standards, is in some odd way not as haphazard and undirected as the critics have said it is, but perhaps subject to its own laws of form and matter" (Moorman 2-3). This statement is especially interesting in regard to the peculiar forms used by Jones and Williams, forms that indeed seem "amorphous" and "haphazard", following no real linearity, possessing no obvious unity. Philip Pacey has claimed that the "strength of the Celtic tradition is its ability to embrace and be embraced by chaos" (Pacey, *Hugh MacDiarmid and David Jones* 12). That Jones's works are indebted to this Celtic aesthetic is posited by Gwyn Williams: "*In Parenthesis* and *The Anathemata* are constructed on an interweaving pattern much like that of the *Gododdin* or Gwalchmai's *Gorhoffedd*" (Williams, *The Burning Tree* 15), and William Blissett states that "David Jones, in a letter to me, and elsewhere, has cited this observation with full approval" (Blissett, "The Welsh Thing in Here" *David Jones: Artist and Poet* 115).

Charles Williams's Arthurian poems can be seen to follow a similar pattern of interweaving motifs and concerns, rather than a strict plot or development. For

---

38 Similarly, MacDiarmid's idea of a "Celtic Front" is reminiscent of Jones's idea of a Celtic underlayer, a fact that MacDiarmid himself acknowledges: "What I am concerned with here, and have been mainly and ever more intensively in all my writing, is, of course, what David Jones in *In Parenthesis* calls 'the Celtic cycle that lies, a subterranean influence […] under every tump of this island […]' Like David Jones, I have always 'had in mind the persistent Celtic theme of armed sleepers under the mounds…'" (MacDiarmid, *Lucky Poet* 186).

example, the two poems "The Calling of Arthur" from *TTL* and "The Calling of Taliessin" from *RSS* are very different in form: the language of "The Calling of Arthur" is highly condensed, the poem has only 10 stanzas with four lines each, while "The Calling of Taliessin" is extremely long (it takes up sixteen pages). Both poems deal, however, with similar topics: Merlin confronting in the one poem Arthur and in the other Taliessin, instructing them to take up their destiny, the founding of Logres. This forms one of the links between the two cycles. "The Calling of Arthur" also introduces the motif of man-as-wolf – Merlin is described as "Wolfish […], coming from the wild, / black with hair, bleak with hunger, defiled / from a bed in the dung of cattle, inhuman his eyes" (*TTL* 14). This then reappears later in the same cycle when Lancelot's madness is called "a delirium of lycanthropy" ("The Son of Lancelot" *TTL* 57), and Merlin in the form of a now white, not black, wolf bears the baby Galahad to Almesbury to protect him from his black wolf-father.[39] Finally, the last stanza of "The Calling of Arthur" runs

> Arthur ran; the people marched; in the snow
> King Cradlemas died in his litter; a screaming few
> fled; Merlin came; Camelot grew.
> In Logres the king's friend landed, Lancelot of Gaul.
> (*TTL* 15)

This moment of the founding of the kingdom (through war), when Lancelot arrives to assist his friend and king, is echoed at the end of the cycle after Lancelot and Arthur have battled over Guinevere, and Lancelot arrives back in Britain too late to assist his former friend against Mordred's treachery (in war):

> In Logres the king's friend landed, Lancelot of Gaul.
> Taliessin at Canterbury met him with the news
> of Arthur's death and the overthrow of Mordred.
> ("The Last Voyage" *TTL* 88)

Through the repetition, the victory at the beginning of Arthur's kingdom is contrasted with the disaster of Camlaan that ends it, bringing the story full

---

39 The poem "The Meditation of Mordred" (*RSS*) would also seem to play on this idea of man-as-wolf and particularly wolf fathers: here it is Arthur who is perceived as the wolf by his bastard son, who in turn envisages himself as a trap: "Like son, like father; *adsum*, / said the steel trap to the wolf when the trap sprang" (*RSS* 48). Interestingly, C.S. Lewis's war poem "French Nocturne" also plays with the idea of men turning into wolves: "I am a wolf. Back to the world again, / And speech of fellow-brutes that once were men. / Our throats can bark for slaughter: cannot sing" (Walsh 37).

cycle. These kind of connections between the various poems create a kind of unity through "an interweaving pattern", a pattern that contrasts with the fragmented narrative and metrical diversity of the cycles as a whole, as is stated by Angelika Schneider: "Durch diese Verbindung wird der metrischen Variation und der narrativen Zersplitterung entgegengewirkt" (Schneider 151).[40] It should be pointed out that these structures of circularity and repetition are also features of myth, that "method" through which many modernists could "control, order, give a shape and significance" (cf. Eliot, "'Ulysses" *Selected Prose* 177) to their material.

A few further words must be said about the Celtic myths used by Jones and Williams and fantasy. As stated above, Williams in his poetry cycles creates a secondary world, "a strong, strange and consistent world" (Lewis, *Arthurian Torso* 198). This world, Logres within an ahistorical Byzantine empire, possesses through its references to Celtic myth and use of figures from that body of mythology, a more Celtic feel both than his precursor Tennyson's *Idylls* or his successor T.H. White's *The Once and Future King*.[41] It is a world of magic and metamorphosis, containing within the "imposed order" of the "organic body" of the Empire ("Prelude" *RSS* 3, "The Vision of the Empire" *TTL* 6) "the darkness of secret-swayed Broceliande" ("The Calling of Taliessin" *RSS* 9), from whence come Merlin, Brisen and their mother Nimue – and within whose bounds lies Carbonek, the place of the Holy Grail. Broceliande is a mythical forest, a "sea-rooted western wood" ("The Fish of Broceliande" *TTL* 24), where sea and land, water and earth, become indistinguishable. This echoes a description by Jones: "The folk tradition of the insular Celts seems to present to the mind a half-aquatic world […] it introduces a feeling of transparency and interpenetration of one element with another, of transposition and metamorphosis" ("The Myth of Arthur" 238-239). When Jones describes no-man's land as "a place of enchantment" (Preface to *In Parenthesis* x), that land takes on some of the features of Williams's Celtic metamorphic Broceliande. The trenches in the mud and rain turn literally into a "half-aquatic world", and the

---

40 Translation: 'These connections counteract metrical variation and narrative discontinuity.'
41 White's tetralogy places not a Celtic-British race and culture against the invading Saxon or Moslem, but a Norman colonial power against the Saxon serfs. Arthur, the "Wart", comes of both races and unites them. There are however some distinctly Celtic characters: the daughters of Cornwall and the "Orkney faction". These figures are either completely evil (Morgause, Morgan le Fay, Agravaine, Mordred) or at best ambiguous (Gawain, Gaheris).

soldiers' corpses indeed "suffer [...] this metamorphosis" (*In Parenthesis* 54); "Solid things dissolve, and vapours ape substantiality" (*In Parenthesis* 179). At certain climactic points in the writing, the Celtic "subterranean influence as a deep water troubling" seems to break through the layers that cover it, and magical creatures appear in no-man's land: "this hour / when unicorns break cover" (*In Parenthesis* 168), and the "Queen of the Woods" crowns the dead soldiers with flowers (cf. *In Parenthesis* 185-186); this would seem to confirm Emig's claim that the palimpsest, the interpenetration of two (or more) layers, represents the extreme experiences of war (cf. Emig, *Krieg* 71). These incursions of fantastic elements into realist descriptions of combat fit in with the writing's overall fusion of the Western Front with the Arthurian magical Waste Land. It would go too far to say that *In Parenthesis* is a fantastic work in Todorov's sense of the word[42] – the realist elements are far too dominant for that, and the fantastic and mythical elements do not, by virtue of the writing's poetic nature, create hesitation in the reader. But the use of Celtic elements creates a distinct similarity between this typically modernist work and Williams's body of fantasy work. In their use of these elements both Jones's and Williams's poetry can be seen as forerunners of much post-World War II Arthurian fiction, which takes up the Celtic theme.[43] However, in Jones and Williams, this Celtic interweaving style, the palimpsest structure, are both conditioned by war.

Waste Lands

> Frodo looked around in horror. Dreadful as the Dead Marshes had been, and the arid moors of the Noman-lands, more loathsome far was the country that the crawling day now slowly unveiled to his shrinking eyes. Even to the Mere of Dead Faces some haggard phantom of spring would come; but here neither

---

42 Tzvetan Todorov's seminal study *The Fantastic* defines the fantastic as the moment of hesitation and uncertainty that lies between the "real" and the supernatural: "In a world which is indeed our world, the one we know, a world without devils, sylphides, or vampires, there occurs an event which cannot be explained by the laws of this same familiar world. The person who experiences the event must opt for one of two possible solutions: either he is the victim of an illusion of the senses, of a product of the imagination – and the laws of the world remain what they are; or else the event has indeed taken place, it is an integral part of reality – but then this reality is controlled by laws unknown to us. [...] The fantastic occupies the duration of this uncertainty" (25).
43 Cf. Adam Roberts, *Silk and Potatoes*, for a thorough discussion of Arthur as a "specifically Celtic hero and freedom-fighter" (14) and the prevailing dialectic between Celt and Saxon used in modern Arthurian fiction.

spring nor summer would ever come again. Here nothing lived, not even the leprous growths that feed on rottenness. The gasping pools were choked with ash and crawling muds, sickly white and grey, as if the mountains had vomited the filth of their entrails upon the lands about. High mounds of crushed and powdered rock, great cones of earth fire-blasted and poison-stained, stood like an obscene graveyard in endless rows, slowly revealed in the reluctant light. They had come to the desolation that lay before Mordor: the lasting monument to the dark labour of its slaves that should endure when all their purposes were made void; a land defiled, diseased beyond all healing – unless the Great Sea should enter in and wash it with oblivion. (Tolkien, *LotR* 617)

The land of Mordor and the area of the Dead Marshes from Tolkien's Middle-earth are probably the most famous examples of 'waste lands' in fantasy literature. A country destroyed by tyranny, relentless industrialisation, and twice the scene of climactic struggles between good and evil (The Last Alliance and the War of the Ring), Mordor has become a symbol of the "global ecological holocaust" (Curry 83), and "the terminus of modernity's merciless logic" (Curry 81).[44] And, as Roger Sale has aptly observed,

> The landscape through which Frodo moves is Sauron's most powerful weapon, a valley of the shadow of death, and we know that there are ways to see the book as being Christian and Frodo as a pilgrim. But the landscape is really much closer [...] to the wasteland, the valley of ashes, and the nightmare cities of Rupert Birkin and Henry Adams than it is to the arbitrary and unclear landscapes of Spenser and Bunyan. (*Modern Heroism* 234)

Sale here draws the connection between Tolkien's fantasy and the modernist D.H. Lawrence, and the waste land is indeed also a recurrent image in modernist literature. It has by now become an almost commonplace statement to say that the mysterious mythical land of Arthurian legend laid waste by the dolorous blow can be seen as a symbol of modern despair and sterility. Eliot's eponymous poem of 1922 makes the most famous use of the waste land myth, charting landscapes of despair, from the "endless plains, [...] cracked earth / Ringed by the flat horizon only" (Eliot, *The Waste Land, Collected Poems* 77), the "dull canal" (70) where the modern Fisher King sits "Fishing, with the arid plain behind me" (79), to the "Unreal City" (65) of loveless sexual encounter and abortion. Likewise, Joyce's Leopold Bloom has an unexpected flash of vision in which he sees contemporary Dublin as a kind of Israel, as

---

[44] Curry brilliantly quotes a description of Auschwitz by Primo Levi which is terrifyingly close to Tolkien's Mordor (Curry 81).

> A barren land, bare waste. Volcanic lake, the dead sea: no fish, weedless, sunk deep in the earth. No wind would lift those waves, grey metal, poisonous foggy waters. Brimstone they called it raining down: the cities of the plain: Sodom, Gomorrah, Edom. All dead names. A dead sea in a dead land, grey and old. Old now. It bore the oldest, the first race. A bent hag crossed from Cassidy's clutching a noggin bottle by the neck. The oldest people. Wandered far away over all the earth, captivity to captivity, multiplying, dying, being born everywhere. It lay there now. Now it could bear no more. Dead: an old woman's: the grey sunken cunt of the world. (*Ulysses* 63)

Fertility has failed, and the Promised Land has turned into a waste, denying the possibility of spiritual redemption. This waste is seen as representative of the modern condition; Edmund Wilson puts it as follows in one of the earliest reviews of Eliot's poem: "The Waste Land is [...] the hero's arid soul and the intolerable world around him, our post-War world of shattered institutions, strained nerves and bankrupt ideals" (cit. Seymour-Jones 291-292). And David Jones, writing of the cultural situation in 1942, stated that "it looks as though the waste land before us is extensive" ("The Myth of Arthur" 242).

Eliot's *Waste Land* in particular is full of references to the Great War just passed, connecting the various waste lands cited above to the destruction wreaked by the War – for example, the allusion to Dante's *Inferno* ("A crowd flowed over London Bridge, so many, / I had not thought death had undone so many", *Waste Land* 65) is often taken to allude to the millions who died in combat between 1914 and 1918 (cf. Fussell 63). The women in the bar discuss the return of one's husband from the War ("He's been in the army four years, he wants a good time", *Waste Land* 68); and the "White bodies naked on the damp ground" from the Fire Sermon section (70) are painfully reminiscent of the corpses of no-man's land. The ravaged landscape of the Front, where all growing things were destroyed and corpses littered the scenery, indeed seemed to be an unreal, ghostly world of desolation like that of the Arthurian myth. David Jones explicitly links the two in his Preface to *In Parenthesis*:

> I think the day by day in the Waste Land, the sudden violences and the long stillnesses, the sharp contours and unformed voids of that mysterious existence, profoundly affected the imaginations of those who suffered it. It was a place of enchantment. It is perhaps best described in Malory, book iv, chapter 15 – that landscape spoke "with a grimly voice". (Preface to *In Parenthesis* x-xi)

The writing itself is full of descriptions of the Front that refer to the Arthurian Waste Land. Part 4 of *In Parenthesis* is actually called "King Pellam's Launde": the footnotes refer the reader to Malory's Book II, Chapter 16, where Balin sees the ruin he has brought on King Pellam and his lands.[45] The section itself opens with a quote from Malory, a dawn scene where Lancelot, sorrowing for his sins after a dream vision of the Grail, "heard the fowls sing; then somewhat was he comforted" (Malory Volume II, 270-271; cit. *In Parenthesis* 59). Similarly, the next lines describe the dawn rising over no-man's land, the birds singing "shrill over from / Biez wood" (59), and the soldiers listening for them. In contrast to Lancelot, the dawn and the accompanying birdsong provides no comfort to the soldiers; it merely reveals the level of devastation anew:

> Very slowly the dissipating mist reveals saturate green-grey flats, and dark up-jutting things; and pollard boles by more than timely wood-craftsman's cunning pruning dockt – these weeping willows shorn.
> And the limber-wheel, whose fractured spokes search upward vainly for the rent-off mortised-rim. (*In Parenthesis* 62)[46]

At dawn and dusk the ritual scanning of the enemy trenches took place; these associations have completely exploded any romantic concepts of these times of day. Paul Fussell writes: "Dawn has never recovered from what the Great War did to it" (Fussell 63).

When it has grown fully light, the soldiers move off and the scenery is described in more detail. This passage links no-man's land, destroyed through industrialised warfare, to the modern urban "waste-land":

> The untidied squalor of the loveless scene spread far horizontally, imaging unnamed discomfort, sordid and deprived as ill-kept hen-runs that back on sidings on wet weekdays where waste-land meets environs and punctured bins ooze canned-meats discarded, tyres to rot, derelict slow-weathered iron-ware disintegrates between factory-end and nettle-bed. Sewage feeds the high grasses and bald clay-crop bears tins and braces, swollen rat-body turned-turtle to the clear morning. (*In Parenthesis* 75)

---

45 "So he rode forth through the fair countries and cities, and found the people dead, slain on every side. And all that were alive cried, 'O Balin, thou has caused great damage in these countries; for the dolorous stroke thou gavest unto King Pellam, three countries are destroyed, and doubt not but the vengeance will fall on thee at the last.'" (Malory, *Morte Darthur* Volume I, 84)

46 Jones's writing dwells time and time again not just on the destruction of men, but of trees: "how piteous the torn small twigs in the charged exposure" (*In Parenthesis* 30). In this he is very similar to Tolkien, whose Treebeard (the Ent, a kind of tree-spirit) mourns that "there are wastes of stump and bramble where once there were singing groves" (Tolkien, *LotR* 463).

Fussell interprets this passage as "implying the war's power to go on forever, however cunningly the postwar world of 1927 to 1937 may try to disguise itself as Paradise" (Fussell 150). The images encountered are similar to those found in Eliot and Joyce. The trench rat, "at night feast on the broken of us" (54), is also a returning motif whose connection to the rats of Eliot's *Waste Land* has often been pointed out (for example in Emig, *Krieg* 195, or Fussell 149). The waste land in Jones, as in Eliot (as indeed in Tolkien's Middle-earth), is a product of modern civilisation and modern war, and the cruelty and futility of both are linked. For if the waste land of the modern condition is created through the ravaging forces of war, it is the mechanics of modern civilization and its spiritual waste land that have made such inhuman warfare possible in the first place. The conclusion would be that these waste lands are the result of "a botched civilization", as Ezra Pound puts it in his own most direct response to the war (Pound, *Hugh Selwyn Mauberley* 101), a civilization that constitutes itself through the very thing that destroys it. This paradoxical structure is, as demonstrated in this chapter's opening section, representative of modernist literature which both condemns war and is dependent on it for its structures; but it also reveals that the image of the waste land in this literature is more problematic than it would seem at first glance. For on the one hand, the waste land is made by war; but on the other, it is made *for* war as well. Adam Piette, discussing desert warfare in the Second World War, calls the desert the "perfect theatre of war" – it is "a place fit only for war" (Piette 13). He cites William Chappell's statement that the "landscapes that suit my war mind must be bare and clear", and his imaginative longing for "negation and wilderness", "sterility" and "silence". In the artistic appropriation of war, the imagination needs the waste land as a necessary precondition of creation: it needs the landscape as its theatre. Piette calls this a "petulant indulgence in space, sterility and silence, a longing for spiritual death" (9), and relates this back to the influence of Eliot: "this indulgence in desert thinking [is] a form of asceticism immaturely learned from *The Wasteland* [sic]" (10). Eliot's poem uses the waste land as the imaginative theatre for its scenes of modern despair. Similarly, Jones in the Preface to *In Parenthesis* (quoted above) admits it was no-man's land, his modern waste land, that fired his imagination in the first place; the waste land is indeed the precondition of creation, and the setting for Jones's soldiers "playing the actor" (Jones, *In Parenthesis* 31). This take on the waste land enables an entirely different interpretation of the boast made by Dai Greatcoat, the centrepiece of *In Parenthesis*: it is Dai, the poet, who "was the spear in Balin's hand / that made waste King Pellam's land" (*In Parenthesis* 79). The poet lays the land waste in order to be able to create.

Charles Williams's cycles do not expressly deal with Balin's dolorous blow; apparently this was to be addressed in later poems that were never written because of Williams's death.[47] This means that we never encounter the waste land proper in his poetry, although Carbonek, the seat of wounded King Pelles, is frequently mentioned. But waste lands there are nonetheless, and they are, as in the modernist texts, the products of a botched civilization, of barbarism and war. Before the founding of Camelot, the country is described: "The waste of snow covers the waste of thorn; / on the waste of the hovels snow falls from a dreary sky; / mallet and scythe are silent; the children die" ("The Calling of Arthur" *TTL* 14). The images of wintry death, the absence of agriculture and squalid housing call up the impression of a land where fertility of any kind has been made impossible. "The Calling of Taliessin" describes "the anarchy of yet unmade Logres" (*RSS* 9), and it is stated that this is a land laid waste by war:

> As he came on the third day down the way to the coast
> he saw on his left a wilderness; Logres lay
> without the form of a Republic, without letters or law,
> a storm of violent kings at war – smoke
> poured from a burning village in the mid-east
> transport had ceased, and all exchange stilled.
> (*RSS* 8-9)

In Williams's poems, war and its waste lands are closely linked to ideas of order and authority. They are the consequence of the lack of a strong leader committed to bringing order to his realm. The opposite of this condition is the "organic body" ("The Vision of the Empire" *TTL* 6) of the Empire, whose representatives are the Emperor in Byzantium, the Pope in Rome and King Arthur in Logres. However, this cultural order is doomed to failure. Arthur puts himself and his own glory above his duty to his people ("the king made for

---

47 "[H]e clearly postponed working on what he thought most important, leaving it till last – largely because he did think it so important, and did not yet feel capable of it. In June 1939, he wrote of 'Balin and the Dolorous Blow. God had better take care of this; I can't.'" (Dodds 7).

the kingdom, or the kingdom made for the king?" "The Crowning of Arthur" *TTL* 21); the consequences of this selfishness are disastrous: "Thwart drove his current against the current of Merlin: / in beleaguered Sophia they sang of the dolorous blow" ("The Crowning of Arthur" *TTL* 21). The tragedy of Balin and the creation of the waste land are here linked to Arthur's personal fall from grace, and both are in turn linked to the original Fall: "Over Camelot and Carbonek a whirling creature hovered / as over Adam in Eden when they found themselves uncovered" ("Lamorack and the Queen Morgause of Orkney" *TTL* 40).[48] Thus it is Arthur's original sin – his pride and self-love, represented by his incest with his sister – that destroys Logres, plunging it and the Empire into war, turning it back into the waste he had made fruitful for a while. And Williams's deliberate connection of the dolorous blow and Arthur's sin allows us to interpret the ruin of Logres as analogous to the creation of the waste land. Williams's final vision of that ruin, "The Prayers of the Pope" is deeply pessimistic; in it, the Pope himself despairs of spiritual redemption from the waste surrounding him: "when the Son of Man comes, he brings no faith in a future" (*RSS* 51). This poem has been interpreted several times as a representation of the Second World War.[49] Here the fall of Logres results in war throughout Europe, laying the entire continent waste:

> A tale that emerged from Logres surged in Europe
> and swelled in the Pope's ears; it held nothing
> of fulfilment of prophecy and the sea-coming of the Grail
> but only of bleak wars between Arthur and Lancelot,
> Gawaine set to seek his heart's vengeance,
> the king's son gone whoring with fantasy,
> and mobs roaring through Camelot; the Pope's letters
> had brought no staying of the slaying nor ceasing of the sin
> nor healed the dichotomy of battle. [...]
> The line faltered along the Danube and the Rhine;
> pale in London and Lutetia grew the tale of peace,
> and bloody the Noel-song; the towns of Logres
> felt the sliding of the raiders' sails,
> and Gaul all the push of Northern woods,

---

48 Williams states this in his essay "Notes on the Arthurian Myth": "The Dolorous Blow is that fact – call it the Fall, as I should, or whatever you like – which has set man in a state of contradiction with and antagonism with himself and the universe. [...] The fatality, the curse, the result of the Dolorous Blow, has to work itself out through the King" (*Image* 175-176).
49 A.M. Hadfield's comment has already been quoted above; C.S. Lewis states "The situation which 'the young Pope Deodatus, Egyptian-born' contemplates is of course very like that which Williams contemplated in 1944 and which we still contemplate in 1946" (Lewis, *Arthurian Torso* 180).

> savage growths, moods infinitely multiplied
> across the bleak plains, where in race
> by sullen marshes separated from race
> virtue is monopolized and grace prized in schism.
> The consuls and the lords fought for the fords and towns,
> but over the Rhine, over the Vistula and Danube
> pressed the grand tribes; the land shook
> as band after band stamped into darkness cities
> whose burning had lamped their path; their wrath grew
> with vengeance and victory; they looked to no returning.
> ("The Prayers of the Pope" *RSS* 51-52)

The figure of Balin who struck the dolorous blow, creating the Waste Land, is highly significant for both Williams and Jones. In Williams, Balin's striking of the dolorous blow is connected to the "mistaken impious hate" ("Lamorack and the Queen Morgause of Orkney" *TTL* 40) through which he unwittingly killed his own brother Balan, and was slain by him. This fratricide is sin of the same order as Arthur and Morgause's incest, and is at the root of the ruin of Logres. Jones links the slaying of brother by brother to the tale of Cain and Abel, and both of these to the soldiers of the Great War. The soldiers setting out to Mametz Wood are compared to innocent Abel, "Who under the green tree / had awareness of his dismembering, and deep-bowelled damage" (*In Parenthesis* 162), but the writing refuses to apportion blame for the slaughter: "who gives a bugger for / the Dolorous Stroke" (*In Parenthesis* 162). Thus Balin and Balan become images for both the Allied and the German-Austrian soldiers, whom Jones calls "THE ENEMY FRONT-FIGHTERS WHO SHARED OUR PAINS AGAINST WHOM WE FOUND OURSELVES BY MISADVENTURE" (Dedication of *In Parenthesis* xvii). *In Parenthesis* refers to "the sweet brothers Balin and Balan / embraced beneath their single monument" (163), and this is echoed in the final "Queen of the Woods" passage of the writing, where a German and a Welsh soldier lie in a similar position beneath a monument of kinds: "Hansel with Gronwy share dog-violets for a palm, where they lie in serious embrace beneath the twisted tripod" (185).[50]

In his Introduction to *In Parenthesis*, David Jones calls no-man's land "a place of enchantment" (x). It is a place of metamorphosis, "the margin of familiar things"

---

[50] The tale of the dolorous stroke and the fratricide of Cain and Abel are already put in close proximity to one another in Malory's *Morte Darthur* Volumes II, Book XVII, Chapter 5 (337-338).

(70). Part 4, "King Pellam's Launde", devotes long passages to the "uncertain flux" (59) and "escaping definitions" (98) of dawn and dusk, and the difficulties of distinguishing between men, machines and vegetation: "Whether that picket-iron moved toward or some other fell away, or after all is it an animate thing just there by the sap-head or only the slight frosted-sway of suspended wire" (98). Likewise Adam Piette, describing the desert, also characterises it as a place of uncertainty and metamorphosis: "This strange and sinister, colourless world of [...] disguised suspicious objects [...] where any smudge or blob in the empty visual field may be enemy, any tree or shrub might turn into a Panzer Mark III or an 88, like vicious looking-glass objects" (Piette 25). In Jones, as we have seen above, the waste land is where the fantastic breaks through into the real; it is the place where the fantastic can come back into its own. This leads us back to the idea of transformation that Rainer Emig claims is central to war literature: war's destruction is really a transformation. The waste land, the scene of war and destruction, is the setting in which transformation and metamorphosis can take place. We have seen how this destruction results in "enchantment" in Jones: the soldiers become "long-barrow sleepers" (51), they are "Oeth and Annoeth's hosts" (187) crowned by the Queen of the Woods. The waste land is, in effect, the place where two worlds intersect, that of realistic and brutal modern warfare, and that of mythical (Celtic) fantasy.[51] In Williams, the waste land is the place where Helayne, the Fisher-King's daughter, is transformed into the likeness of Guinevere to trick Lancelot into procreating Galahad; it is the place where Lancelot and Merlin turn into wolves. More ghastly metamorphoses take place when spectre-soldiers are called up in the final assault on the Empire (cf. "The Prayers of the Pope" *RSS* 50-61). In both *In Parenthesis* and the Arthurian poems of Williams, these transformations taking place in the waste lands – and the transformation of fruitful landscape into waste land – can be related back to the ravages of war.

One aspect in which Jones's and Williams's waste lands differ from their most famous contemporary, Eliot's *Waste Land*, is that in contrast to Eliot, spiritual redemption can ultimately be achieved, if only redemption of a

---

[51] A similar idea is found in Alan Garner's *Elidor* (1965), a fantasy novel that takes up the notion of a waste land – in this case a site of urban dereliction – as the place of transit between the world of Elidor and our own: "Wasteland and boundaries: places that are neither one thing nor the other, neither here nor there – these are the gates of Elidor" (50-51).

limited kind. *The Waste Land* closes without the final "Om", forming a closed circle of despair and denial. But in Williams, the healing of Pelles by Galahad and the achievement of the Grail hold the fall and death of Arthur in balance: "At the hour of the healing of Pelles / the two kings were one, by exchange of death and healing" ("The Last Voyage" *TTL* 88), although this healing cannot prevent the destruction of Logres. And even after the fall of the Empire, hope remains through the prayers of the Pope:

> consuls and lords within the Empire,
> for all the darkening of the Empire and the loss of Logres
> and the hiding of the High Prince [Galahad], felt the Empire
> revive in a live hope of the Sacred City.
> ("The Prayers of the Pope" *RSS* 61)

In Jones, the ritual acts of military command, of companionship and sacrifice give meaning and a spiritual dimension to the experience of war (the importance of liturgy for both Jones and Williams will be discussed later). The waste land is not made fruitful, for as Dai Greatcoat says "You don't ask, / although the spear-shaft / drips" (*In Parenthesis* 84); nevertheless short-term relief is possible: "They [the soldiers] would make order, for however brief a time, and in whatever wilderness" (22).[52]

Bodies and Corpses

One of the most horrible features of war's waste lands are the bodies that lie about it and underneath it, structuring its landscape. These bodies are sometimes dead, sometimes dying, sometimes alive: the distinctions between life and death become fluid.

> Soldiers' descriptions of corpses make clear that dead bodies at the front were simultaneously understood as both animate subjects and inanimate objects. The disturbing susceptibility of bodies to become indistinguishable from the landscape of mud and objects through which they moved is documented over and over again in accounts of war. (Booth 53)

---

52 This is another aspect of the writing that I believe is misinterpreted by Fussell: when he insists that Jones's use of the Arthurian myth is an attempt to bring the action on the Western Front into line with mediaeval chivalry, but that "the Western Front is not King Pellam's Land, [...] it will not be restored and made whole, ever, by the expiatory magic of the Grail" (Fussell 154) he does not take into account that this may be precisely the point Jones is trying to make.

One war book that thematises this impossibility to distinguish between human body and landscape, life and death is Remarque's *Im Westen Nichts Neues*, where the narrator states: "Unsere Hände sind Erde, unsere Körper Lehm und unsere Augen Regentümpel. Wir wissen nicht, ob wir noch leben" (236).[53] Modernist literature takes up the motif of the corpse given such horrible contemporary resonance by the war; Joyce's *Finnegans Wake*, with the burial and resurrection of HCE, is one example, and Eliot's *The Waste Land* another. Eliot's poem's opening section, "The Burial of the Dead", is actually written, as Michael Levenson has pointed out, from the point of view of a buried corpse – but a corpse not yet really dead (cf. Levenson, *Genealogy* 172). Thus it plays on the fusion of life and death, body and landscape prevalent in many war texts.

Jones's *In Parenthesis* has many examples of this. The passage of the soldiers in the section "Starlight Order" is impeded by flooding of the trenches caused by corpses blocking the water, necessitating a "dreadful lifting-out of obstacles" (43). In this passage the soldiers lifting out the corpses are themselves described as "Lazarus figures", confusing the alive and the dead:

> Appear more Lazarus figures, where water gleamed between dilapidated breastworks, blue slime coated, ladling with wooden ladles; rising, bending, at their trench dredging. They speak low. Cold gurgling followed their labours. They lift things, and a bundle-thing out; its shapelessness sags. From this muck-raking are singular stenches, long decay leavened; compounding this clay, with that more precious, patient of baptism; chemical-corrupted once-bodies. (*In Parenthesis* 43)

Not only Lazarus, but also the Celtic "long-barrow sleepers" and Arthur himself are of course figures that confuse the distinction between life and death. They are buried, yet they are not dead: they merely sleep and will return at some appointed time. It is only natural that Jones should find them apt images for his wartime bodies.

Jones's writing also makes mention of the corpse become unrecognizable because blown to pieces in the passage on Aneirin Lewis's death cited above, "unwholer,

---

53 Translation: 'Our hands are earth, our bodies clay and our eyes pools of rain. We do not know whether we are still alive.'

limb from limb, than any fallen at Catraeth" (*In Parenthesis* 155).⁵⁴ A vain hope that the shattered corpses, like Lazarus, might somehow be brought back to life is expressed, playing on the biblical Book of Ezekiel and the prophet's vision of the valley of dry bones, another waste land made up of corpses:⁵⁵ "you mustn't spill the precious fragments, for perhaps these raw bones live. / They can cover him again with skin – in their candid coats, / in their clinical shrines and parade the miraculi" (175). The allusion to Ezekiel and the bones brought back to life through prophecy occurs already at the beginning of "King Pellam's Launde", where the soldiers are aroused from their night's sleep, the word of command "making rise again the grey bundles where they lie. / Sodden night-bones vivify, wet bones live" (60). The description of the soldiers as "grey bundles" refers of course to the "bundle-thing" of the corpse uncovered in the dredging of the previous section. This corpse-like state is emphasised even further on the following pages:

> They stretched encumbered limbs to take their rifles, listless, bemused, to slowly scrape away the thicker mire caked, with deadness in their eyes and hands as each to each they spoke – like damned-corpse-gossiping, of hopeless bleedin' dawns – then laugh't to see themselves so straitened, tricked out in mudded stiffening. (*In Parenthesis* 63)

All these passages reaffirm that in the waste lands of war, the barriers between life and death become permeable, and live and dead bodies are shattered, disintegrate and become part of the waste surrounding them: "their bodies grope the mazy charnel-ways – / seek to distinguish men from walking trees and branchy moving like a Birnam copse" (179).⁵⁶

That not just modernists, but fantasy authors are aware of these problems of distinction caused by war becomes clear in one of the most striking examples

---

54 Neil Corcoran assumes that when the Queen of the Woods cannot find Dai Greatcoat at the end of "The Five Unmistakable Marks" it is because, like Aneirin Lewis, "he has been blown unrecognizably to pieces" ("Spilled Bitterness" 224). I prefer to read it as Dai, the changeling, not dying but having faded away like at the end of his boast: "Old soljers never die they / Simply fade away" (*In Parenthesis* 84).
55 "The hand of the Lord was upon me, and carried me out in the spirit of the Lord, and set me down in the midst of a valley which was full of bones, And caused me to pass by them round about: and, behold, there were very many in the open valley; an, lo, they were very dry. And he said unto me: Son of man, can these bones live? And I answered, O Lord God, thou knowest." (AV: Ezekiel 37, 1-3)
56 Even in modernist works that ostensibly have nothing to do with the war bodies become increasingly fragmented, perceived as disjunct parts rather than belonging to a whole. This can be seen for example in Eliot's "The Love Song of J. Alfred Prufrock", where we have "eyes", "arms [...] downed with light brown hair", but no complete bodies (cf. Eliot, "The Love Song of J. Alfred Prufrock" 15).

of a waste land made up of (undead) corpses: The Dead Marshes in Tolkien's *The Lord of the Rings*. The Dead Marshes that lie before Mordor were once the plain of Dagorlad, scene of the great battles of the Last Alliance against Sauron. By the time of the War of the Ring, they have become marshland, but the dead of that earlier conflict can still be seen:

> "There are dead things, dead faces in the water," [Sam] said with horror. "Dead faces!" Gollum laughed. "The Dead Marshes, yes, yes: that is their name," he cackled. "You should not look in when the candles are lit." "Who are they? What are they?" asked Sam shuddering, turning to Frodo [...]. "I don't know," said Frodo in a dreamlike voice. "But I have seen them too. In the pools when the candles were lit. They lie in all the pools, pale faces, deep deep under the dark water. I saw them: grim faces and evil, and noble faces and sad. Many faces proud and fair, and weeds in their silver hair. But all foul, all rotting, all dead. A fell light is in them." Frodo hid his eyes in his hands. "I know not who they are; but I thought I saw there Men and Elves, and Orcs beside them." "Yes, yes," said Gollum. "All dead, all rotten. Elves and Men and Orcs. [...] There was a great battle long ago, yes, so they told him when Sméagol was young, when I was young before the Precious came. It was a great battle. Tall Men with long swords, and terrible Elves, and Orcses shrieking. They fought on the plain for days and months at the Black Gates. But the Marshes have grown since then, swallowed up the graves; always creeping, creeping." (*LotR* 613-614)

Williams's Arthurian poems use a complex symbolism of the body, which fuses body and landscape, body and zodiac. The Empire is conceived in terms of a female body: Camelot and Logres are the head, the seat of language (represented by Taliessin), the breasts are Gaul where are the universities, the fountains of learning, the hands are Rome where the Pope performs his "heart-breaking manual acts [the performance of Mass]" ("The Vision of the Empire" *TTL* 9), Jerusalem, the birth-place of Christianity, is the genitals, the buttocks symbolising sensual pleasure are Caucasia. Byzantium, the Empire's centre, is of course the navel. The poem "The Vision of the Empire" explains this "organic body" (*TTL* 12). Every human body is thus a microcosm which in its physicality symbolically represents the glories of creation: "the crowned form of anatomized man, / bones, nerves, sinews, / the diagram of the style of the Logos" ("Taliessin in the School of Poets" *TTL* 30). It corresponds to mathematics and music, and to poetry; it is, in the words of Lewis, "an ideal geometry mediated through an actual arrangement of living curves" (Lewis, *Arthurian Torso* 119). This is why Taliessin can say that he "sigh[s] for the zodiac in flesh" ("Taliessin in the Rose-Garden" *RSS* 23), and Palomides, falling in love with Iseult, sees

> how curves of golden life define
> the straightness of a perfect line,
> till the queen's blessed arm became
> a rigid bar of golden flame
> where well might Archimedes prove
> the doctrine of Euclidean love.
> ("The Coming of Palomides" *TTL* 34-35)

But if the body represents the Empire in all its glory, it can also represent landscapes of ruin and destruction. The most striking example of this is the figure of Morgause, the Queen of Orkney and Arthur's sister with whom he commits incest. Lamorack, her lover, comes first to Orkney and sees it as a harsh, barren place where sea, sky and rock war on each other:

> Caves and hollows in the crags were filled with the scream
> of seamews nesting and fleeting; the extreme theme
> of Logres rose in harsh cries and hungry storms,
> and there, hewn in a cleft, were hideous huge forms. [...]
> Ship and sculpture shuddered; the crag's scream
> mingled with the seamews'; Logres' convulsed theme
> wailed in the whirlwind; we fled before the storms,
> and behind us loosed in the air flew giant inhuman forms.
> ("Lamorack and the Queen Morgause of Orkney" *TTL* 38-39)

When Lamorack first sets eyes on Morgause, he sees her as the embodiment of this violent landscape: "I saw in her long eyes the humanized shapes of the cleft" (39). She herself is the living sculpture of rock:

> I am the queen's servant; while I live
> down my eyes the cliff, the carving, the winged things drive,
> since the rock, in those fleet lids of rock's hue,
> the sculpture, the living sculpture, rose and flew.
> (41)

Morgause's body and the wild waste land of Orkney become one; it is unclear whether she is made by the landscape or the landscape made by her, "the source of all stone" (38). The hardness and barrenness of rock mirrors her harshness and her spiritual, not physical, barrenness. Morgause is of course the mother of Mordred, the bastard who brings ruin on Arthur's kingdom: "Her hand discharged catastrophe" (38), and Lewis describes her as "the most Celtic, and most terrible, person in the poem", going on to quote Yeats's description of Queen Aoife from *On Baile's Strand*: "There was one / In Scotland, where you had learnt the trade of war, / That had a stone-pale cheek and red-brown hair" (cit. Lewis, *Arthurian Torso* 128), very likely a model for Williams's queen. Morgause, who is partly the reason Logres turns back into a waste, is herself described in terms of a desolate landscape, her body merging with the Orkney Isles in a way similar to the merging of body and landscape in war literature.

The Queen of Orkney, while made of rock, is neverthless alive, a "living sculpture". But (un)dead bodies also appear in Williams's cycles. Taliessin returning to Logres from Byzantium passes through Broceliande, "the wood / that had lost the man's mind" ("Taliessin's Return to Logres" *TTL* 4), and is there confronted with ghostly figures: "on a path harder than death / spectral shapes stood / propped against trees; / they gazed as I rode by" (4). These spectres seem corpse-like in their lack of agency: they are "propped", they can gaze at Taliessin but not actively harm him; they are neither alive nor dead. A passage in *In Parenthesis* is remarkably like this: "The trees of the wood beware each other / and under each a man sitting; [...] For the pale flares extinction you don't know if under his close lids, his eye-balls watch you" (184-185).[57]

More gruesome than these bodies under the trees are Williams's zombies, called up by necromancers to make war on the Empire. Here we have the typically modernist merging of death and life, of bodies and earth, and both in a setting of war:

> Then, in that power, they called and enthralled the dead,
> the poor, long-dead, long-buried, decomposing
> shapes of humanity; the earthy shapes stirred,
> [...] the poor bodies
> were drawn again slowly up through the earth,
> and, held steady on their feet, stood and answered.
> With rods of desecrated hazel the sorcerers
> touched them and bade them walk; bloodless, automatized,
> precursors of the tribes in a necromancy of justice,
> those mechanized bodies stalked across the fords,

---

57 This is also similar to the "Paths of the Dead" episode in Tolkien's *The Lord of the Rings*.

and the hordes of the heathen followed the corpses to battle.
("The Prayers of the Pope" *RSS* 53-54)[58]

The use of the words "automatized" and "mechanized" would seem to hint at the horror of modern mechanized warfare, that turns its soldiers into killing machines. While much war literature deals with the dehumanization of the soldier at the front, the greater part of it describes the soldiers as beasts – Remarque's narrator for example says "Wir [...] sind Menschentiere geworden" (Remarque 79),[59] and C.S. Lewis's "French Nocturne", cited above, turns the soldiers into wolves. Williams, whose soldiers are magically mechanized corpses, has taken this one step further. Jones's writing hints ironically at a similar process: but instead of magic, the wonders of modern technology are used to put the soldiers back together (who were of course blown to bits by modern technology in the first place): "Give them glass eyes to see / and synthetic spare parts to walk in the Triumphs, without anyone feeling awkward and O, O, O, its a lovely war with poppies on the up-platform for a perpetual memorial of his body" (*In Parenthesis* 176). Both Jones's *In Parenthesis* and Williams's Arthuriad thus make use of bodies, corpses and fuse the two with landscape in a particularly modernist way – a way that was conditioned through the experience of the battle-fields of World War I. Both poets deplore the destruction of life, body and landscape, and use the perceived permeability of the boundaries between life and death, body and landscape to invoke horror in the reader (rather than use it to a more comic effect as Joyce does in *Finnegans Wake*). This can perhaps be attributed to their Christianity, for if man is made in God's image, a symbol of divine perfection as Williams sees it, the fragmenting of his body is a destruction of divine order. That the corpses cannot rest in peace after their death but are dug up again, that they seem not even to have died properly, is also a form of sacrilege. This desecration of the body mirrors the desecration of creation in the ruined landscapes of war, and carries the same implications of spiritual aridity and despair: there is no Christ to restore Lazarus to full life and health, no Spirit of God to fill the dry bones with living breath, so

---

[58] A somewhat similar episode occurs on Williams's novel *All Hallow's Eve*, where the magician Simon the Clerk forms a golem-like body out of paste into which he invokes the spirits of the dead.
[59] Translation: 'We have become human animals.'

a return to life is impossible; but a proper death also seems impossible, and if one cannot die, one cannot reach Heaven and salvation.

Heroes

The hero figure in modernist literature marked by the tension is, as Rainer Emig claims, one of the central features of modernism.[60] Modernist works constantly refer back to mythic heroes, such as Odysseus in Joyce's *Ulysses* and Pound's *Cantos*, only to establish the failure of these old models in the modern world. Old heroes are invoked only to be rejected, yet frequently modernist protagonists – like Stephen Dedalus – are incapacitated by the persistence of the old ideals, which they know they will never be able to live up to. Eliot's Prufrock cries "No! I am not Prince Hamlet, nor was meant to be" ("The Love Song of J. Alfred Prufrock" 17), only to be so paralysed he cannot even "dare eat a peach" (17), let alone "disturb the universe" (14).

It is often stated that it was the First World War that destroyed conventional notions of heroism; the most blunt expression of this is famously expressed in Wilfred Owen's "Dulce et Decorum": "the old Lie: Dulce et decorum est / Pro patria mori" (*Poems* 140). While it may be true, as Paul Fussell claims, that the young soldier "going up to the line to his destiny cannot help [feeling like] a hero of medieval romance if his imagination has been steeped in actual literary romances or their equivalent" (Fussell 135), that concept must have been violently shattered once they reached the front by the impersonal brutality of mechanised modern war. The use of old models of heroic action in literature of the First World War is thus often ironic (as in Owen's poem).[61]

David Jones's *In Parenthesis*, however, differs from this: he usually uses his references to chivalric literature to create an atmosphere of pity rather than one of irony, stressing aspects of defeat and sacrifice rather than heroic action. When he refers to the knights of the Malorian Arthuriad, for example, he

---

60 "[T]he essential character of the modernist work [is] tension" (Emig, *Modernism* 241).
61 Fussell notes that this irony is itself a means of conferring significance on the war: "By applying to the past a paradigm of ironic action, a rememberer is enabled to locate, draw forth, and finally shape into significance an event or a moment which otherwise would merge without meaning into the general undifferentiated stream" (Fussell 30).

quotes passages in which the heroes despair – as in the case of Lancelot in the Waste Land – or where they are already dead: "like those others who fructify the land / like Tristram / Lamorak de Galis / Alisand de Orphelin / Beaumains who was the youngest" (*In Parenthesis* 163). His attempt seems to me less to "elevate the new Matter of Flanders and Picardy to the status of the old Matter of Britain" (Fussell 153), than to humanize those heroes, bring them "down" to the level of the soldiers. His writing is not a celebration of heroism, but "the song of the Battle of Camlann – the song of treachery and of the undoing of all things" (Jones, Preface to *In Parenthesis* xiii). The condition of mankind is not that of the hero, but that of the low-ranking soldier: "We find ourselves privates in foot regiments" (Preface to *In Parenthesis* xiii). This is not to say that this is an unproblematic stance to take, for it betrays the assumption that war is the "normal" condition of man, and in its passive acceptance of war's horror comes close to what Rainer Emig terms "eine Ästhetik des Todes und der Zerstörung" (Emig, *Krieg* 316).[62]

An alternative heroic model is offered in Jones, as in several other works of the Great War. Discussing Ford Madox Ford's *Parade's End*, Bergonzi states: "The word 'martyr' is, indeed, significant. [...] Tietjens is a passive and suffering hero, whose triumphs arise, not from violent action, but from *patience* (derived, ultimately, from *patior*, to suffer)" (Bergonzi, *Heroes' Twilight* 180). This model of the hero as martyr, as sacrificial, also informs *In Parenthesis*. The soldiers are "appointed scape-beasts come to the waste-lands" (70). This refers to Leviticus XVI (which is also quoted at the end of the writing, 226), where a beast is appointed "sin offering" (Leviticus XVI, 11): "And the goat shall bear upon him all their iniquities unto a land not inhabited: and he shall let go the goat in the wilderness" (Authorized Version: Leviticus XVI, 22). The soldiers, described as "the lambs of the flock" (*In Parenthesis* 6), are thus sacrificed for the sins of others. In this they obviously take on a function similar to that of Christ, the lamb who takes upon himself the sins of the world. Yet they are sacrificers as well as the sacrificed, killers as well as the killed, in spite of their unwillingness to indulge in slaughter: "you scramble forward and pretend not to see, / but ruby drops from young beech-sprigs / are bright on your hands and face. / And the other one cries from the breaking-buckthorn" (169). It should not be

---

62 Translation: 'an aesthetic of death and destruction'.

forgotten that the spear that strikes the dolorous blow is that which pierced the side of Christ as he hung on the cross, and Dai Greatcoat in his boast claims to be that very spear – the soldiers are not simply sacrificed like Christ, they are also the ones that cause his death. Jones is too wise – and too good a Christian – to subscribe fully to the sacrificial heroic model without being aware of the problems it brings with it. In this, he seems close to Tolkien, whose protagonist Frodo, while obviously a sacrificial hero, is not unproblematic (ultimately he has to be forced to his sacrifice by Gollum).

The problem of valid heroic models is one central to the genre of fantasy besides that of modern(ist) war literature, because the archaic worlds of fantasy seem to call for ancient heroes that are however no longer credible to a modern readership. This dilemma is expressed especially well in T.H. White's Arthurian fantasy *The Once and Future King*:

> "Do you know that Homo sapiens is almost the only animal which wages war? [...] True warfare is rarer in Nature than cannibalism. Don't you think that it is a little unfortunate?"
> "Personally," said the Wart, "I should have liked to go to war, if I could have been made a knight. I should have liked the banners and the trumpets, the flashing armour and the glorious charges. And oh, I should have liked to do great deeds, and be brave, and conquer my own fears. Don't you have courage in warfare, Badger, and endurance, and comrades whom you love?" (193)

White manages to condemn war while acknowledging the human longing for bravery and heroism. In the works of the Inklings, we are faced with a strange assortment of protagonists, none of which really conform fully to any traditional model (although Tolkien's *Silmarillion*, modelled very strongly on Norse and Finnish legend, is something of an exception). Both in Tolkien's *The Hobbit* and *The Lord of the Rings*, the hero is split: on the one hand, we have traditional figures such as Aragorn or the dragon-slayer Bard, and on the other the slightly comic hobbits. Lewis's Elwin Ransom (whose surname again implies a sacrificial function) is an academic, although he later takes on the function of the Arthurian Pendragon and Fisher-King. Generally, while the need for heroism and brave action is acknowledged, there is never an uncritical adoption of traditional models, and frequently the heroes fail in the end: Frodo cannot survive in Middle-earth, neither can Ransom on our planet.

The ambivalence of the figure of Arthur as a hero has been mentioned earlier: he establishes a kingdom, but fails to hold it, ultimately undone by his own wrongdoing in the form of his bastard son. Williams's poems make these two sides to Arthur quite clear, far more so than other versions of the myth do, and Arthur is given full responsibility for the incest he commits with Morgause: "Arthur tossed loves with a woman and split his fate" ("Lamorack and the Queen Morgause of Orkney" *TTL* 40). Again, this stands in marked contrast to other versions (such as White's) where Morgause is portrayed as an evil seductress and Arthur as her young and innocent victim. Nevertheless, Arthur is the one who manages to establish Logres, the head of the Empire, and when the kingdom is first founded it is an ideal state: "hierarchic, republican, the glory of Logres, / patterns of the Logos in the depth of the sun" ("The Crowning of Arthur" *TTL* 20). Thus he is, as David Jones puts it in his Notes to *In Parenthesis*, "Arthur the Protector of the Land, the Leader, the Saviour, the Lord of Order carrying a raid into the place of Chaos" (Jones, *In Parenthesis* 201). This notion of Arthur as conveyor of order seems typically modernist, for modernism was very much concerned with ideas of order. As Williams's Bors asks: "What can be saved without order? and how order?" ("Bors to Elayne: on the King's Coins" *TTL* 45). Yet Arthur fails: in the version of the myth used by David Jones, he digs up the head of Brân the Blessed, which protected Britain from invasion, wishing to "defend the Land by his might alone" (Jones, *In Parenthesis* 209). This is mentioned in Dai Greatcoat's boast: "The Bear of the Island: he broke it in his huge pride, and over-reach of his imperium" (*In Parenthesis* 82). Similarly, in Williams Arthur becomes more concerned for himself than for his kingdom. One cannot help seeing parallels in this pride of Arthur's to some of the leaders and monarchs involved in the Great War, whether or not Williams and Jones intended them. The alternative hero figure offered by Williams is Taliessin, the king's bard.

Charles Williams's Arthurian poems are unusual in that they centre round the figure of the poet Taliessin rather than the king or one of the knights. The writer or poet as hero has of course been current since the *Künstlerroman* of the late eighteenth century, but Williams's poems are the first Arthurian works that place the Welsh bard at their centre. In the twentieth century, especially in modernism, the figure of the artist is taken up and reworked through the typically self-reflexive modernist preoccupation with art and language, and

Williams's Taliessin can be seen as an example of this. Two poems from *Taliessin through Logres* – "Taliessin's Song of the Unicorn" and "Taliessin on the Death of Virgil" – are actually songs by Taliessin, and "Taliessin in the School of Poets" (*TTL*) and "Taliessin in the Rose-Garden" (*RSS*) are poetological works, where the bard reflects on the nature of poetry and the mode of its composition. His reflections betray concerns that seem more modernist than mediaeval: Taliessin is acutely aware of the slippage between word and meaning in language, and sees verse as a way of bringing order to language, that otherwise threatens to collapse into chaos; thus he warns Sir Kay at the introduction of coins into the kingdom (that is, the introduction of symbols):

> Sir, if you made verse you would doubt symbols.
> I am afraid of the little loosed dragons.
> When the means are autonomous, they are deadly; when words
> escape from verse they hurry to rape souls; [...]
> We have taught our images to be free; are we glad?
> ("Bors to Elayne: on the King's Coins" *TTL* 44)

The task of the poet, then, is to bring order: thus Taliessin "defined the organisms of hell" ("Taliessin in the School of Poets" *TTL* 29), binding them, and under his tutelage "the young poets studied precision" (30). In the order of his verse the structure of the world becomes apparent:

> they saw the macrocosm drawn;
> they heard the universal sigh
> in the balance of changing levels
> and complemented sound.
> (*TTL* 30)

Poetry thus is another reflection of that order evident in the human body and the body of the Empire; it is to Byzantium, the centre of the Empire, that Taliessin must go to learn verse, for beforehand his poetry is "lacking the formulae and the grand backing of the Empire" ("The Calling of Taliessin" *RSS* 6). Poetry is a similar "imposed order" ("Prelude" *RSS* 3) on the chaos of language as the Empire is on the chaos of the world. This concern with imposing order on language and reality is again typically modernist.

That it is poetry that confers order not just on language, but on reality itself, becomes clear in the poem "Mount Badon" from *Taliessin through Logres*. This poem deals with Arthur's final victory over the Saxons after which (in Williams's version of the myth) he is crowned king of Logres. Taliessin is Arthur's captain of the horse, and while waiting to charge to the aid of Arthur and the other knights, he has a vision of the Roman poet Virgil composing the *Aeneid*, and this act of poetic composition reveals to him how he himself must charge. "Mount Badon" thus establishes a parallel between writing and war:

> Taliessin saw the flash of his style
> dash at the wax; he saw the hexameter spring
> and the king's sword swing; he saw, in the long field,
> the point where the pirate chaos might suddenly yield,
> the place for the law of grace to strike.
> He stood in his stirrups; he stretched his hand;
> he fetched the pen of his spear from its bearer;
> his staff behind signed to their men. [...]
> The tor of Badon heard the analytical word;
> the grand art mastered the thudding hammer of Thor,
> and the heart of our lord Taliessin determined the war.
> (*TTL* 17-18)

Again it is the typically modernist method of the palimpsest, the layering of various writings and, through them, various realities, that represents the battle. Taliessin's epiphanic vision which conflates different times and situations is also very modern. As to the poem's hero: it is not the king, nor any of his knights, but the poet who saves the day and wins the battle that enables Arthur to be crowned – a remarkable innovation to the myth on Williams's part. The poem is also remarkable in that it basically claims war can be won through language; here language controls war, instead of war fragmenting language, as is usually the case, and the poet becomes the hero instead of the king. The fact that Taliessin is called by Merlin to assist at the founding of Logres (cf. "The Calling of Taliessin" *RSS* 5-20) places him close to that ideal of Joyce's Stephen, "forg[ing] in the smithy of [his] soul the uncreated conscience of [his] race" (Joyce, *Portrait* 276) – the poet as founding father of a nation as well as a king.

Nevertheless, Taliessin remains a strange heroic figure. As a poet, he does not seem quite human: "It is a doubt whether my body is flesh or fish, / therefore no woman will ever wish to bed me" ("The Calling of Taliessin" *RSS* 7). He is condemned to remain sterile, without an heir, and his one true love Blanchefleur (or Dindrane, as she is called in *The Region of the Summer Stars*) enters a convent. In this he is similar to Tolkien's Frodo or Lewis's Ransom, who also die (or rather, leave the world) without founding a family. His final fate after the collapse of the Empire and the death of Arthur is tragic (rather than ironic as in the case of Stephen Dedalus): Taliessin ends up "the tongue tired of song, the brain fey" ("The Prayers of the Pope" *RSS* 56). In the end, although he once decided a battle through his "analytical word", he is himself undone by the tragedies of war that destroy Logres. He fades out of the poems, losing his own identity: in the last stanzas of "Taliessin at Lancelot's Mass" he is referred to as "That which had been Taliessin", and is last seen "rid[ing] to the barrows of Wales" (*TTL* 91). His language and its power have disappeared.

The figure of the poet does not appear directly in *In Parenthesis*. In the Welsh epics whose fragments the writing appropriates, the poet usually speaks in praise of the fallen; in the *Gododdin* the poet is actually one of the few survivors of the attack on Catraeth:

> Of those who met over flowing drink
> only three escaped from the fury of battle,
> Aeron's two wardogs and Cynon came back,
> and I from my bleeding for my song's sake.
> (Aneirin, "The Gododdin" transl. Ifor Williams; *The Burning Tree* 23)

In Parenthesis mourns the absence of a bard to sing of the soldiers' battles: "no maker to contrive his funerary song" (155) – no one is left, possibly there are no survivors at all. The figure of Dai Greatcoat, the figure often taken to represent the poet and *In Parenthesis*'s parallel (through the boast) to Taliessin, has disappeared at the end (like Taliessin in Williams's poems, and like the predominant centre of consciousness in *In Parenthesis*, John Ball). Nevertheless, the quote from the *Gododdin* heading Part 7 reads: "It is our duty to sing", and obviously the poem has been written as we are able to read it, despite the apparent absence of a poet; the lament over "no maker" is itself the "funerary song" supposedly made impossible by the missing singer. This is a prime example of the paradoxical modernist technique of creating presence (of text) through absence (of a producer) and continuity (of the traditional lament for the fallen) through loss (of the poet carrying on the tradition). It evinces the aesthetics of absence and loss created and represented by war which were adopted by modernism.

Ultimately, the Great War conditions the ways in which both *In Parenthesis* and Williams's Arthurian poetry question traditional heroic models. The alternatives offered are tentative and do not stand unquestioned; and in the end, the central "heroes" of the writings do not merely fail, they disappear: "Old soljers never die they / Simply fade away" (*In Parenthesis* 84).

War, Language and Liturgy

One of the central concerns of modernist literature was the crisis of language and its failure to connect adequately to an increasingly bewildering reality, and the failure of language to describe the extreme experiences of war is just the most blatant example of this. Modernist texts repeatedly thematise this failure; T.S. Eliot in his *Four Quartets* described writing poetry as "a raid on the inarticulate" (Eliot, "Burnt Norton" *Collected Poems* 203) and despairs as

> Words strain,
> Crack and sometimes break, under the burden,
> Under the tension, slip, slide, perish,
> Decay with imprecision, will not stay in place,
> Will not stay still.
> ("Burnt Norton" 194)

Many modernist works are highly self-reflexive ones that thematise language, thus emphasising the material of their own construction, and simultaneously, by deploring the inadequacy of that material, destabilising their own status.

Similarly, Williams's secondary Arthurian world is a highly self-reflexive one, that constantly thematises the material of its construction, language. The multiple layers of its reality, in which Empire, body, zodiac, mathematics and music correspond each to the other, are created through language:

> The organic body sang together;
> dialects of the world sprang in Byzantium;
> back they rang to sing in Byzantium;
> the streets repeat the sound of the throne.
> ("The Vision of the Empire" *TTL* 6)

Logres is the organic body's head, and Camelot, where Taliessin lives, is its mouth; Camelot (through Taliessin) is the centre of poetry, ordered language. Indeed, in "The Vision of the Empire", it is stated that Logres is made of language: "if there be worlds of language beyond Logres" (*TTL* 13). The fact that the cycles centre around a poet and contain poetological poems naturally contributes to the metatextuality of the Arthuriad. However, the very insecurity of this medium is emphasised in the poems in a very modernist way; the Empire of language is threatened by the headless (and thus language-less) Emperor of antipodean P'o-lu, "Inarticulate always on an inarticulate sea" ("The Vision of the Empire" *TTL* 12), and Taliessin himself, as shown earlier, is aware of the possibility of language collapsing into chaos at any moment, for the order of the Empire, the order of language, is but an "imposed" one ("Prelude" *RSS* 3). In the end, of course, that order is destroyed by war: the zombie-soldiers marching on Rome are conjured up by "half-broken and half-spoken syllables" ("The Prayers of the Pope" *RSS* 53) which represent their half-decomposed and undead state. Williams's poems however present a means by which language can (supposedly) counteract this disintegration: through ritual language, especially liturgical language. Linguistic disorder is confronted by the most ordered language possible: that of the rite of Mass. Mass, in which the host is through the ritual words transformed into the body of Christ, is performative, efficacious language, language in which the spoken word exercises immediate power over reality through transubstantiation.[63]

Both *Taliessin through Logres* and *The Region of the Summer Stars* close with the celebration of Mass. In "The Prayers of the Pope", the Pope's prayers finally defeat the corpse army:

> at the junction of communion
> he offered his soul's health for the living corpses [...]
> the Body salvaged the bodies
> in the fair, sweet strength of the Pope's prayer. [...]
> Before the host on the rivers, the automatized corpses
> stopped, dropped, disintegrated to dust;
> (*RSS* 61)

Here ritual language is able to transcend and, like the Eucharistic transubstantiation, transubstantiate war.[64] The poem itself creates its own liturgy: the Pope's prayer, ironically alluding to the Magnificat, "Send not, send not

---

[63] More of Williams's ideas on the divine Logos are to be found in his history of the workings of the Holy Ghost, *The Descent of the Dove*.
[64] In fact, it is more of a reverse transubstantiation that takes place: instead of bread being turned into flesh, flesh is turned back to dust.

the rich empty away" is repeated at the end of the stanzas until through the very repetition it is endowed with symbolic power (for of course objectively speaking it is this act of repetition that gives liturgical language power rather than any meaning inherent in the words themselves). "Taliessin at Lancelot's Mass" takes this transformation even further: at this Mass, the dead knights of the Round Table killed at Camlaan reappear, Galahad ascends to heaven, and Arthur and the (now healed) Fisher-King Pelles become one in one supreme moment of heavenly vision in which Taliessin himself loses his identity:

> In the ritual before the altar Lancelot began to pass;
> all the dead lords of the Table were drawn from their graves
> to the Mass; [...]
> singly seen in the Mass, owning the double crown,
> going to the altar Pelles, and Arthur moving down.
> Lancelot and Arthur wove the web; the sky
> opened on moon and sun; between them, light-traced on high,
> the unseen knight of terror stood as a friend;
> invisible things and visible waited the end. [...]
> That which had been Taliessin rose in the rood;
> in the house of Galahad over the altar he stood,
> manacled by the web, by the web made free;
> there was no capable song for the joy in me:
> joy to new joy piercing from paths forgone;
> that which had been Taliessin made joy to a Joy unknown;
> manifest Joy speeding in a Joy unmanifest.
> Lancelot's voice below sang: *Ite; missa est.*
> (*TTL* 89-91)

The misery of defeat at Camlaan and the collapse of Logres are through this ritual transformed into joy. The interrelation of war and this joy it has been turned into are betrayed by the fact that neither war nor this supreme happiness can supposedly be expressed in words: again, we have the same paradox of expression that appears constantly in war literature that Taliessin has "no capable song for the joy" in him, yet of course the poem is there, attempting to express it. The strict form of the poem itself, with its consistent use of pair rhymes and its quoting of the Latin Mass at its climax, attempts to recreate the liturgical order of the ritual in itself, a stark contrast to the cycle's preceding poem, "The Last Voyage", which describes Galahad's journey with the Grail to Sarras and the final wars ending Logres, and whose stanzas and lines are irregular, making no use of rhyme.

David Jones's *In Parenthesis* also stresses the importance of liturgy. The orders of army movement are seen as similar to ritual: "the concerted movement of arms in which the spoken word effected what it signified" (3), and equated with liturgy: "The liturgy of a regiment departing has been sung" (4). For Jones, the ritual of command is a way in which the destruction of meaning in war can be counteracted; it is a language which still describes reality and has an immediate effect on it: "ritual words made newly real [...] brought intelligibility and effectiveness to the used formulae of command; the liturgy of their going-up assumed a primitive creativeness, an apostolic actuality, a correspondence to the object, a flexibility" (28).

Much of army life is compared to (Christian) religion: thus the soldiers are given lectures in a barn that is reminiscent of a church "with its great roof, sprung, upreaching, humane, and redolent of a vanished order" (13), and Lance-Corporal Lewis giving out rations takes on the character of a priest dispensing the host at Mass:

> Dispense salvation,
> strictly apportion it,
> let us taste it and see,
> let us be renewed,
> for christ's sake let us be warm.
> O have a care – don't spill the precious
> O don't jog his hand – ministering.
> (*In Parenthesis* 73)

And Part 5, "Squat Garlands for White Knights", contains an actual service (cf. 107). The writing itself repeatedly makes use of liturgical language. Part 3, "Starlight Order", begins with the liturgy of Good Friday, and Part 7, "The Five Unmistakeable Marks", uses the Tenebrae, texts from the Lamentations recited in a special ritual the night before Good Friday. As Rainer Emig states, this Good Friday liturgy appears as a strategy to create the highest meaning out of the greatest absence of meaning.[65] Ritual language brings order, even to the chaos and meaninglessness of war.

---

65 "Das Karfreitagsritual erscheint im Text als Versicherungsstrategie, um aus der größten Sinnleere die größtmögliche Sinnfülle zu schaffen" (Emig, *Krieg* 187). Translation: 'The Good Friday ritual appears in the text as a strategy, creating the greatest possible meaning from the greatest possible absence of meaning.'

The writing's strategy – besides the actual quoting of liturgy – is, similarly to Williams's "The Prayers of the Pope", to create its own ritual patterns through repetition. Jones stresses the ritual character that even the cursing in the army took on: "The very repetition of them made them seem liturgical" (Preface to *In Parenthesis* xii). Part 1, "The many men so beautiful", constantly circles around passages such as "Keep those sections of four. / Pick those knees up" (4), "Kipt' that step there. / Keep that proper distance. / Keept' y'r siction o' four" (6), where the repetition recreates the order of marching in the text itself, the word corresponding to actuality. Later, we come across the passage:

> The repeated passing back of aidful messages assumes a cadency.
> Mind the hole
> mind the hole
> mind the hole to left
> hole right
> step over
> keep left, left.
> (*In Parenthesis* 36)

The hole warnings take on an aesthetic "cadency" through repetition; the text manages to become a ritual – "im wahrsten Sinn des Wortes ein Ritual über die Leere" (Emig, *Krieg* 195).[66] The ritual constitutes itself through holes, through absence. The ritual use of language is thus seen as a method of getting around the chaos of war: the writing can take even the lack of meaning generated by war and create a ritualistic form from it.

There is one fundamental difference between Jones's and Williams's texts: while in *In Parenthesis* the soldiers appear to be largely unaware that they are participating in a ritual of sorts, the liturgical effect building up unintentionally through repetition, in Williams's poems liturgy is used consciously, and the ritual words uttered by Lancelot and the Pope have a specific effect (the destruction of the zombie armies, the reconciliation of Arthur and Pelles).

The central strategy of this use of ritual language is to subsume and transfigure war itself; war is taken up and contained by liturgy, supposedly even changed into something else. War can be contained within the sacramental work of art. Both Williams's and Jones's texts attempt to do this. Whether they are truly

---

66 Translation: 'a ritual of emptiness in the truest sense of the word.'

successful is doubtful, for they still depend on the fragments and relics generated by war – whether it be corpses, the spirits of slain knights and kings, or fragments of language to create their ritual forms. Ultimately, the transfigured forms betray the same structures as war itself – a paradoxical presence constituted out of absence, a form typical of war literature and of modernism.

Chapter Three

History

Modernist Histories: Yeats's Historical Models

The word "history" is one of the most controversial terms in modernist discourse, and it has been claimed that "the problematic of history, rather than that of literary form, is at the very heart of what modernism is" (DeCoste 769). Stephen Dedalus's famous comment (quoting Nietzsche) at the beginning of *Ulysses*, "History [...] is a nightmare from which I am trying to awake" (Joyce, *Ulysses* 40), is often taken as representative of modernism's vexed relation to the past, a past which the modernist work of art simultaneously tries to escape and yet finds impossible to leave behind. As described earlier in this study, much of canonical modernism can be seen as veering between a rejection of history and the call for a new beginning on the one hand, and on the other hand a return to ancient works and the creation of a historical canon of "high culture" into which their own work could be fitted. Wyndham Lewis declared of the Vorticist movement: "Our Vortex is not afraid of the Past. It has forgotten its existence" (in *Blast*; cit. Hapgood and Paxton 23), and T.S. Eliot in his review of *Ulysses* denounced "contemporary history" as an "immense panorama of futility and anarchy", a chaos that could only be "order[ed]" and "controll[ed]" by art ("'Ulysses', Order and Myth", *Selected Prose of T.S. Eliot* 177). Likewise, Ezra Pound called for his contemporaries to forget the past and "make it new" ("Canto 53", *Cantos* 275). However, while he had rejected the decadent Victorian style of his earliest works, Pound was using diverse historical literary models from ancient China to the twelfth-century troubadours of the Provence to "make it new", and his monumental *Cantos* are described by their author as "a long poem including history". As Bernard Bergonzi states, modernism "repudiated the present and the recent past" only to "establish contact with a more authentic remote past" (Bergonzi, *The Myth of Modernism* xi). Alongside concepts of ruptures between past and present, we find that "modernism sought to correct the apparently amnesiac tendencies of modernity by reconnecting it to a valued cultural tradition" (Nicholls 167). One of modernism's central tensions is thus, as Paul de Man claims, the tension between the desire for a tabula rasa and the impossibility of overcoming history (cf. de Man150).

One explanation for the emphasis laid on history by the modernists is of course that they lived through challenging times – the World Wars, the rise of totalitarianism, the collapse of the British Empire, and so forth: these events clearly influenced their work (as has been shown in the previous chapter). However, towards the end of the nineteenth century the entire way history and historiography was perceived had been fundamentally challenged by the work of the philosopher Nietzsche: now history, rather than being seen as an absolute, was unmasked as a fiction like any other. As Nietzsche stated, "die Geschichte [...] ist die stille Arbeit des Dramatikers" (Nietzsche, *Historie* 57).[1] This led to "the rejection of the presuppositions about the nature of historical knowledge that make the construction of any sort of teleological or even linear history possible" (Longenbach 6). Now, the artist had become a historian as legitimate as the historiographer; perhaps an even more important one, for by his (or her) more visionary use of the past, the past could come alive again for the present. This change in the perception of history and the artist's role in creating it accounts for the central position of history in modernism, and the variety of ways (both affirmed and negated) in which it appears. For example, writers such as Yeats, Pound and Eliot consciously try to incorporate the past into their work in order to achieve a sense of both historicity and tradition and contemporaneity of past and present; their works make use of the palimpsest method, layering up historical and mythical events against contemporary ones. In this way both past and present are constructed imaginatively, rather than objectively as in linear positivistic historiography. "End fact. Try fiction" Pound writes in his poem "Near Perigord", which deals with the Provençal troubadours of the twelfth century (*Selected Poems* 60).

This rejection of a linear history coincided with the collapse of the Victorian meliorist view of the past. This idea of history as unstoppable progress was questioned particularly by the traumatic events of the First and Second World Wars, and shown to be, in Yeats's words, "the newspaper['s] happy counter-

---

1 Translation: 'History [...] is the silent work of the dramatist.'

myth of progress" (Yeats, *Vision* 262). One of the earliest critics of the idea of progress was once again Nietzsche, who stated:

> Die Menschheit stellt *nicht* eine Entwicklung zum Besseren oder Stärkeren oder Höheren dar, in der Weise, wie dies heute geglaubt wird. Der "Fortschritt" ist bloss eine moderne Idee, das heisst eine falsche Idee.
> ("Der Antichrist" *Götzendämmerung* 193)[2]

Nietzsche takes the grammatical term "imperfect", designating the past tense, as representative of the past and "historical" human beings' ties to it; in order to become perfect *Übermenschen* mankind would have to overcome history and become "superhistorical".[3] Here history is seen not as progress, but as a tragedy to be overcome – a prophetic view that was to become painfully true after the atrocities of the World Wars.[4] Some of the most famous modern images of history were created in the aftermath of the Great War: Walter Benjamin's "angel of history" describes the past as a gigantic pile of ruins and progress as a driving storm:

> Es gibt ein Bild von Klee, das Angelus Novus heißt. Ein Engel ist darauf dargestellt [...] Der Engel der Geschichte muß so aussehen. Er hat das Antlitz der Vergangenheit zugewendet. Wo eine Kette von Begebenheiten vor *uns* erscheint, da sieht *er* eine einzige Katastrophe, die unablässig Trümmer auf Trümmer häuft und sie ihm vor die Füße schleudert. Er möchte wohl verweilen, die Toten wecken und das Zerschlagene zusammenfügen. Aber ein Sturm weht vom Paradiese her [...] Dieser Sturm treibt ihn unaufhaltsam in die Zukunft, der er den Rücken kehrt, während der Trümmerhaufen vor ihm zum Himmel wächst. Das was wir Fortschritt nennen, ist *dieser* Sturm.
> ("Über den Begriff der Geschichte" 697-698)[5]

---

[2] Translation: 'Humanity does not represent progression towards something better or stronger or higher, the way it is believed today. "Progress" is only a modern idea, that is a wrong idea.'
[3] Cf. Nietzsche, *Historie* 16-17.
[4] Interestingly, Wyndham Lewis writing on the First World War interprets it as a war *against* history: "The nations allied against Germany are in reality opposing the interference of the past. Europe today dislikes history. [...] The past is a murderous drug whose use should be forbidden and is being vetoed now." Lewis, "A Later Arm than Barbarity" *Outlook* 24 (5 Sept. 1914) 298.
[5] Translation: 'There is a Klee picture called Angelus Novus. On it there is an angel [...] The angel of history must look like this. His face is turned towards the past. Where we see a chain of events, he sees only a catastrophe ceaselessly piling up wreckage and throwing it at his feet. He wants to stay, to put the broken pieces back together and awaken the dead. But a storm is blowing from Paradise [...] This storm drives him relentlessly into the future, while the pile of rubble at his feet grows to the sky. This storm is what we call progress.'

And writing during the Second World War, Theodor Adorno saw the Romantic Hegel's progressive philosophy of history violently refuted by the current *Weltgeist*:

> Hätte Hegels Geschichtsphilosophie diese Zeit eingeschlossen, so hätten Hitlers Robotbomben, neben dem frühen Tod Alexanders und ähnlichen Bildern, ihre Stelle gefunden unter den ausgewählten empirischen Tatsachen, in denen der Stand des Weltgeists unmittelbar symbolisch sich ausdrückt. [...] "Ich habe den Weltgeist gesehen", nicht zu Pferde, aber auf Flügeln und ohne Kopf, und das widerlegt zugleich Hegels Geschichtsphilosophie. (*Minima Moralia* 64)[6]

While modernism thus rejects the view of history as progress, it (re)discovers other models of history. Some criticism sees a sense of deterioration evinced in modern thought, related to the old classical model of history as constant decline (exemplified in Ovid's *Metamorphoses*) where the earliest Golden Age is followed by the Silver, the Bronze, and the Iron. Thus Leon Surette states that modernism's view of the past derives from "the antique view of history as a story of decline from some pure origin" (253). Indeed, Art Berman claims that this sense of historical decline is central to modernism: "this decline is modernism's subject: there would be no modernism without it" (212). Pound's *Hugh Selwyn Mauberley* laments that

> The tea-rose tea-gown, etc.
> Supplants the mousseline of Cos,
> The pianola "replaces"
> Sappho's barbitos.
> (*Selected Poems* 99)

The return to this ancient model of history can of course be seen in itself as a typically modernist paradox, exemplifying Bergonzi's claim that modernism repudiates the past only to return to a more ancient version of it.

Besides this view of history as a constant decline from an earlier golden age, we find an equally influential model of history as a repetition of cycles; indeed the two models often cannot be clearly separated. In modernism, these cycles are usually ones of violence and destruction. In *Minima Moralia*, quoted

---

6 Translation: 'If Hegel's philosophy of history had included our times, then Hitler's robot bombs, besides the early death of Alexander and similar images, would have found their place among the select empirical facts through which the spirit of the world expresses itself symbolically. [...] "I saw the world spirit", not on horseback, but with wings and no head, and this in itself refutes Hegel's philosophy of history.'

above, Theodor Adorno reflects: "Die Logik der Geschichte ist so destruktiv wie die Menschen, die sie zeitigt: wo immer sie ihre Schwerkraft hintendiert, reproduziert sie das Äquivalent des vergangenen Unheils", concluding gloomily, "Normal ist der Tod" (65)[7] – the collapse of the progressive view of history leads the philosopher to conclude that history is a continuous repetition of past atrocities. Damon Marcel DeCoste states that "the hallmark works of Anglo-American modernism [contain] a dread of the present not as a break with tradition, but as the bloody rehearsal of a corrupt Western history" (770). DeCoste interprets Eliot's *The Waste Land* accordingly, pointing out that the loveless sex of the typist and young man carbuncular has its earlier violent counterpart in the rape and mutilation of Philomel, who "still [...] cried / and still the world pursues, / 'Jug Jug' to dirty ears" (Eliot, *Collected Poems* 66), and that London's unreal state is paralleled by that of "Jerusalem Athens Alexandria / Vienna" (Eliot, *Collected Poems* 77). *The Waste Land* shows that previous ages were in no way superior to the modern, but are equally "waste": the poem then "is indeed a lamentation, but one made over a culture ostensibly corrupt from its very inception, and not sadly fallen from an earlier age of grandeur" (DeCoste 770). Even Stephen Dedalus's famous utterance quoted above is preceded by a statement that implies the idea of recurrence: "History [is] a tale like any other too often heard" (Joyce, *Ulysses* 31). Once again, it is Nietzsche who with his idea of "ewige Wiederkehr", eternal recurrence, laid the foundation for much of modernist thought on this matter (cf. Nietzsche, *Götzendämmerung*).[8]

Writing on the modernists' vexed relationship with history, Louise Blakeney Williams summarizes that they "used history, and in particular the idea of cycles, as a means not only to discover order in the face of disorder, but also to innovate their own creative writing" (3). While most prominent modernist writers wrote on history and their theories of it, William Butler Yeats is definitely the one who went furthest in systematising his ideas. Yeats came up with a controversial esoteric model of history documented in *A Vision* (published 1925), which sees all history – indeed, all existence – as the eternal spiralling and unwinding of antithetical gyres that represent various stages of human, cultural

---

[7] Translation: 'The logic of history is as destructive as the humans it brings forth. Wherever its gravity tends to, it reproduces the equivalent of past disaster [...] The normal condition is death.'
[8] For a thorough discussion of the cyclical view of history in literary modernism, cf. Louise Blakeney Williams, *Modernism and the Ideology of History* (Cambridge: Cambridge University Press, 2002).

and intellectual development. History can thus be seen as the cyclical rise and fall of opposite states, the one declining while the other gains in strength. Yeats describes these two intersecting gyres as "one always narrowing, one always expanding, and yet bound to one another forever" (Yeats, *Vision* 131). He was introduced to the figure of the cone or gyre by supernatural "spirit-teachers" during a séance in which his wife acted as a medium; these spirit-teachers applied the gyre to history:

> Two such cones were drawn and related neither to judgement nor to incarnations but to European history. They drew their first symbolical map of that history, and marked upon it the principal years of crisis, early in July 1918, some days before the publication of the first German edition of Spengler's *Decline of the West*, which, though founded on a different philosophy, gives the same years of crisis and draws the same general conclusions. (*Vision* 11)

Accordingly Yeats applied the double gyre to his own time:

> This figure is also true of history, for the end of an age, which always receives the revelation of the character of the next age, is represented by the coming of one gyre to its place of greatest expansion and of the other to its greatest contraction. At the present moment the life gyre is sweeping outward, unlike that before the birth of Christ which was narrowing, and has almost reached its greatest expansion. The revelation which approaches will however take its character from the contrary movement of the interior gyre. (Yeats, *Michael Robartes and the Dancer*; cit. in *Yeats's Poems* 573)

This model is also taken up in Yeats's poetry. The poem that illustrates Yeats's concept of the gyres of history best is "The Second Coming", where the order of the "life gyre" "fall[s] apart; [its] centre cannot hold" and instead "mere anarchy is loosed upon the world"; the revelation of the interior gyre is the "Second Coming" of the "rough beast", antithetical to Christ whose advent marked the character of the opposite gyre (*Yeats's Poems* 294-295).

Yeats's system of gyres represents an interesting attempt to come to terms with the chaos and uncertainties of a non-linear history. It also manages to encompass the models of history as progress and decline by seeing them as antithetical states that follow after each other, as well as the view of history as cyclical. While Yeats himself remained aware of its constructed state, calling his gyres "stylistic arrangements of experience comparable to the cubes in the drawing of Wyndham Lewis and to the ovoids in the sculpture of Brancusi" (*Vision* 25), that did not stop him believing in the symbolic truth of his system;

he wrote to Dorothy Wellesley that he saw "things double – doubled in history, world history, personal history" (Yeats, cit. in Kirschner 12). He used his gyres to try and make sense of the "mere anarchy" that surrounded him at his own particular point in history: the Fenian bid for Irish independence, the Anglo-Irish War and the Irish Civil War, played out against the larger backdrop of the First World War and the beginning dissolution of the British Empire.

Fantastic Cycles: Tolkien's History of Middle-earth

J.R.R. Tolkien's world of Middle-earth is as singular among the work of the Inklings as Yeats's symbolic historical system is in modernism. While most fantasy authors invent fantastic secondary worlds, Tolkien's Middle-earth in its complexity, its wealth of history and mythology, and above all its languages, goes far beyond what any writer had come up with before him, and indeed beyond what most writers of fantasy have developed since. W.H. Auden's statements about *The Lord of the Rings* from the year 1955 still hold true:

> no previous writer has […] created an imaginary world and a feigned history in such detail. By the time the reader has finished the trilogy, including the appendices to the last volume, he knows as much about Mr. Tolkien's Middle-earth, its landscape, its flora and fauna, its peoples, their languages, their history, their cultural habits, as, outside his special field, he knows about the actual world. (Auden, "At the End of the Quest, Victory" 45-46)

The words "feigned history" are echoed by Tolkien himself, who stated in the Foreword to the second edition of *The Lord of the Rings*: "I cordially dislike allegory […] I much prefer history, true or feigned" (*LotR* xv). As critics have pointed out, *The Lord of the Rings* is itself "feigned history" (cf. Friedman, "Fabricating History").[9]

---

9 Taking into account this emphasis on history, a case might be made for reading *The Lord of the Rings* (and, to a lesser extent, *The Hobbit*) as forms of the historical novel. This genre, according to general definition, "not only takes its setting and some characters and events from history, but makes the historical events and issues crucial for the central characters and narrative, […] reveal[ing] what the author regards as the deep forces that impel the historical process" (Abrams, *Glossary* 194). Unfortunately the scope of the present study does not allow for further investigation of this idea; but many fantasy novels, not just Tolkien's, place a strong emphasis on (feigned) history that results in many similarities to the historical novel, and perhaps a more general claim for interrelation could be made.

Tolkien's *The Lord of the Rings* began as a simple sequel to his children's story, *The Hobbit*. He himself wrote: "This tale grew in the telling, until it became a history of the Great War of the Ring and included many glimpses of the yet more ancient history that preceded it" (*LotR* xiii). For many years before he wrote *The Hobbit*, Tolkien had been constructing an elaborate system of languages, and had made up an imaginary world and a history to go with them. His first book was not really intended to take place in the context of this world, Middle-earth, but, as he writes in the Foreword to *The Lord of the Rings*, "[in *The Hobbit*] there were already some references to the older matter: Elrond, Gondolin, the High-elves, and the orcs, as well as glimpses that had arisen unbidden of things higher or deeper or darker than its surface: Durin, Moria, Gandalf, the Necromancer, the Ring" (*LotR* xiii). The history of Middle-earth was already refusing to be contained. This process continued on into *The Lord of the Rings*, and Tolkien concluded despairingly at its completion: "My work has escaped from my control, and I have produced a monster: an immensely long, complex, rather bitter, and very terrifying romance, quite unfit for children (if fit for anyone)"; his mythology, the historical background of Middle-earth, had "bubbled up, infiltrated and probably spoiled everything" (Tolkien, *Letters* 136). Luckily for Tolkien, millions of readers have since proved him wrong, and critics have declared that it is precisely the scope and breadth of Tolkien's creation that creates its appeal (as does Auden, quoted above).

Middle-earth's history is recounted in *The Silmarillion*.[10] We are told of Middle-earth's creation at the dawn of time in the "Ainulindalë", which tells of the Valar ("the Powers of the World", *Silmarillion* 21) and the Fall of the wicked Vala Melkor, who desires to dominate the created world (in the course of the narration Middle-earth's cosmology is set firmly in place). *The Silmarillion* then goes on to give an account of the events of the First Age of Middle-earth: the creation of the Great Jewels, the Silmarils, by the elf Fëanor, their rape by Melkor, and the ceaseless war made on Melkor by the elves in order to

---

10 A purposeful decision has been made to use *The Silmarillion* as a kind of "definitive" history of Middle-earth – for the simple reason that considering the changes that occurred in Tolkien's mythology and cosmology, as documented in the many volumes of *The History of Middle-earth*, would go beyond the scope of this chapter and study overall. These developments are discussed in detail in Elizabeth Whittingham's *The Evolution of Tolkien's Mythology: A Study of the History of Middle-earth* (Jefferson, NC: McFarland, 2008) and in Dimitra Fimi's *Tolkien, Race and History: From Faeries to Hobbits* (Basingstoke: Palgrave Macmillan, 2009).

regain the Silmarils with all its tragic consequences, finally culminating in the apocalyptic War of Wrath in which the Valar cast Melkor out into the Void. The Second Age follows, in which the island of Men, Númenor, is established and destroyed through their own folly; the Númenoreans return to Middle-earth and there face Sauron, Melkor's old ally, who was instrumental in the downfall of their isle, in a great battle that ends the Second Age. *The Lord of the Rings* then deals with the Third Age of Middle-earth and its ending in the War of the Ring, in which Sauron is finally destroyed.

This summary of Middle-earth's history, though extremely brief, should make it clear that Tolkien is here working with a cyclical model of history. Each of the ages of his world begins with the establishment of great kingdoms or realms: in the First Age, the various elven kingdoms in Beleriand, in the Second Age, Númenor, in the Third, Arnor and Gondor. The beginning of the Fourth Age as recounted in *The Lord of the Rings* likewise sees the re-establishment of Númenorean rule in Gondor after the interim government of the stewards. Each age ends with a cataclysmic war, in which even the shape of the world is changed: Beleriand sinks beneath the sea, Númenor is swallowed by a gigantic wave, and the western shores of Middle-earth are changed time and time again. Each age reenacts the central struggle of good against evil, a struggle that can never be won, for "the lies that Melkor, the mighty and accursed, Morgoth Bauglir, the Power of Terror and of Hate, sowed in the hearts of elves and men are a seed that does not die and cannot be destroyed; and ever and anon it sprouts anew, and will bear dark fruit even unto the latest days" (*Silmarillion* 307). The neverending nature of this struggle ensures that the cycle will be repeated over and over again. To think that it will ever be broken is a fallacy, as Elrond states when he recalls of the Battle of the Last Alliance at the end of the Second Age and the War of Wrath at the end of the First:

> I remember well the splendour of their banners[.] It recalled to me the glory of the Elder Days and the hosts of Beleriand, so many great princes and captains were assembled. And yet not so many, nor so fair, as when Thangorodrim was broken, and the Elves deemed that evil was ended for ever, and it was not so. (*LotR* 237)

The quote used here indicates that Middle-earth's history can be read not just as cyclical, but equally well as a history of constant decline. The splendour of Elendil and Gil-galad's troops is not as great as the army facing Melkor in the War of Wrath; and the host of Aragorn that sets out to challenge Sauron in the War of the Ring numbers only seven thousand warriors, "scarce as many as the vanguard of [Gondor's] army in the days of its power" (*LotR* 864). Middle-earth is in decline, from the "Golden Age" at the beginning of Middle-earth, where the elves created their own kingdoms in the world and those kingdoms, one after the other, are destroyed, to the final waning of the elves and the "time [...] of the dominion of Men" (*LotR* 950) at the end of the Third Age. The symbol that would represent this historical model best, combining the downward and the circular movement, is the downward spiral – or, in Yeatsian terms, the gyre. "Quenta Silmarillion" concludes: "the SILMARILLION [...] has passed from the high and beautiful into darkness and ruin" (*Silmarillion* 307), Númenor "fell and went down into the darkness, and is no more" (336), and at the end of the Third Age "an end was come for the Eldar of story and of song" (367).

Tolkien is particularly fond of this image of songs fading or ending; thus in *The Return of the King* we encounter the passage "the Third Age was over, and the Days of the Rings were passed, and an end was come of the story and song of those times" (*LotR* 1006). Similarly, his poem "The Last Ship" from *The Adventures of Tom Bombadil* concludes: "never more / westward ships have waded / in mortal waters as before, / and their song has faded" (*Adventures* 64). In *The Lord of the Rings* itself we constantly come across songs "that none now remember aright as [they] were told of old" (*LotR* 187). Middle-earth's decline engenders slow and inexorable cultural loss – a sense of which is also given in many modernist works of art, such as Pound's *Hugh Selwyn Mauberley*, cited above, which deplores the passing of "Sappho's barbitos" and its replacement by "the pianola". As Yeats laments in "Nineteen Hundred and Nineteen",

> Many ingenious lovely things are gone
> That seemed sheer miracle to the multitude,
> Protected from the circle of the moon
> That pitches common things about. There stood
> Amid the ornamental bronze and stone
> An ancient image made of olive wood –

> And gone are Phidias' famous ivories
> And all the golden grasshoppers and bees.
> (*Yeats's Poems* 314)

Thus we can see that in his constructed history of Middle-earth, Tolkien uses historical models precisely of the kind espoused by modernist writers of his time: both cyclical and declining. It is to be doubted that he did this completely consciously; rather, his use of them testifies to their currency in general thought during the early twentieth century. To what end these models are used will be examined in the following sections of this chapter.

Myth and History

Closely connected to the term "history" is that of "myth", both of them central terms in the study of modernism and fantasy. For both literatures, drawing the line between the two can prove difficult, but examining the connections between them can reveal textual strategies that both fantasy and modernism have in common. That both Tolkien and Yeats saw connections between history and myth is borne out in their writings; thus Tolkien stated: "History often resembles 'Myth', because they are both ultimately of the same stuff" ("On Fairy-stories" 127), and Yeats reveals his mythical view of ancient history: "Our history speaks of opinions and discoveries, but in ancient times [...] history spoke of commandments and revelations. [Men] looked as carefully and as patiently towards Sinai and its thunders as we look towards parliaments and laboratories" (*Essays and Introductions* 44).

General definitions of myth stress the aura of truth and timelessness that surround it, and above all its attempt to explain the world, trying to provide a type of world-formula in the form of a story.[11] In the words of Nietzsche, myth is "das zusammengezogene Weltbild, [die] Abbreviatur der Erscheinung" (*Geburt der Tragödie* 171)[12] – it is the world reduced to its essentials. Nietzsche sees history as the polar opposite of myth, as it creates alienated instead of unified individuals.[13] Myth, on the contrary, claims universal validity and

---

11 Cf. for example M.H. Abrams, *A Glossary of Literary Terms* 170.
12 Translation: 'The contracted image of the world, the abbreviation of appearances.'
13 "fast jeder, bei strenger Prüfung, [fühlt] sich so durch den kritisch-historischen Geist unserer Bildung zersetzt [...], um nur etwa auf gelehrtem Wege, durch vermittelnde Abstraktionen, sich

renders history unnecessary: "der Mythus will als ein einziges Exempel einer ins Unendliche hineinstarrenden Allgemeinheit und Wahrheit anschaulich empfunden werden" (*Geburt der Tragödie* 131).[14] However, in order to do this it becomes necessary to exclude anything pointing beyond the myth itself from its picture of the world.

The structural mechanisms through which myth establishes this claim and pushes history aside have been demonstrated by Claude Lévi-Strauss and Roland Barthes, both of whom study myth as a signifying system. Lévi-Strauss's seminal *Structural Anthropology* (first published in 1958) points out that "myth is language: to be known, myth has to be told; it is a part of human speech" (Lévi-Strauss 209). It can thus be interpreted according to the linguistic model of Saussure, with the difference that myth, while starting off from the basic differentiation between *langue* and *parole*, progresses to a third level which belongs "to a higher and more complex order" (Lévi-Strauss 211), and which lies "*above* the ordinary linguistic level" (Lévi-Strauss 210). This is how myth can escape history and time: it becomes a type of language "where meaning succeeds practically at 'taking off' from the linguistic ground on which it keeps rolling" (Lévi-Strauss 210). Barthes in his book *Mythologies* develops Lévi-Strauss's ideas of the double linguistic layers of myth further, defining myth as "a type of speech defined by its intention [or concept] much more than by its literal sense [or meaning]; and [...] in spite of this, its intention is somehow frozen, purified, *made absent* by this literal sense" (Barthes, *Mythologies* 124). The presence of the literal sense suggests the absence of an obvious motivation, and presents the myth as something unmotivated and thus something natural

---

die einmalige Existenz des Mythus glaublich zu machen. Ohne Mythus aber geht jede Kultur ihrer gesunden schöpferischen Naturkraft verlustig: erst ein mit Mythen umstellter Horizont schließt eine ganze Kulturbewegung zur Einheit ab. [...] Worauf weist das ungeheure historische Bedürfnis der unbefriedigten modernen Kultur, das Umsichsammeln zahlloser anderer Kulturen, das verzehrende Erkennenwollen, wenn nicht auf den Verlust des Mythus, auf den Verlust der mythischen Heimat, des mythischen Mutterschoßes?" (*Geburt der Tragödie* 172). Translation: 'Nearly everyone, if he examines himself closely, will feel demoralised by the critical-historical spirit of our education [...], which attempts to render myth credible only through scholarship, through abstractions. Without myth, however, every culture loses its inherent, healthy, creative natural powers: only a horizon spanned by myths can unify a cultural movement. [...] The incredible historical need of our unsatisfied modern culture, its tendency to gather countless other cultures around itself, its consuming desire to know, what does this point to but to the loss of myth, the loss of our mythic home, our mythic mother's womb?'

14 Translation: 'Myth wants to be understood as the sole example of truth and universality, pointing towards the infinite.'

and self-justifying. This, Barthes says, is the very principle of myth: "it transforms history into nature" (129). It transforms historical reality into a natural, self-justifying image of this reality. This is one of the important connections between history and myth: while history must perforce be arbitrary, myth has the power to (supposedly) transform that history into an absolute, an essence, denying any relativity, valid everywhere and at all times, escaping time. This is what makes it so attractive to modernism.

The German critic and philosopher Hans Blumenberg, following Nietzsche, sees historiography as only another way of artificially structuring the past in a way similar to that of myth:

> Das Geschichtsbedürfnis tendiert auf Markierungen von der Deutlichkeit des mythischen Typs, die Bestimmungen darüber erlauben, wie sich das individuelle Subjekt mit seiner endlichen Zeit zu den es weit übergreifenden Großraumstrukturen der Geschichtszeit ins Verhältnis setzen darf. Aus ihrer lebensweltlichen Motivation heraus arbeitet auch die Geschichtsschreibung der Indifferenz der Zeit entgegen. Deshalb kann sie den Epochenbegriff nicht preisgeben, so oft er ihr streitig gemacht wird. (Blumenberg, *Mythos* 113)[15]

Thus history depends on mythical structures for its meaning, and both myth and history are informed by the same desire to overcome what Blumenberg calls *Indifferenz der Zeit*, the indifference of time. This definition of both myth and history is essentially modern, as it recognises both as artificial constructs.

The importance of myth in modernism as a structural tool was first acknowledged by T.S. Eliot in his review of Joyce's *Ulysses*, which has already been quoted several times. Joyce, who in his work creates a parallel between the voyages of Ulysses and the wanderings of Stephen Dedalus and Leopold Bloom through contemporary Dublin, is hailed by Eliot as a literary pioneer:

> In using the myth, in manipulating a continuous parallel between contemporaneity and antiquity, Mr. Joyce is pursuing a method which others must pursue after him. [...] It is simply a way of controlling, of ordering, of giving a shape and significance to the immense panorama of futility and anarchy which is contemporary history. It is a method already adumbrated by Mr.

---

15 Translation: 'What we need from history tends towards indicators with the clarity of mythical models, indicators that enable the individual subject, with his finite time, to determine how he can set himself in a relationship to the large-scale structures that reach far beyond him. The life-world motivation of historiography means that it also works against the indifference of time. That is why it cannot give up the concept of epochs, even though this concept is constantly contested.'

> Yeats, and the need for which I believe Mr. Yeats to have been the first contemporary to be conscious. It is a method for which the horoscope is auspicious. [...] Instead of narrative method, we may now use mythical method. ("'Ulysses', Order and Myth", *Selected Prose of T.S. Eliot* 177-178)

According to Eliot, myth is a way of (artificially) imposing order and asserting authority both in the modernist work and its interpretation of reality. Two central problems of modernist writing could effectively be dealt with through myth: the problems of subjectivity and of time. Through the use of myth, which is "by definition both impersonal and ahistorical" (Emig, *Modernism* 90), a text could be given timelessness, a validity surpassing the mere concerns of the era, and its voice given an (apparent) authority through the parallels or direct quotation of ancient myth. Myth also becomes a means of giving unity to both a text and the world, the unity Nietzsche declares modern man has lost – it is, in fact, the way "historical" man can escape history and become "superhistorical". For if myth is the timeless essence of the world, then it must represent also that superhistorical moment in which "die Welt in jedem Augenblicke fertig ist und ihr Ende erreicht" (Nietzsche, *Historie* 16-17).[16] The consequence of this escape from history is that the universal validity claimed by the texts negates the possibility of anything else beside the text. The prime examples of this are Ezra Pound's *Cantos*: called "a long poem including history" by its maker, the *Cantos* become in fact not

> an account of history, culture and language; they are history, culture and language in language. [...] What it creates instead is an all-inclusive meta-myth that is identical with the text itself and an all-powerful identity that neither requires justification nor has to fear fate. (Emig, *Modernism* 117-118)

The fact that modernism remains aware of the artificial nature of myth, that it uses it as a "method", is symptomatic of what Michael Bell calls the "double awareness" of modernism (Bell 12): it uses one artifice (myth) to overcome another (history); as Bell states, "[myth's] most important meaning was as an emblem of the human world as self-created" (14).

It is significant that Eliot cites Yeats as being the first to adopt "mythical method". Yeats had made use of myth, especially Celtic myth, since he started writing, and the desire to replace history or at least control it with myth is apparent even

---

16 Translation: 'The world is completed every single moment, and reaches its end.'

in his earliest works. Thus in *The Wanderings of Oisin* of 1889 the legendary Gaelic warrior Oisin encounters the historical St. Patrick (himself of course by Yeats's time the subject of much popular legend), rejecting the latter's offer of salvation in order to "dwell in the house of the Fenians, be they in flames or at feast" (*Yeats's Poems* 35).[17] The vision of mythical Ireland in his early work is one that attempts to place Ireland outside of history and time: "your mother Eire is always young", he claims, while "time and the world are ever in flight" ("Into the Twilight" *Yeats's Poems* 93). Yet his nationalist ambitions made him keen to connect this vision of Eire to his concrete historical surroundings. It was his historical system that offered him a way of connecting myth and history, his own "mythical method" with which to impose order on the chaos and anarchy of contemporary history. Yeats uses the cyclical patterns of myth to order his own version of world history, confirming Blumenberg's claim that both rely on the same artificial structures. According to his system, the Trojan War is the end of a cycle that began with the union of Leda and Zeus (as described in "Leda and the Swan"). In *A Vision*, Yeats calls this "the annunciation that founded Greece[,] made to Leda" (268). He thus links the mythic Zeus and Agamemnon to the concrete Greece of "Homer, civil life" (269), and to other historical figures such as Anaxagoras, Aeschylus, Pausanias (cf. 269-270). He sees his cyclical view confirmed by history itself:

> Before Phidias, and his westward-moving art, Persia fell, and [...] when full moon came round again, amid eastward-moving thought, and brought Byzantine glory, Rome fell; and [...] at the outset of our westward-moving Renaissance Byzantium fell; all things dying each other's life, living each other's death. (Yeats, *A Vision* 271)

Thus for Yeats, history becomes subsumed under his system; historical events and people (even contemporaries of his such as Ezra Pound) are taken out of their context and appropriated by it. This system can be called mythical as it provides a kind of world-formula, relating everything to its own structure,

---

17 It should be pointed out that much of Irish history and mythology is confused as it is. Ireland's mythical rulers, from the Tuatha de Danaan to the Firbolg, Fomorians etc., can all be traced back to actual invasions of the island; the Tuatha de Danaan were probably invaders from Aegean Greece who later became elevated to the mythical status of gods. The Fenians Oisin calls upon were an actual war band led by Finn Mac Cumhail, Oisin's father, who was killed AD 283. Their exploits are narrated in the Ossianic cycle of tales, which presents them as supernatural heroes, and they have since entered Irish mythology. It is this mythic aspect Yeats makes use of in his work. The Fenian revival of the nineteenth century of course adds another historical dimension to this already complex intertwining of myth and history.

allowing meaning only within its own bounds. It is mythic in the Barthesian sense, for it "transforms history into nature"; concrete historical happenings and characters become expressions of the myth, rather than possessing significance in their own right. History functions as the primary signifying system for Yeats, which is appropriated and emptied of meaning, becoming mere form; yet its existence justifies the mythic secondary system. Yeats makes it appear as if history has come into being because of the myth, not the myth because of it.

In its claim to universal validity, from mythic times to the present, Yeats's mythology also functions as a prime example of a modernist cosmic model: a work of art that attempts to incorporate reality and human history in its entirety. It is, as Rainer Emig says of Pound's *Cantos*, "an all-inclusive metamyth" (*Modernism* 118). But as Barthes points out, the way myth creates its own universal validity is by hiding its constructed nature and posing as natural. Blumenberg (and, as quoted above, Nietzsche) states that one of the fundamental traits of myth is to deny any reality outside itself: "Isolierung des Realitätsgrades bis zur Ausschließlichkeit gegen jede andere Realität" (Blumenberg 80).[18] It can only claim to be real and universally applicable by excluding other competing narratives of reality. Yeats's *A Vision* is no exception. At its beginning, Yeats gives a detailed explanation of how the system he develops is not his personal construction, but a form of higher knowledge revealed to him by spirit teachers. He is keen to avoid the impression that his mythology is in any way arbitrary and obviously wishes to claim an impersonal authority for it. When he goes into closer historical detail in Part III, "The Twenty-eight Incarnations", Yeats gives examples of people he sees expressing the phases of the moon that correspond with phases of human civilisation. Thus Walt Whitman is an expression of Phase Six, Alexandre Dumas and Thomas Carlyle of Phase Seven. The latter phase supposedly is one in which "men have a passion for history, for the scene, for the adventure" (Yeats, *Vision* 116). Yeats writes "Alexandre Dumas was the phase in its perfection", but then "Carlyle [...] showed the phase at its worst. He neither could nor should have cared for anything but the personalities of history, but he used them as so many metaphors in a vast popular rhetoric, for the expression of thoughts that seeming his own were the work of preachers

---

18 Translation: 'The isolation of the degree of reality to the extent that every competing reality is excluded.'

and angry ignorant congregations" (Yeats, *A Vision* 116). Carlyle is allowed no other interest than that of the historian, that accords to Yeats's phase; but his supposedly "popular" tone and matter make him less worthy an exponent of Phase Seven than Dumas. Both writers are denied any true originality, as they are merely expressing the spirit of their times. But here the incongruity of Yeats's system becomes clear: why Carlyle should be regarded as more "popular" than Dumas, who was one of the most successful best-selling authors of the nineteenth century, is left unsaid (Dumas's merits are also left unmentioned). Yeats's myth completely excludes alternative histories – ones that would, for example, show another side to Thomas Carlyle, or recognise Walt Whitman and Alexandre Dumas as writers in their own right, rather than mere expressions of his phases. If Yeats lambasts Carlyle for using "the personalities of history [...] as so many metaphors" he himself is surely not doing otherwise. One also feels driven to ask where Yeats would place himself among his incarnations, or whether he somehow mysteriously stands outside his own cosmic model.

However, *A Vision* perhaps shows Yeats's myth at its worst, where the author rigidly tries to prove the validity of his system. It is Yeats's poetry where his vision of historic cycles and their connection to myth is at its most convincing. "Leda and the Swan", already mentioned before, offers a sweeping panoramic view of the cycle beginning with Leda and Zeus's mating and culminating in the Trojan War. Leda's seduction is here portrayed as a rape, and the ensuing cycle is one whose catastrophic end mirrors the violence of its inception – a violence also formally reproduced in the sonnet's broken eleventh line, which concludes abruptly with the word "dead":

> A shudder in the loins engenders there
> The broken wall, the burning roof and tower
> And Agamemnon dead.
> (*Yeats's Poems* 322)

This is indeed, as DeCoste states, an "inevitable rehearsal of a cyclical, indeed unredeemable [...] violence" (768). In "The Second Coming", also quoted above, the myth is carried into Yeat's own day and age, where the end of the 2000-year Christian cycle is heralded by the vision of a "second coming", not of Christ, but of his polar opposite: "A shape with lion body and the head of a man, / A gaze blank and pitiless as the sun" (*Yeats's Poems* 294). In contrast to

"Leda and the Swan", which is set entirely in the realm of Greek mythology (although Yeats, as demonstrated above, connected it to actual history) and narrated impersonally, "The Second Coming" has a distinct lyrical I privy to the mythic vision of history, although he himself appears to remain enclosed within its cosmic model. The poem reveals a tension between the personal and the universal, as the speaker's images come from "*Spiritus Mundi*" and thus command a higher, objective authority; yet the speaker seems to insist on the elect nature of his vision: "my sight", "I know" (*Yeats's Poems* 294-295): he is, as Yeats himself claimed to be, the mouthpiece of a higher knowledge similar to that of Zeus in "Leda and the Swan" – a wisdom that Nietzsche calls superhistorical (cf. *Historie* 17). This superhistorical knowledge is how the historical human being can overcome history and turn it into myth – and this is precisely what Yeats affects to do through the system supposedly revealed to him through his spirit teachers. Perhaps to be privy to the secret structure behind the historical model is to escape it: as Thomas Whitaker traces Yeats's thought: "the mastery of that vision of history might lead to a transcendence of history" (21).

At first glance, Tolkien's Middle-earth, apart from its similar cyclical historical structure, might seem to have little in common with Yeats's mythic system and its attempts to turn history into myth. For within the boundaries of Tolkien's secondary world, myth is history: *The Silmarillion*, which functions as Middle-earth's mythology, is simultaneously the history of its First Age. Middle-earth's gods, the Valar, are not removed from their world (at least not at first) and the elves meet them and indeed live with them in the realm of Valinor. The events narrated in *The Silmarillion* seem incredibly remote by the time of the narrative of *The Lord of the Rings*. Yet there are connections that prove its reality, such as the figures of Galadriel and Elrond, or the direct descent of Aragorn from Beren and Lúthien. The Elves that wander the woods of Middle-earth in the Third Age, exiled from Valinor, are telling the truth literally when they sing:

> O Elbereth! Gilthoniel!
> We still remember, we who dwell
> in this far land beneath the trees,
> Thy starlight on the Western Seas.
> (*LotR* 76)

This "myth-realization" (Basney 183) is one of the patterns repeated most often in *The Lord of the Rings*, and it has been noted that "Tolkien's narrative [...] evoke[s] the remote past, thereby establishing an all but cosmic context for Frodo's quest and implying the conflation of myth and history" (Friedman, "Fabricating History" 128).

The individual characters in Tolkien's works never lose the sense that they are acting before a vast historic backdrop, and that their actions are related to it. For example Sam, on the steps of Morgul Vale, remembers the tale of Beren, and relates their quest to his (in a way that again shows the merging of mythic legend and actual history in Middle-earth):

> Beren now, he never thought he was going to get that Silmaril from the Iron Crown in Thangorodrim, and yet he did, and that was a worse place and a blacker danger than ours. But that's a long tale, of course, and goes on past the happiness and into grief and beyond it – and the Silmaril went on and came to Eärendil. And why, sir, I never thought of that before! We've got – you've got some of the light of it in that star-glass that the Lady gave you! Why, to think of it, we're in the same tale still! It's going on. Don't the great tales ever end? (*LotR* 696-697)

Thus we see that myth and history are, in Middle-earth, the same thing[19] – unlike the primary world, where they cannot be connected except through an artificial cosmic model of history such as Yeats's.

However, when the relationship of Middle-earth to the primary world is examined, it becomes clear that here, too, we are dealing with an expertly crafted cosmic model. Tolkien stated: "Middle-earth is *our* world" (cit. Carpenter, *Tolkien* 98), and "Middle-earth is not an imaginary world" (Tolkien, *Letters* 239), and claimed that in his creation of Middle-earth and its tales he wanted to create a mythology for England (cf. *Letters* 144-145, 231). These statements, if taken seriously, place Middle-earth in an uneasy position somewhere between the imaginary and the real. He seems to be fusing (created) mythology with concrete historical reality in a way similar to the way Yeats's system does. We can see here the kind of mythic expansion prominent in so many modernist texts – among them Yeats's works. Tolkien wrote that in his works he wished

---

[19] This could be seen to be working similarly to the way that Irish pre-history and myth become conflated, as pointed out in a previous footnote.

"to restore to the English an epic tradition and present them with a mythology of their own" (Tolkien, *Letters* 231). If Tolkien's mythology is really to be a mythology for England, then it claims validity not only in the secondary world, but in the primary one as well. In positing that Middle-earth, his creation, is actually the primary world, Tolkien expands his creation beyond just a secondary world. It attempts to encompass our modern reality and to incorporate our world in its reality. In the Prologue to *The Lord of the Rings* and in its many Appendices the narrator, editor or translator appears to be writing in our time, discussing the changes that have taken place in the world since the recording of the events of the War of the Ring. For example, the calendar of the Shire is said to have "differed in several features from *ours*" (*LotR* 1080; my emphasis). This "ours" clearly refers to the Gregorian calendar used in England and Western Europe. There are several more links of elements of Middle-earth to our primary world. In the Prologue "Concerning Hobbits", the reader is told that "Even in *the ancient days* they were, as a rule, shy of 'the Big Folk', as they call *us*, and *now* they avoid *us* with dismay" (*LotR* 1; my emphases). The use of "us" creates identity of reader and narrator, and "now", used in contrast to "the ancient days" of the story, seems to imply our own day and age. This position taken by the narrator seems to imply that the happenings portrayed in *The Lord of the Rings* are actually real in the primary world as well, and that in the primary world, too, myth and history converge. In merging the history of Middle-earth with that of the primary world, Tolkien is incorporating our world into the reality of his secondary world. This link can be seen as a mythic attempt to hide the constructed nature of the secondary world. If it poses as a kind of pre-history of our own world, it is less obviously imaginary, it claims to be nature. And thus it claims validity in our primary world. It tries to show that our primary world only makes sense in relation to the mythic secondary world, which explains why the primary world we live in has become what it is – modernised and disenchanted, as the elves have departed and the hobbits "avoid us with dismay". This fusion of the two worlds into one large cosmic model forms the basis of Tolkien's critique of modernity that has been noted by many critics. Thus we can see that in ways very similar to Yeats's, Tolkien's work posits a continuum between myth and history, structures them in a similar way, and finally subsumes actual history under his mythology, creating a cosmic model like his modernist contemporaries. Middle-earth is indeed a feigned history – but not just of the secondary world: it is actually a feigned history of the primary world, that incorporates the primary world into its own myth.[20]

Myth claims to render history redundant, as seen above, and to transform it into nature, that is, part of its own system. However, we have already seen in the chapter on War and the Arthurian myth the difficulty of keeping the actual historical reality of war contained safely within the myth, for in its most apocalyptic form war breaks free of myth, with the consequence that "history began" (Williams, "Prelude" *TTL* 1). History breaks free of the myth that tries to contain it; a fact we shall encounter repeatedly in Yeats's and Tolkien's works.

Nationalist Histories

While works like Pound's *Cantos* or Eliot's *Waste Land* create mythic cosmic models of a truly cosmopolitan nature, incorporating allusions and quotes from a cultural background ranging from mediaeval Provence and ancient China to Renaissance England, mythic Greece, and nineteenth-century Gemany, it should have become evident above that the focus of Yeats and Tolkien is purposely narrower. While the displaced Americans Eliot and Pound cultivated an international modernism (at least at first), Yeats is usually associated with a specifically Irish brand of modernism, and Tolkien's self-declared allegiance to England and his distrust (rather than active dislike) of Romance culture is well-documented. The works of both these writers can be seen as trying to create a (mythic) history for their respective countries, attempting to establish a distinct national identity. Both were writing in times of historical upheaval in which this identity was challenged and a re-writing of history was becoming necessary: for Yeats, the turmoils surrounding Irish independence, and for Tolkien, the collapse of the British Empire that had up to then been the focus

---

20 Both Simonson (2008) and Fimi (2009) discuss the relationship between myth and history in narratological terms; Fimi describes how "*The Hobbit* […] inaugurated a new way of writing. Tolkien was not writing a mythology anymore, he was writing a novel" (119). Simonson reads the Mines of Moria episode in *The Lord of the Rings* as an "intrusion" of the novel into a text previously dominated by myth (cf. 185-88).

of constructions of British identity. Both authors write against the idea of a united Britain and seek to return to a national past preceding union.

The problems faced by Yeats as he struggled with Irish history and concepts of Irishness throughout his career have been discussed in a number of studies.[21] Ireland's history, at least since English occupation,[22] was one of defeat by and repeated failed rebellions against a colonial oppressor who systematically attempted to destroy the Irish language, identity, and culture. By the time independence was finally achieved, the colonisers had created, through the long history of occupation, an Irish nation divided against itself. As Michael North writes: "The most general cultural appeal of all is usually to history, but Ireland's is a history of discontinuity, of revolts and defeats. [...] the very attempts to conceive of a unified Irish culture exacerbated the divisions that made such a culture" (31-32).

The solution seemed to be to return to a period before the occupation, in which a unified Irish identity could be found: "By delving into Celtic pre-history, the political and historical divisions that had come to define the Irish situation could be elided and annealed into a mythic and heroic cultural archive which would allow Irish people to take pride in their own culture" (O'Brien 128). Yeats, along with writers such as Synge and Lady Gregory, thus indulged in a "redemptive Revivalism" (Castle 248). Ancient myth was seen as the way in which history could be overcome, and by returning to it, the period of English/British oppression could be, at least in theory, written out of Ireland's history. However, this proved, at least in the case of Yeats, to be impossible to carry out in practice.

As we have seen above, Yeats's early plays and poetry return to a mythic, pre-historic Ireland in an attempt to create a specifically Celtic literature and identity. In a way very similar to Tolkien's cosmic model, his writings establish

---

21 This chapter is indebted particularly to Elizabeth Cullingford, *Yeats, Ireland and Fascism* (London: Macmillan, 1981) and *Gender and History in Yeats's Love Poetry* (Cambridge: Cambridge University Press, 1993); Michael North, *The Political Aesthetic of Yeats, Eliot and Pound* (Cambridge: Cambridge University Press, 1991); Marjorie Howes, *Yeats's Nations: Gender, Class, and Irishness* (Cambridge: Cambridge University Press, 1996); and Eugene O'Brien, *The Question of Irish Identity in the Writings of William Butler Yeats and James Joyce* (Lampeter: Edwin Mellen, 1998).
22 To be historically accurate, Ireland's occupation was English from the 12th to 16th century and British from the 17th to 21st century (including the present day occupation).

a dichotomy between a mythic, enchanted Irish past and its grey, disenchanted and oppressed present; thus in "The Dedication to a Book of Stories selected from the Irish Novelists" (*Yeats's Poems* 80-81) from the 1893 collection *The Rose*, Yeats writes:

> There was a green branch hung with many a bell
> When her own people ruled this tragic Eire;
> And from its murmuring greenness, calm of Faery,
> A Druid kindness, on all hearers fell.

Now, however, those green branches are "the barren boughs of Eire", and Ireland is

> That country where a man can be so crossed;
> Can be so battered, badgered and destroyed
> That he's a loveless man;

The poet's ambition to re-establish that enchanted past becomes clear when he states "I also bear a bell-branch full of ease", namely the book this dedication is written for. This poem makes it clear that the way to make Eire new is through writing it new. Similarly, in "Into the Twilight" (*Yeats's Poems* 93) from *The Wind among the Reeds* (1899), the poet distinguishes between a dull historical present ("a time out-worn") and an enchanted vision of Ireland that almost stands outside of time and space ("time and the world are ever in flight"):

> Out-worn heart, in a time out-worn,
> Come clear of the nets of wrong and right;
> Laugh, heart, again in the grey twilight,
> Sigh, heart, again in the dew of the morn.
> Your mother Eire is always young,
> Dew ever shining and twilight grey;
> Though hope fall from you and love decay,
> Burning in fires of a slanderous tongue. [...]
>
> And God stands winding his lonely horn,
> And time and the world are ever in flight;
> And love is less kind than the grey twilight,
> And hope is less dear than the dew of the morn.

The fusion of this enchanted past with the present and the poet's hope for Irish freedom is expressed in strongly symbolic language in "The Secret Rose" (*Yeats's Poems* 105):

> I, too, await
> The hour of thy great wind of love and hate. [...]
> Surely thine hour has come, thy great wind blows,
> Far-off, most secret, and inviolate Rose?

These early poems of Yeats's make use of a Celticism that is problematic in that it seems to a large extent to repeat the colonialist discourse it sets out to replace. Ireland is largely personified as a beautiful woman, much as colonialism frequently represents conquered countries as women to be ruled and dominated. "Our mother Eire" is the subject of the poet's devotion, and claims his absolute loyalty; but it becomes clear that a large part of her attraction lies in the fact that she is oppressed. The poet "would accounted be / True brother of a company / That sang, to sweeten Ireland's wrong" ("To Ireland in the Coming Times" *Yeats's Poems* 85) – if she were not wronged, he would have nothing to sing about. Also Yeats's definition of Celticism rests in part on Matthew Arnold's (immensely influential) view of the Celt, which posited a complementary relationship between a feminine, artistic but ultimately mentally and physically inferior Celt and the male, rational and hence superior Saxon.[23] Yeats's view of the Irish poet seems to subscribe to this imagery: the poet writes "fitful Danaan rhymes", his "heart would brim with dreams" ("To Some I have Talked with by the Fire" *Yeats's Poems* 84). In Yeats, as in Arnold, this sensitive and creative nature of the Celt depends largely on his oppression; thus he writes: "It is hardly an exaggeration to say that the spiritual history of the world has been the history of conquered races" (*Uncollected Prose* II, 70). In this way oppression and colonial exploitation actually become prerequisites for the creativity that marks out the Celts as special: the "double-edged virtues of Celts" are "idealism, self-sacrifice and spiritual victory through material defeat and impoverishment" (Howes, *Yeats's Nations* 45). Yeats's early nationalistic works reinscribe oppression as a key factor in "the history of conquered peoples". "Mother Eire" demands a blood price from those who love her: they must sacrifice themselves for a cause that is hopeless and never-ending: "It is a hard service they take that help me. [...] They that had red cheeks will have pale cheeks for my sake; and for all that they will think they are well paid. They shall be remembered for ever" (Yeats, *Cathleen Ni Houlihan*, in *Selected Plays* 11). The reward is posthumous

---

23 Matthew Arnold, *On the Study of Celtic Literature* (London: Smith, Elder and Co., 1867).

sanctification as an Irish hero, to be the inspiration for the next generation of sacrificial victims, who in their turn become heroes, and so on and so forth.[24] With this "history of conquered peoples", Yeats actually describes and participates in the construction of an Irish history that is a cyclical rehearsal of defeat after defeat, and thus also a national identity that makes a virtue of oppression and so becomes dependent on it:

> [Yeats] defines his land as "tragic Eire" and plainly has no wish to change its character. The standpoint may be expressed as a question: What would be the good of a politically victorious Ireland which had lost its specifically Irish culture, tinged – and often more than tinged – with melancholy? (May 29)

Even the hope for freedom supposedly expressed in "The Secret Rose" is undermined by the fact that the Rose is "far-off" and "most secret". Thus Yeats's works become a Celtic literature of defeat, as exemplified in the previous chapter of this study: a literature "of a people under duress, who *in extremis* are attempting collectively to bring together and preserve the elements of their common past and so produce what might be called a literature of defeat, of displacement and dispossession and disinheritance" (Moorman 7). The "elements of [a] common past" in Ireland are however oppression and exploitation, and Yeats's works are thus doubly inscribed with defeat, displacement, dispossession and disinheritance – while overtly aiming at establishing unity.

It is Yeats's poetry and his plays dealing with the Easter Rising that mark a change in his attitude towards this version of Irish history and Celticism, that now begins to doubt the ideology of self-sacrifice and the possibility of joining a mythic, heroic Celtic past with the concrete historical present. Famously, he questions the heroism of the 1916 rebels in "Easter 1916" (*Yeats's Poems* 288-289), wondering whether their passionate love for their country, verging on fanaticism, was the result of confused values:

---

24 Richard Kearney points out the relation of this sacrifice to pre-historical terror cults, and their relation to history: "The terror cult grants man a victory over history by permitting him to return to its origin, where he may be contemporaneous with his heroic forbears." This supposed sacrifice is intrinsically linked to (colonial) oppression/terrorism and its dark twin, (nationalist) terrorism, as the "experience of impotence gives rise to feelings of revenge and resentment which ultimately express themselves in violent rites of terror. Just as this 'cruel and ineluctable destiny' was the cosmic evil of demons for early man, [...] it was and is British Imperialism for many Irish Republicans" (169-170). He concludes that "without this mythological hermeneutic, our understanding of the Northern Ireland crisis remains incomplete" (177).

> Too long a sacrifice
> Can make a stone of the heart. [...]
> Was it needless death after all?
> For England may keep faith
> For all that is done and said.
> We know their dream; enough
> To know they dreamed and are dead;
> And what if excess of love
> Bewildered them till they died?

The rebels, through this self-sacrifice, are "changed utterly", taking on a "terrible beauty": the "terrible beauty" of Cathleen Ni Houlihan who demands death as her due, and for which Yeats felt a "mixture of admiration and contempt" (DeCoste 771). In the play *The Dreaming of the Bones* (1919), the Easter Rising is seen as a part of the vicious circle of Irish history. The sentiments expressed here, condemning violence and doubting the worth of self-sacrifice, stand in almost diametric opposition to those in *Cathleen Ni Houlihan* cited above. In *The Dreaming* a participant in the Rising fleeing from Dublin meets two enchanted spirits, the ghosts of Diarmuid and Devorgilla that first called the Normans into Ireland and so set off its history of violence. If "somebody of their race at last would say, / 'I have forgiven them'" (*Selected Plays* 118), the ghosts would be at peace and, by implication, the violence in Ireland would cease. The young man however, fresh from the latest bloodshed, cannot bring himself to find mercy for them: "O, never, never / Shall Diarmuid and Devorgilla be forgiven" (118). Thus Ireland is doomed to repeat its violent history again. This play is interesting as it stresses both the necessity of forgiveness and the impossibility of it; as the young man says after the ghosts have left him, "I had almost yielded and forgiven it all – / Terrible the temptation and the place!" (120). The play also points out that it was the Irish themselves who brought the Norman invasion upon their country. In his last play, *The Death of Cuchulain* (1939), Yeats draws a parallel between the mythic hero Cuchulain and the men involved in the Easter Rising; however, this version of Cuchulain does not die fighting the waves, "mak[ing] a myth of himself" (Friedman, *Adventures* 21) as in Yeats's earlier play *On Baile's Strand*; he dies "blinded by heroism, butchered by a clown" (Jeffares, Introduction to *Selected Plays* xviii). Thus when the play concludes with the song

> What stood in the Post Office
> With Pearse and Connolly? [...]
> Who thought Cuchulain till it seemed
> He stood where they had stood?
> (230)

it is not Pearse and Connolly's heroism that is stressed by the parallel with Cuchulain so much as their blindness and even the absurdity of their actions. These are further discredited by the final lines of the song: "So ends the tale the harlot / Sang to the beggar-man" (230). It becomes impossible to reconcile mythic Eire with modern Ireland; to attempt to do so must reveal both as fundamentally flawed, worthy not of heroic ballads but only the songs of the low-life on the streets.[25] Yeats expressed his growing concern with what he viewed as his own complicity with the myth of heroic sacrifice for Ireland presented in works such as *Cathleen Ni Houlihan* in his drafts for *A Vision*: "Now I begin running through the years from my youth up & measure my responsibility for an event that has been a great grief to me & many mother[s]" (Typescript of *A Vision*, transcribed Richard Ellmann; qtd. Cullingford, *Gender and History* 69).

Yeats saw the continuing bloodshed of the Irish Civil War as part of the "mere anarchy [...] loosed upon the world" as the two thousand year Christian cycle drew to its end. In *Plays and Controversies* he writes that pre-Civil War Ireland was already "preparing, in that dark portion of the mind which is like the dark side of the moon, for insurrection and anarchic violence" (Whitaker 52). Once again, Ireland's history is seen to be one of inescapable violence; problematically, Yeats's historical cosmic model seems to offer no peaceful alternative as the gyre widens and all spirals out of control. This is the key problem of his cyclical view of Irish history: it is doomed to repeat itself for ever, and there seems to be no escape from the vicious circle:

---

[25] Similarly, Yeats's poem "The Circus Animals' Desertion", written around the same time as *The Death of Cuchulain*, sees his "masterful images", Oisin, Cuchulain, and Countess Cathleen, grown out of "A mound of refuse or the sweepings of a street, / Old kettles, old bottles, and a broken can, / Old iron, old bones, old rags, that raving slut / Who keeps the till" (*Yeats's Poems* 471-472). The impossibility of constructing an adequate modern-day version of Cuchulain is taken up by the contemporary Irish poet Michael O'Loughlin in his poem "Cuchulain": "If I lived in this place for a thousand years / I could never construe you, Cuchulain." O'Loughlin's Cuchulain eventually appears as a science-fiction character: "An obvious Martian in human disguise / You stomped about in big boots / With a face perpetually puzzled and strained / And your deep voice booms full of capital letters: / What Is This Thing You Earthlings Speak Of" (Fallon and Mahon 427).

> Violence upon the roads: violence of horses;
> [...] wearied running round and round in their courses
> All break and vanish, and evil gathers head:
> Herodias' daughters have returned again,
> A sudden blast of dusty wind and after
> Thunder of feet, tumult of images,
> Their purpose in the labyrinth of the wind;
> ("Nineteen Hundred and Nineteen" *Yeats's Poems* 317)

This "dusty wind" is a pessimistic re-writing of the "great wind of love and hate" of Ireland's fight for independence celebrated in "The Secret Rose".[26] We can see that essentially, Yeats's view of Irish history as cyclical and marked by defeat has remained the same, but it is evaluated differently and in an increasingly negative way, as his aspirations to construct a unified national identity failed to bear fruit.[27]

Yeats's alienation in the Irish Free State, which subscribed to "a monological view of Irishness as Celtic, Gaelic, and Catholic" (O'Brien 29), in which he, the non-Gaelic-speaking Protestant allied with the Ascendancy, was increasingly marginalised, is expressed in his Anglo-Irish "Big House" poems. These poems construct Anglo-Irishness as "a nationality in crisis", expressing "an ambivalence about foundations and essences, repeatedly enacting their desirability, necessity, and functions only to confront their chimerical nature" (Howes, *Yeats's Nations* 104, 130). Any possibility of a unified nationality connected to a mythic past has been completely abandoned. Instead, history figures only as ruins, such as the broken tower of Yeats's own house in Ballylee. Myth fails to control history in the face of its brutal actuality.[28]

---

26 The "violence of horses" is also reminiscent of Yeats's earlier poem "He bids his Beloved be at Peace", where "The Horses of Disaster plunge in the heavy clay" (*Yeats's Poems* 96). The trope of the horse as disastrous portent appears – possibly in reference to Yeats, and certainly in reference to the Civil War – in the work of the contemporary Irish poet Eavan Boland: "Iron of his shoes as he stamps death / Like a mint on the innocent coinage of earth. [...] That rose he smashed frays / Ribboned across our hedge, recalling days / Of burned countryside, illicit braid: / A cause ruined before, a world betrayed." ("The War Horse" in Fallon and Mahon 258-259).

27 This view is of course besides being typically modernist also typical of the (post)colonial condition. For readings of Yeats as postcolonial, cf. Terry Eagleton et al., *Nationalism, Colonialism, and Literature* (Minneapolis: University of Minnesota Press, 1990), esp. Edward Said's contribution "Yeats and Decolonization" 69-95.

28 Yeats's Protestantism can be seen as a key factor in his inability to reconcile myth and history. As Kiberd notes, "While Roman Catholic writers of the revival period seemed obsessed with the history of their land, to Protestant artists that history could only be, as Lady Gregory insisted, a painful accusation against their own people" (107).

As already mentioned above, J.R.R. Tolkien wished in his legendarium of Middle-earth to write a mythology for England. In a long letter he described this in detail:

> I was from early days grieved by the poverty of my own beloved country: it had no stories of its own (bound up with its tongue and soil), not of the quality which I sought, and found (as an ingredient) in legends of other lands. [...] Do not laugh! But once upon a time (my crest has long since fallen) I had a mind to make a body of more or less connected legend, ranging from the large and cosmogonic, to the level of romantic fairy-story – the larger founded on the lesser in contact with the earth, the lesser drawing splendour from the vast backcloths – which I could dedicate simply to: to England; to my country. [...] I would draw some of the great tales in fullness, and leave many only placed in the scheme, and sketched. The cycles should be linked to a majestic whole, and yet leave scope for other minds and hands, wielding paint and music and drama. Absurd. (*Letters* 144-145)

Tolkien notes a dearth or lack of continuity in English legend and myth, and it is indeed the case that the English (in marked contrast to the Irish they occupied for centuries) have no mythology of their own, the closest being the Arthurian "Matter of Britain", which is however a mix of Celtic and Romance influence, besides being distinctly Christian in character.[29] This dearth is the result of the repeated invasions of the island of Britain in early history, when one people after another drove the previous inhabitants out. The Celtic fringe of Britain persists in seeing the English as a Saxon race (still seen for example in the contemporary Gaelic term of "Sassenach", Saxon, for an English person), although the English even before the Norman conquest were not a homogenous Germanic race in possession of their own mythology, but a mixture of Saxon, Celt, Norseman, and Roman. Tolkien himself appears to subscribe to the (not entirely accurate) view of Englishness as essentially Saxon, placing himself in a tradition of "Saxonism" that begins in the 17th century with Milton's *History of Britain*.[30] Perhaps his Saxon ideal and insistence on Englishness, rather than Britishness, is also what makes the Arthurian myth problematic for Tolkien, as in it the Saxons are portrayed as

---

[29] Tolkien was not the only one to think so. Forster in *Howard's End* writes: "Why has England not a great mythology? Our folklore has never advanced beyond daintiness, and the greater melodies about our countryside have all been issued through the pipes of Greece. Deep and true as the native imagination can be, is seems to have failed here" (262).

[30] The rise of Anglo-Saxon studies significantly also begins around this time. Thus it is also an academic tradition of "Saxonism" that Tolkien places himself in. How indebted Tolkien's creation of Middle-earth is to his academic background in Old English philology in particular is described in detail in Shippey's *Road to Middle-earth*.

enemy barbarians. Conversely, this is, as we have seen, the very fact that makes Arthurian legend ideal for appropriation by the Welshman David Jones.[31]

1066 saw the complete destruction of the "Saxon" culture and the imposition of a French Norman system of society and the French language. Tolkien himself saw the Battle of Hastings as one of the most tragic events in his country's history, the worst result of which in the eyes of Tolkien the philologist was the virtual extinction of Old English, which lost all status, becoming the language of the serfs, then gradually merging with French to become what we know today as Early Modern English. Tolkien's passion for Anglo-Saxon made him ever suspicious of French, the language that had displaced and (as he felt) deformed the tongue he felt to be inherently his own.[32]

When Tolkien went about creating his mythology, he consciously made use of those fragments of Anglo-Saxon that had survived the Norman Conquest and into his own day, building them into his subcreation and weaving them into his own ideas. For example, the very first inspiration of what was to become *The Silmarillion* was an Old English poem from the *Exeter Book*, which runs

> Eala earendel, engla beorhtast,
> ofer middangeard monnum sended...

This means "Oh, Earendel, brightest of angels, sent to men above Middle-earth..." (both poem and translation are taken from Shippey, *Road* 218). And thus the concept of Eärendil the Mariner, whose star (the Silmaril) rose over Middle-earth as a sign of hope to men and elves at the end of the First Age, was born. The Rohirrim, the race of men in *The Lord of the Rings* who are basically Anglo-Saxons on horses,[33] are inspired both by the Anglo-Saxon language (they speak a lost form of Old English, Mercian) and by the pre-Norman images of

---

31 This does not mean to say that there are no Celtic influences on Tolkien's work. Examining the genesis of Tolkien's legendarium, Dimitra Fimi writes that "in *The Book of Lost Tales* the emphasis was on England's Anglo-Saxon past, in contrast with 'Britain' and the 'Celtic' tradition of Wales and Ireland. By the 1950s this opposition had lost its significance. ['Things Celtic'] had crept into his legendarium from the beginning [and] were later consciously interlinked with the Anglo-Saxon tradition" (129). Cf. Fimi's study and Marjorie Burns's *Perilous Realms* (2005) for a thorough discussion of Celtic elements in Tolkien's work.
32 Humphrey Carpenter describes the passionate personal feelings Tolkien had for Anglo-Saxon in his *J.R.R. Tolkien. A Biography*, esp. in the chapter "He had been inside language" (136-46).
33 See Thomas Honegger "The Rohirrim: "Anglo-Saxons on Horseback?" An Inquiry into Tolkien's Use of Sources" in Jason Fisher (ed.), *Tolkien and the Study of his Sources* (2011).

horses cut into England's chalky soil, one of which is close to Oxford and which Tolkien doubtlessly saw often. The Old English epic *Beowulf* also plays a significant role in imagining the Riddermark (as the Rohirrim call their land in their own language); at one point it is even quoted directly (although in translation) when describing the Golden Hall of Meduseld: "The light of it shines far over the land" (*LotR* 496).³⁴ It is also of note how the expressly English or Anglo-Saxon nature of Tolkien's subcreation is reflected in his choice of language; for example, the simple name "Bag End", the dwelling-place of the Baggins family, is at the dead end of a road that would in conventional English be called a "cul-de-sac" – a French term (although not used in France!) of which "Bag End" is a literal translation – and in Tom Shippey's eyes is "a defiantly English reaction" (*Road* 66). The Baggins's nasty relatives, the Sackville-Bagginses, have by contrast "severed their connection with Bag End by calling it *cul-de-sac(k)* and tagging on the French suffix –*ville*!" (Shippey, *Road* 66). Amusing as this particular instance of insistent Englishness may seem, Tolkien was serious about keeping French influence to a minimum in his works.

Through its use of actual historic sources, Tolkien's Middle-earth is clearly related to the England it wishes to provide a mythology for. But the deliberate avoidance of any post-Conquest material and language reveals that Tolkien's endeavour to create a specially "English" mythology represents an attempt to write foreign (i.e. Norman) invasion out of his country's history, just as Yeats looks back to Celtic myth to erase British occupation from his country's history. It attempts to establish a specifically "English" identity that equated Englishness with the Anglo-Saxon culture and language, dismissing any Norman and French influence. Perhaps it can thus be seen, strangely enough, as a postcolonial literature written 900 years after colonisation.³⁵

The historical context explaining Tolkien's insistent Englishness and perhaps also his work's connection to (post)colonialism can be seen in the preliminary

---

34 These examples are all taken from Shippey, *Road* (111-113).
35 The application of the term "postcolonial" is hotly contested, especially when used to refer to imperial states such as Great Britain. I here use it as suggested by Peter Hulme, who writes: "If 'postcolonial' is a useful word, then it refers to a *process* of disengagement from the whole colonial syndrome, which takes many forms and is probably inescapable for all those whose worlds have been marked by that set of phenomena." He also points out that "a country can be postcolonial and colonizing at the same time" (120-122).

dissolution of the British Empire following the World Wars. Far from this being universally perceived as a dramatic decline, Jed Esty notes that "English intellectuals translated the end of empire into a resurgent concept of national culture", and that some "canonical English writers [...] measured the passing of British hegemony not solely in terms of vitiated imperial humanism but also in terms of a recovered cultural particularity, that is, at least potentially, the basis for both social and aesthetic renewal" (2, 3). Among these writers cited by Esty are the canonized modernists T.S. Eliot, Virginia Woolf, and E.M. Forster, but also Tolkien himself. The renewed insistence apparent in the later works of these modernists on a specifically English culture, as opposed to the diversity of imperial Britishness, becomes increasingly important as that diversity breaks up.[36] This insistence on Englishness does not necessarily mean that their writings become provincial and narrowed down; their aim is to "implicitly reinscribe universalism into the language of English particularism [...] so that Englishness represents not just a type, but the very archetype" (Esty 14). Eliot for example cites Yeats as his model, noting that "in becoming more Irish [...] he became more universal" (Eliot, "Yeats" *Selected Prose* 252). Esty points out that in doing this, "Eliot and his London contemporaries were beginning to borrow the logic of cultural nationalism back from the colonies" (14).[37] Postcolonial cultural nationalism, as seen in the case of Yeats, searches for a unified and integrated national culture and identity; accordingly, the "metaphor of lost totality" that characterises both imperial and modernist literature might be overcome in a postimperial England, and "the end of empire might be taken to augur a basic repair or reintegration of English culture itself" (7). However the example of Yeats and Ireland has shown that this (re)integrated culture is well-nigh impossible to achieve, which bodes ill for the English version of the same project.

---

36 Esty notes the change in the modernists' works from metropolitanism to Anglocentrism: "Virginia Woolf, for example, wrote her first novel, *The Voyage Out* (1915), about a colonial journey and her last, *Between the Acts* (1941), about a country ritual; Eliot's multicultural metropolis in *The Waste Land* gave way to the nationalist sacred sites of "Little Gidding"; Forster moved from the hot states of Italian and Indian culture in his major fiction to the delibidinalized insularity of his midcentury pageants and country rambles" (7).

37 This universality of the particular is also taken up by Patrick Kavanagh, who writes: "The parochial mentality [...] is never in any doubt about social and artistic validity of his parish. All great civilizations are based on parochialism – Greek, Israelite, English. Parochialism is universal; it deals with fundamentals" (cit. Fallon and Mahon xviii). It is interesting that Kavanagh lists *English* parochialism here as a model for the Irish to follow, and not the other way round.

Tolkien fits perfectly into Esty's reading of late modernism and resurgent nationalism in post-imperial England. As seen above, his work can in a way be seen as postcolonial, albeit postcolonial in a very peculiar (if not necessarily unique) form. His letters reveal a dislike and indeed condemnation of imperialism, a fear of cosmopolitanism (particularly in the guise of Americanization), and a self-declared love of England, rather than (modern) Britain.³⁸ His works, particularly *The Hobbit* and *The Lord of the Rings*, can be seen as partaking in "a national pastoral fantasy" (Curry 37) that takes the Shire as its starting and its end point – the Shire that is, in Tolkien's own words, "based on rural England" (*Letters* 250). As Fimi writes:

> In the inter-war period Englishness came to be associated with the simple ways of the English countryside, rather than with England's glorified Anglo-Saxon past. Tolkien's hobbits and their provincial Englishness can be read as a move towards this alternative portrayal of England. (129)

Interestingly, it was only when he conceived of the Shire and used the hobbits as protagonists that Tolkien found himself able to write a coherent narrative about Middle-earth. Tolkien's masterpiece, *The Lord of the Rings*, which forms the greater part of his mythology for England, also puts Englishness at the heart of its created world. Indeed, as Esty notes, with the Shire Tolkien manages to simultaneously "reenchant England and recover its ordinariness" (122).

However, it must remain doubtful whether this vision of a unified English culture and mythology is actually achieved in Tolkien's works. The vision of the past given in *The Lord of the Rings* is not one of a continuous history, but one where noble lines are broken, heirlooms are lost, and ancient citadels and fortresses are destroyed or fall into ruin. The elves have dwindled until only four of their dwelling-places remain: Rivendell, Lórien, Mirkwood and the Grey Havens; and this last is only really a place of departure. While these places and indeed the elves encountered in the narrative have their importance as points where the action is slowed down and the motivations behind it are made clear (as in the Council of Elrond and the mirror-gazing in Lórien), it is actually elvish relics that take on a vital role in the narrative, such as the elvish swords from the lost

---

38 For example, "I do find this Americo-cosmopolitanism very terrifying. [...] For I love England (not Great Britain and certainly not the British Commonwealth (grr!)" (*Letters* 65); or, "I know nothing about British or American imperialism in the Far East that does not fill me with regret and disgust" (115).

kingdom of Gondolin, Gandalf's Glamdring and Bilbo and later Frodo's Sting. The line of the kings of Gondor, the South Kingdom of the Númenoreans, is broken when their king Eärnur falls in Minas Morgul (cf. *LotR* 1062), while although in the North Kingdom of Arnor the line is kept intact, the kingdom itself is lost and the heirs of Númenor become Rangers of the wild. It is of course symbolic that the heirloom of these kings is a broken sword. The great realm of the dwarves, Khazad-dûm, is destroyed by the Balrog and the lesser one in Erebor also by the dragon Smaug (in a similar fashion, too: both evil powers are fire-monsters). While the latter realm is eventually re-established, an attempt to recolonise Moria ends in a repetition of its first downfall. While travelling across Middle-earth, the Fellowship of the Ring repeatedly encounters the remains and ruins of these past kingdoms: first of all, the hobbits traverse the Barrowdowns, the graves of the old kings and queens of Arnor, then encounter what used to be the "great watch-tower [called] Amon Sûl" upon Weathertop (181); after an interlude in Rivendell, the Fellowship passes through Hollin, where elves used to dwell. Now, however, the only trace of the elves is the stones they carved; as Legolas says, "the trees and the grass do not remember them. Only I hear the stones lament them: *deep they delved us, fair they wrought us, high they builded us; but they are gone*" (276). The companions then pass through the ruined dwarf kingdom, now called Moria, and finally cross into Gondor, the border marked by two ancient statues of Isildur and Anárion and the hills of Amon Hen and Amon Lhaw, upon which there used to be "high seats [...] and watch was kept" (384). The journeys of the Fellowship are thus almost like an archaeological trip, cataloguing the ancient ruins of Middle-earth's history.[39] Significantly, each of these sites of ruin becomes a place of threat or danger: the hobbits are trapped in the Downs by the Barrow-wight, the Nazgûl attack Aragorn and the hobbits on Amon Sûl, in Hollin flocks of black crows and a mysterious flying shadow "moving fast [...] and not with the wind" (279) disturb the travellers, in Moria they re-encounter "Durin's Bane" the Balrog and lose their leader Gandalf, and finally the Fellowship is attacked and breaks up on Amon Hen. History is not only ruinous; it seems to possess a malevolent power that dooms those passing through its ruins to re-enact the destruction that laid them waste in the first place. In some cases this is almost

---

39 Richard Lehan (33) points out the importance of archaeology for modernism and modern thought, particularly after Schliemann's discovery of the nine layers of Troy.

a literal repetition of the initial disaster: for example, Amon Sûl was destroyed by the Witch-King of Angmar (cf. *LotR* 1060), who becomes the Lord of the Nazgûl and leads the attack upon Weathertop in which Frodo is wounded. Even more striking is the episode in Moria. In Moria's Chamber of Records the Fellowship discover a book that, although partly slashed and stained and thus rendered illegible, tells them the fate of the dwarves that lived there:

> "It is grim reading," [Gandalf] said. "I fear their end was cruel. Listen! *We cannot get out. We cannot get out. They have taken the Bridge and second hall. Frár and Lóni and Náli fell there.* Then there are four lines smeared so that I can only read *went 5 days ago.* The last lines run *the pool is up to the wall at Westgate. The Watcher in the Water took Óin. We cannot get out. The end comes,* and then *drums, drums in the deep.* I wonder what that means. The last thing is written is in a trailing scrawl of elf-letters: *they are coming.* There is nothing more." (*LotR* 314)

It may seem strange that a dwarf should have made a record of his colony and kept it, very practically for the Fellowship, up till the moment he died (though maybe not so strange if one gives credit to Tolkien's statement that he wrote parts of his mythology "down in dugouts under shell fire"; Tolkien, *Letters* 78). However, it is important for the novel not just because it fills in information; it sets the scene for a repetition of that very tragedy:

> Gandalf had hardly spoken these words, when there came a great noise: a rolling Boom that seemed to come from the depths far below, and to tremble in the stone at their feet. They sprang towards the door in alarm. *Doom, doom* it rolled again, as if huge hands were turning the very caverns of Moria into a vast drum. [...] "They are coming!" cried Legolas. "We cannot get out," said Gimli. "Trapped!" cried Gandalf. "Why did I delay? Here we are, caught, just as they were before." (*LotR* 315)

It is not just by chance that Legolas and Gimli repeat the sentences they have just heard Gandalf read out. Thus we can see that in Middle-earth, as in Yeats's Ireland, history becomes the perpetuation of violence.

Of course, one can argue that with the reestablishment of Gondor and Arnor and the return of the king (and the symbolic reforging of the sword), this pessimistic view of history is proved wrong and a new order is set up. Similarly, the Shire, threatened with industrialisation and modernisation, is saved and its rural order preserved. This seeming restoration is however undermined by the fact that it can no longer satisfy the very ones who laboured to bring it about – Frodo departs from Middle-earth, and as we hear in the Appendices, so does Sam (cf. *LotR* 1072). "The Tale of Aragorn and Arwen", also found in the Appendices, casts a note of gloom even upon Aragorn's success, for he, as all mortals, must die, and Arwen ends her days alone in abandoned Lórien, to be "utterly forgotten" after her death (*LotR* 1038).[40] The hope that with the end of the Third Age, wholeness and unity is established, is actually belied by the very form of *The Lord of the Rings*, which, although it contains a long coherent narrative, is actually in its entirety made up of (supposedly historical) fragments. Of all Middle-earth's rich and varied history, all that remains are these fragments, embodying in their incomplete state the "loss and the silence" that is thematised repeatedly in Tolkien's tales. Thus we can see that Middle-earth, the mythological England, actually repeats England's loss of a unified cultural heritage instead of reestablishing it. It is founded on the fragments that survived the Norman Conquest, but instead of truly erasing that part of English history as it sets out to do, Tolkien's sub-creation repeats the history of destruction and fragmentation. As within the narrative of *The Lord of the Rings*, the weight of history unavoidably results in destruction, even when – or perhaps particularly when – its power is denied.

In the cases of both Tolkien and Yeats, then, their attempts to rewrite their nations' history to produce a unified national culture based on a (traditional or newly created) mythology ultimately end by acknowledging the impossibility of doing so. The attempt to contain the forces of history within a constructed mythology, as both writers try to do, results in failure when that construct is harnessed to a nationalist agenda. Yeats cannot rewrite Ireland's past and create a unified national culture, and the myth to which he has recourse collapses into "the song the harlot / Sang to the beggar-man", into a "circus animal". Whenever actual history appears in his works, it asserts its destructive power. Tolkien's mythology for England, based upon an Anglo-Saxon concept of Englishness, wishes to contribute to a nationalist English culture, but ultimately repeats

---

40 In addition, the one attempt Tolkien made at writing a story set after the passing of the Ring he quickly abandoned, but it has been published as a fragment in *The History of Middle-earth*. The tale, set in Gondor during the reign of Eldarion, Aragorn's son, deals with a cult worshipping the dark powers and plotting to overthrow Eldarion. Tolkien wrote: "I could have written a 'thriller' about the plot and its discovery and overthrow – but it would have been just that. Not worth doing" (*Letters* 344). In this fragment it becomes obvious, however, that Tolkien could envisage no long-term happy solution even after the restoration of the line of kings.

the inherent fragmentation that makes a unified Englishness impossible. Both writers' myths, attempting to contain history, fail in the face of its reality.

In Joyce's *Ulysses*, Stephen, during the history class he gives the schoolboys, reflects on the limitations that history presents: "Had Pyrrhus not fallen by a beldam's hand in Argos or Julius Caesar not been knifed to death? They are not to be thought away. Time has branded them and fettered they are lodged in the room of the infinite possibilities they have ousted" (31). In their attempts to rewrite the histories of their respective nations, both Tolkien and Yeats are trying to create new versions of their countries from those "infinite possibilities". If they ultimately fail to do so, their failure can perhaps be read through Stephen's following musings: "But can those [infinite possibilities] have been possible seeing that they never were? Or was that only possible which came to pass? Weave, weaver of the wind" (31). Perhaps one cannot rewrite that which has come to pass, write that which the passage of time has made impossible: a return to a time before colonial conquest. In contemporary postcolonial literature and criticism, it is generally acknowledged that the colonial experience must be recognised in order for its trauma to be dealt with; as Chinua Achebe writes, "The storyteller creates the memory that the survivors must have – otherwise their surviving would have no meaning" (cit. Gikandi 10). A literature that tries to wipe the mind blank, destroy memory rather than create it – even with the best of intentions – must be seen as escapist. It falls into the trap of repeating history and reproducing its structures instead of moving on.

Escapes from History and Time

The escapist urge is evident in Stephen Dedalus's famous statement that follows on the passage quoted above: "History [...] is a nightmare from which I am trying to awake" (Joyce, *Ulysses* 40). This desire to "wake from" history obviously represents a desire to escape from it and its burdens. Unsurprisingly, the theme of escape from history and time itself is prominent in the works of both Yeats and Tolkien, who writes in "On Fairy-stories": "[Fairy-stories] open a door on Other Time, and if we pass through, though only for a moment, we stand outside our own time, outside Time itself, maybe" (129). Tolkien and Yeats are not alone in this: the concern with time and escape from it is central in much modernist and fantastic fiction (and science fiction) of their day. H.G. Wells's *The Time Machine* is perhaps the most famous example of this in popular fiction, but works such as Eliot's *Four Quartets* also focus on the perception of time and ways to perhaps stand outside of it, "At the still point of the turning world" where "past and future are gathered" ("Burnt Norton" *Collected Poems* 191). Eliot's poem mourns the inevitable passing of time: "Time and the bell have buried the day, / The black cloud carries the sun away" (193). "East Coker" (*Collected Poems* 196-204) is perhaps the quartet most concerned with the inevitable consequence of this passing: Death. "O dark dark dark. They all go into the dark" mourns the speaker. Tolkien and Yeats share this concern with death.[41]

Tolkien wrote that he saw "Death and Immortality" as the "real theme" of *The Lord of the Rings* (*Letters* 246). Many critics have pointed out the predominant atmosphere of mortality and loss that characterises Middle-earth, and the relentless passing of time is emphasised again and again in Tolkien's works:

> *Where now the horse and rider? Where is the horn that was blowing?*
> *Where is the helm and the hauberk, and the bright hair flowing? [...]*
> *They have passed like rain on the mountain, like a wind in the meadow;*
> *The days have gone down in the West behind the hills into shadow.*
> (*LotR* 497)

What awaits is the "shadow", the "dark dark dark" of Eliot's poem. Yeats's late poems in particular betray an overwhelming concern with age and death, but even his early works thematise these topics. Thus "The Lamentation of the Old Pensioner" from the 1893 collection *The Rose* (*Yeats's Poems* 81) concludes full of rage, "I spit into the face of Time / that has transfigured me". And the final piece from Yeats's *Last Poems* (1938-39), "Politics" (*Yeats's Poems* 472) laments "But O that I were young again".

The escape from time often takes the form of a journey to Faërie or Other Time. As Tolkien states in "On Fairy-stories", fairy-tales allow their readers to

---

[41] Rosemary Jackson states that "Behind the 'high' fantasy of Kingsley, MacDonald, Morris, Tolkien, Lewis, etc., there is a recognizable 'death wish', which has been identified as one recurrent feature of fantasy literature. [...] these more conservative fantasies simply go along with a desire to cease 'to be', a longing to transcend or escape the human" (156). While this awareness of death and finality is undeniably characteristic of fantasy, I find Jackson's view of the genre fantasy over-simplified; I hope the passages on Tolkien's "Escape from Deathlessness" and on transmission in this chapter will give a more diverse view on this matter.

escape from the primary world and indeed time itself (cf. 129). Yeats's dramatic poem *The Shadowy Waters* asks the question in the beginning "*Is Eden out of space and time?*" (*Yeats's Poems* 144), and its hero Forgael discovers that "There is a country at the end of the world / Where no child's born but to outlive the moon" (174), a fairyland where he and his beloved Dectora can escape time and death: "knitted mesh to mesh, we grow immortal" (179). The fact that time is of no consequence or passes differently in Faërie is a topos found in many fairy-tales and taken over into literature such as Irving's *Rip van Winkle*. It also becomes an issue in C.S. Lewis's Narnia stories, where the Pevensies return to Narnia to find that in their absence of one year's count in their time, hundreds of years have passed in Narnia. In Tolkien, mortal beings' encounter with the elves often confronts them with a sense of being outside of time, as Sam says during the Fellowship's stay in Lórien: "Anyone would think that time did not count in there!" (*LotR* 379). The ultimate escape from time is of course the journey to the Undying Lands of Valinor, which the elves can make and which is given to Frodo as a reward for his labours in destroying the Ring. If Frodo is wounded by the malevolent forces of history, his journey to Valinor which presumably heals him of those wounds can be seen as an escape from history itself, into a place where time loses its meaning. Tolkien however sees this "Escape from Death" as problematic: it is made clear that Frodo does not leave the Shire willingly and would rather have led a normal life there. Also Tolkien introduces the concept of the "Escape from Deathlessness": "Fairy-stories provide many examples and modes of [the Escape from Death]. But [...] Fairy-stories are made by men not by fairies. The human stories of the elves are doubtless full of the Escape from Deathlessness" ("On Fairy-stories" 153). For the elves, having to leave Middle-earth even for Valinor is not seen as something entirely positive, as Galadriel declares: "The love of the Elves for their land and their works is deeper than the deeps of the sea, and their regret is undying and cannot ever be wholly assuaged" (*LotR* 356). They "regard [Middle-earth] as a paradise, loss of which is not even fully compensated by immortality" (Shippey, *Author* 248). This sentiment seems somewhat similar to that found in Yeats's poem "The Stolen Child" (*Yeats's Poems* 53-54), where the fairies' world contrasts with the mortal world "*more full of weeping than you can understand*", but in choosing their (presumably immortal) life, the child forfeits the comfort of his homely environment:

> He'll hear no more the lowing
> Of the calves on the warm hillside
> Or the kettle on the hob
> Sing peace into his breast,
> Or see the brown mice bob
> Round and round the oatmeal chest.

While both writers see the escape from time as one into Faërie, Yeats and Tolkien seem to share the opinion that giving up a mortal life may not always be as straightforwardly positive as it would seem at first glance.[42]

There are also examples of escapes gone wrong. One of Tolkien's finest poems, "The Sea-Bell" (*Adventures* 57-60), deals with a mortal's trip to Faërie and into Other Time but also his (enforced) return from it. Walking by the sea, the speaker finds "a white shell like a sea-bell", and listening to it hears "a ding within, [...] a call ringing" out like the sound of a bell. The sound of the bell of course measures time: when he hears it the speaker cries "It is later than late!", and he sets off, both to follow the elusive call and to escape the time whose passing the bell measures. A boat takes him on an enchanted voyage to Faërie, "wetted with spray, / wrapped in a mist, wound in a sleep". Once in Elfland the speaker vainly tries to make contact with its inhabitants; in the end, falling victim to his own hubris, he declares himself "king of this land" and is imprisoned "wandering in wit" for the traditional magical period of a year and a day, after which he searches for his boat in order to return to his own country until his "hair [is] hanging grey" and "years [are] heavy on [his] back". Through his own folly he has squandered the possibility of evading time and age in Faërie, and time's revenge is all the more bitter for it. When he finally reaches his home his sea-shell is "silent and dead", and he concludes despairingly:

> Never will my ear that bell hear,
> never my feet that shore tread,
> Never again, as in sad lane,
> in blind alley and in long street
> ragged I walk. To myself I talk;

---

42 Once again, the "escape" from time and a fixed locality can be read as emblematic of the colonial situation. Thus Terry Eagleton writes of "the 'no-time' and 'no-place' of the disregarded colony, with its fractured history and marginalized space" (*Heathcliff and the Great Hunger* 298).

for still they speak not, men that I meet.
(*Adventures* 60)

The image of the sea-bell and the strange time it keeps is also found in Eliot's "The Dry Salvages", the third part of the *Four Quartets*. Some passages are remarkably similar to Tolkien; thus Tolkien's

> Birds came sailing, mewing, wailing;
> I heard voices in cold caves,
> Seals barking, and rocks snarling,
> And in spout-holes the gulping of waves.
> (*Adventures* 59)

is paralleled by Eliot's

> The sea howl
> And the sea yelp, are different voices
> Often together heard: the whine in the rigging,
> The menace and caress of wave that breaks on water,
> The distant rote of granite teeth,
> And the wailing warning from the approaching headland
> Are all sea voices, and the heaving groaner
> Rounded homewards, and the seagull[.]
> (*Collected Poems* 206)

Eliot then goes on to number the voice of the sea-bell among his voices:

> And under the oppression of the silent fog
> The tolling bell
> Measures time not our time, rung by the unhurried
> Ground swell, a time
> Older than the time of chronometers[.]
> (*Collected Poems* 206)

Eliot's sea-bell, like Tolkien's, measures fantastic Other Time. The bell's call eventually becomes "the sound of the sea bell's / Perpetual angelus", reassuring the hearer with a call to prayer, resting in the certainty that however time passes security can be found in religious faith – in this case, the Christian faith (the Angelus is a devotion in honour of the Incarnation). Tolkien's bell carries no such reassurance, and its voice in the end is silenced.

In this Tolkien's poem is actually remarkably like a set of poems by Yeats, "The Happy Shepherd" and "The Sad Shepherd" from Yeats's 1889 collection *Crossways* (*Yeats's Poems* 41-43), where a sea shell plays a similar role to the one in Tolkien. In Yeats's first poem the shepherd laments "the many changing things / In dreary dancing past us whirled, / To the cracked tune that Chronos sings" – in short, the passing of time. No one's truths have withstood the test of time; the shepherd then counsels:

> Go gather by the humming sea
> Some twisted, echo-harbouring shell,
> And to its lips thy story tell,
> And they thy comforters will be,
> Rewording in melodious guile
> Thy fretful words a little while,
> Till they shall singing fade in ruth
> And die a pearly brotherhood;
> For words alone are certain good[.]
> (*Yeats's Poems* 42)

It is words – the words of the poet – that alone can comfort. However, this conversation with one's own echoes traps the speaker in a kind of vicious circle as every utterance is turned inwards upon itself. This is made clear in the second poem, where the sea shell distorts the words: "But the sad dweller by the sea-ways lone / Changed all he sang to inarticulate moan / Among her wildering whirls." This end is similar to that of Tolkien's speaker in "The Sea-Bell", whose magic shell is not only "silent" but "dead", and who can also speak only to himself: "to myself I talk; / for still they speak not, men that I meet" (this strengthened by the fact there is no apparent narratee to whom the speaker's tale is being told). What then to do, if, as Yeats claims, "Words alone are certain good" but communication breaks down as it does in "The Sea-Bell" and the "Shepherd" poems?

Eliot's *Four Quartets* hint at an answer. "Words, after speech, reach / Into the silence" through "the form, the pattern" ("Burnt Norton" *Collected Poems* 194). It is the written word rather than the spoken one that lasts and that can brave time, perhaps even escaping it. As Yeats's fellow Irishman and Tolkien's fellow fantasist Lord Dunsany writes:

> And little he knew of the things that ink may do, how it can mark a dead man's thoughts for the wonder of later years, and tell of happenings that are gone clean away, and be a voice for us out of the dark of time, and save many a fragile thing from the pounding of heavy ages; or carry to us, over the rolling centuries, even a song from lips long dead on forgotten hills.
> (*The King of Elfland's Daughter* 105)

Ink withstands the ravages of time, and the work of art itself with its "form" and "pattern" apparently becomes the way to escape it.

This is also the solution found in Yeats's Byzantium poems. Yeats describes the city of Byzantium in *A Vision*:

> I think that in early Byzantium, maybe never before or never since in recorded history, religious, aesthetic and practical life were one [...]. The painter, the mosaic worker, the worker in gold and silver, the illuminator of sacred books, were almost impersonal, almost perhaps without subject-matter and that the vision of a whole people [was woven] all into a vast design, the work of many seemed the work of one, that made building, picture, pattern, metal-work of rail and lamp, seem but a single image. (279-280)

The city becomes one "single image", combining spirituality, beauty and utility and becoming, although situated in history, a timeless symbol for artistic perfection. In Yeats's poems, Byzantium actually appears to be located outside history and the mortal world altogether. In "Sailing to Byzantium" (*Yeats's Poems* 301-302), the speaker finds himself confronted with the neverending cycle of "Whatever is begotten, born, and dies". He himself is an "aged man", "a paltry thing" doomed to die; this age is contrasted with the "Monuments of unageing intellect" that are part of "the artifice of eternity". The escape from time thus lies in the work of art, and eternity itself becomes an "artifice". In the poem this is symbolized by the contrast between the country the speaker comes from (Ireland, maybe), a place of "dying generations", and "the holy city of Byzantium" where the speaker has travelled upon an enchanted journey into Other Time. The speaker longs to leave his "mortal dress": "Consume my heart away; sick with desire / And fastened to a dying animal / It knows not what it is." Once he has thus been cleansed, he declares

> Once out of nature I shall never take
> My bodily form from any natural thing,
> But such a form as Grecian goldsmiths make
> Of hammered gold and gold enamelling
> To keep a drowsy Emperor awake;
> Or set upon a golden bough to sing
> To lords and ladies of Byzantium
> Of what is past, or passing, or to come.
> (*Yeats's Poems* 302)

The way to immortality for the speaker lies in becoming an artifice himself, in this particular case a golden bird. This bird reappears in the poem "Byzantium"

> scorn[ing] aloud
> In glory of changeless metal
> Common bird or petal
> And all complexities of mire and blood.
> (*Yeats's Poems* 363-64)

As an artifice, the bird is "changeless" and (apparently) vastly superior to the natural, "common" bird subject to the changes of time. Similarly, the great cathedral dome "disdains / All that man is"; rejecting the human, the speaker of "Byzantium" "hail[s] the superhuman". This term of course refers to Nietzsche and his concept of the *Übermensch* who stands outside history. In Byzantium, the human "blood-begotten spirits" are transformed (as the speaker wishes to be in "Sailing to Byzantium"), "Dying into a dance" to become "Marbles of the dancing floor", mosaics that become part of Byzantium's "single image" (*Vision* 280). Mortality is overcome through being transformed into art.

But it is not just the human spirits or speakers within the poems that are made artifices of eternity. The poems themselves aim to escape time, they embody the artifices of eternity they thematise. It is the symbol, in the case of these poems the symbol of Byzantium, through which Yeats detaches the work of art – the poem itself – from time. The symbol, which acts as a pointer to something larger and beyond itself, connects the concrete and personal to the impersonal and universal, to the timeless. As Paul Kirschner states, for Yeats "the symbol is a way out of the flux of time" ("Yeats and Time" 10). In making Byzantium a symbol for "almost impersonal" art, Yeats connects the historical city with a place outside time: as he writes, Byzantium has "an architecture that suggests the Sacred City in the Apocalypse of St. John" (*Vision* 279). By using this symbol the poems attempt to pass into the Other Time they are about, enabling the written word to escape history.

In Tolkien's *The Lord of the Rings*, we also encounter "ink" as the means through which time can be overcome. If songs passed down orally fade (as pointed out earlier), the written word endures. Although this has hitherto not been recognised in criticism, perhaps the most significant role the hobbits take on is that of recorders of history and song. As historians, they write down their own versions of the end of the Third Age, they note down elvish songs and translate them besides writing down their own songs. It is never mentioned anywhere that the elves write down their tales and songs – they require the hobbits to do this for them. And if we hear of some manuscripts of men (such as Isildur's parchment where he writes of the finding of the Ring), it is also made clear that Aragorn has his own copies made of the hobbits' Red Book, their account of the War of the Ring, showing the high value placed upon the hobbits' historical accounts. The Red Book takes on particular significance: Bilbo leaves it to Frodo, and he in turn leaves it to Sam to complete: "I have quite finished, Sam. [...] The last pages are for you" (*LotR* 1004). While the Baggins family disappears from Middle-earth at the end of the novel, they leave behind their book which makes sure that their legacy endures even though they themselves have gone, acting as a kind of Ersatz child. As Frodo says to Sam: "But you are my heir: all that I had and might have had I leave to you. [...] you will read from the Red Book, and keep alive the memory of the age that is gone" (*LotR* 1006). This the Red Book does: as has been demonstrated above, the Red Book endures into our own time, eventually becoming *The Lord of the Rings* itself, all that remains of (pre)historical Middle-earth in our day and age. Thus we can see that paradoxically, the writing down of history in the Red Book actually tries to overcome history and time, becoming in its own way an artifice of eternity; perhaps one can read the Red Book as a "monument of unageing intellect" that stands outside time.

So we see a tension can be detected in the form of *The Lord of the Rings*, in that it both pretends to record history and, by virtue of its detachment from the primary world, stand outside it. However, if the book were to stand fully outside time it could have no subject-matter: there is no history in undying Valinor, and no need for historians. Similarly, Yeats's Byzantium poems cannot detach themselves entirely from the time they wish to escape: even the golden bird must sing of "What is past, or passing, or to come", that is, of time. As in *The Lord of the Rings*, without time, no theme: the bird's utterance would have to fall silent. Rainer Emig points out the tension in Yeats's symbolism, the search for the perfect symbol that threatens to render poetic utterance impossible (cf. *Modernism* 42-43): to reach impersonality through the symbol would destroy the personality needed to create the poem. For example, the shell in "The Sad Shepherd" should transform the personal utterance into an impersonal one: but thus the shepherd's personality is eradicated totally: "He vanishes from the symbolic stage of the poem so radically that he even ceases to be its grammatical subject" (*Modernism* 43). Both Tolkien and Yeats's works are characterised by a tension that is typically modernist: that between the desire to escape history and the necessity of history for creation, between escaping time and standing rooted in it. Their mythic systems try to place their works outside history, they attempt to rewrite history and try to escape from it; and yet simultaneously their works cannot but acknowledge that they need the historical and the personal to come into being. Ultimately, there can be no escape: "A people without history / Is not redeemed from time" (Eliot, "Little Gidding" *Collected Poems* 222).

"Lateness"

The final section of this chapter proposes to reread the claims made here in the light of a specific theory: that of "late style" developed by Theodor Adorno and Edward Said. This concept, while hardly an established literary theory, is particularly well suited to examine the questions of time and history raised in this chapter, for as its very name implies, late style is concerned with temporality, a sense of lateness or belatedness. Late style is a concept developed by Adorno in his writings on the composer Ludwig van Beethoven. Two essays on late style survive: one is complete and polished, the second more tentative and fragmentary. It is Beethoven's late symphonies in particular that interest Adorno, for they have always posed formal problems as they break with the traditional classical convention of the sonata form. Critics have sought to find an explanation for their structural oddity ever since their first performances: Adorno's essays represent one of the more interesting attempts to come to terms with them.

Adorno sees the difficulty of Beethoven's forms as following a pattern typically found in the mature works of major artists. These works break with the traditions of their time, and the new style they advance often appears inharmonious, obscure and incomprehensible:

> The maturity of the late works of important artists is not like the ripeness of fruit. As a rule, these works are not well rounded, but wrinkled, even fissured. [...] They lack all that harmony which the classicist aesthetic is accustomed to demand from the work of art, showing more traces of history than of growth. ("Late Style I" 123)

This "maturity" Adorno relates to "reflection on death" ("Late Style I" 125) or a sense of decline. While according to Adorno, it is the awareness of death that causes "lateness", he calls it a metaphysical mistake to attempt to locate the creating subject's awareness of death in the work itself (for example, to try and interpret the late work psychologically). For Adorno states that late works' difficult form should be attributed to the *lack* of subjectivity in them:

> [Subjectivity], as something mortal, and in the name of death, vanishes from the work of art in reality. The force of subjectivity in late works is the irascible gesture with which it leaves them. It bursts them asunder, not in order to express itself but, expressionlessly, to cast off the illusion of art. Of the works it leaves only fragments behind [...]. Touched by death, the masterly hand sets free the matter it previously formed. [...] the work falls silent as it is deserted, turning its hollowness outwards. ("Late Style I" 125)

The late work is thus characterised by a disappearance of subjectivity rather than a heightened subjectivity. In his second essay, Adorno reflects further on what the disappearance of subjectivity from the work entails for it: "The late Beethoven *covers its traces*. [...] Does he, in order to enable tonality, and so on, to emerge in this way, obliterate the traces of *composition*? Is this supposed to sound as if it had not been composed?" ("Late Style II" 154). For him, Beethoven's late works take on a self-generated appearance. He concludes that in its strange and fragmented form, "Beethoven's polyphony [...] presents the lost totality of the alienated world" ("Late Style II" 157).

Adorno's theory of a late style is taken up by Edward Said. It is Said who claims that "lateness" can be related to modernism and modernity; carrying on from Adorno's statement quoted last, Said concludes that "Beethoven's late style, remorselessly alienated and obscure, is the prototypical modern aesthetic form" (5). Said states that the characteristics of late style are identical with the alienation and formal disruption typical of the early twentieth century; in this sense all modern or modernist works are "late" (in his article, Said interprets for example works by the modernist writers Lampedusa and Cavafy as late works).

Adorno relates lateness to a sense of decline and death, and much of modernism, as we have seen, is concerned with historical decline and both individual and cultural decline and death, which it thematises in its works and expresses in its unconventional and fragmented forms. Accordingly, Said finds in the modern works he calls late a "particular melancholy associated with senescence, loss and death" and a "sense of all-pervading mortality" ("Thoughts on Late Style" 5). Said's claims are borne out by modernist texts that show forth what Hardy termed the "ache of modernism" (*Tess of the D'Urbervilles* 147): "This late age of world's experience had bred in them all, all men and women, a well of tears" (Woolf 8) – Woolf's use of the word "late" takes on especial significance in this context, showing a sense of belatedness related specifically to history.

For both Adorno and Said, late style's most special characteristic is that it is capable of expressing contradictions without having to resolve them. Thus Adorno describes Beethoven's music as "a process, but not as a development; its process is an ignition between extremes which no longer tolerate a safe means or a spontaneous harmony" ("Late Style I" 126): oppositions are not reconciled, nor is it felt necessary to do so. Said sees this lack of a "spontaneous harmony between extremes" as "equal forces straining in opposite directions" ("Thoughts on Late Style" 7) that hold one another in tension. Tension thus becomes a further characteristic of the late work, and once again it is a characteristic typical of the modernist work of art as well; as Rainer Emig states, "the essential character of the modernist work [is] tension" (*Modernism* 241). Said sees this as the factor which above all others makes late style special and noteworthy: "This is the prerogative of late style: it has the power to render disenchantment and pleasure without resolving the contradiction between them" ("Thoughts on Late Style" 7). Late works are those that can accommodate contradictions both thematic and structural without having to resolve them.

A sense of historical decline and belatedness, a concern with mortality and death, and inner tension can all be found in Yeats and Tolkien's works. As we have seen above, their writings espouse a pessimistic view of history as decline, and are characterised by the desire both to make history new and to escape history and death. These desires which are frustrated by the intrusion of historical reality into the mythic models they create, fill these works with unresolved tension. Lateness is perhaps most obvious in the mature poems of Yeats such as "Sailing to Byzantium", where the poet sees himself exiled from the "new" Ireland as a result of his age ("That is no country for old men") and wishes to escape into "the artifice of eternity" only to find that even in Byzantium he must sing "Of what is past, or passing, or to come" (*Yeats's Poems* 301-302). This is a work obsessed with decline and death, that simultaneously manages to escape and remain trapped within time; the oppositions between youth and age, time and eternity, are explicitly not reconciled, showing Yeats's poem to be representative of lateness. However, Said's claim that late works have a "sense of all-pervading mortality", and a "particular melancholy associated with senescence, loss and death", reminds one equally of *The Lord of the Rings*. Many critics have noted the sense of melancholy and loss that characterises the Third Age of Middle-earth, the setting for Tolkien's masterpiece; thus W.A. Senior for example claims that its "most pervasive and unifying component of atmosphere and mood [is] the sustained and grieved sense of loss" (173). Tolkien's topics of the Escape from and the Escape to Death, mentioned above, can also be read within the context of lateness.

Lateness can also reveal how the attempts to come to terms with history manifest themselves in the forms of Yeats and Tolkien's works. Beginning with Tolkien and *The Lord of the Rings*, the book's form is basically a large epic narrative made up of six books. However, surrounding the main narrative is a mass of extra editorial material – a long prologue and six appendices. Even the main narrative itself is interspersed with footnotes referring the reader to the Appendices: all in all, a highly unusual form whose strangeness is seldom commented upon as such. This mass of critical material, if taken seriously by the reader (as was the author's intention), disrupts the conventional reading process as it encourages him or her to interrupt reading the main story by looking up the footnotes in the Appendices; the unity of the narrative is broken up. This disruption is a first hint that the form of Tolkien's tale is, as Adorno states of late works, "not well rounded" ("Late Style I" 123), not as unified a narrative as it might appear at first glance. Further, with all the extra material encompassing the main story, *The Lord of the Rings* very strongly resembles an academic critical edition. And in fact this is exactly what the book pretends to be – an edition of the Red Book, whose significance has already been pointed out above. In the Prologue, *The Hobbit* is referred to as a "selection from the

Red Book of Westmarch" (*LotR* 1), and it is stated that "[t]his account of the end of the Third Ages is drawn from the Red Book of Westmarch" (*LotR* 14). In the Prologue to *The Lord of the Rings*, we are given an overview of the main hobbit manuscripts and the history of their transmission. All the material in the Appendices is said to derive from these sources, such as the "Thain's Book of Minas Tirith", which is Aragorn's copy of the Red Book, or "Herblore of the Shire", written by Merry. These various sources and their copies are carefully compared and their differences listed. This is the kind of documentation one would certainly expect to find in the edition of an ancient text preserved in various manuscript forms (of course, Tolkien himself made several such editions). *The Lord of the Rings* itself thus appears as a selection of material from the fictional Red Book, presented in a scholarly edition. Similarly, the poetry collection *The Adventures of Tom Bombadil* carries the sub-title "verses from The Red Book" (*Adventures* 3), and in a Preface its poems are ascribed to Bilbo and Sam, among others. The implications of this fictitious transmission history are far-reaching. When Tolkien changed the story of *The Hobbit* for the 1947 edition to accommodate the sinister nature of the Ring, a hint of the original was preserved as the story Bilbo made up about his encounter with Gollum (that he found the Ring, and Gollum showed him the way out of the mountains). Now, in the Prologue of *The Lord of the Rings*, we are told that this false account

> still appeared in the original Red Book, as it did in several copies and abstracts. But many copies contain the true account (as an alternative), derived no doubt from notes by Frodo and Samwise, both of whom learned the truth, though they seem to have been unwilling to delete anything actually written by the old hobbit himself. (*LotR* 12-13)

Of course, this is nothing but a disguised history of the various editions of *The Hobbit*. Tolkien's desire to present the tales of Middle-earth as actual documents is so strong that he makes up a transmission history to account for his own changes to his stories! The end result is one that Adorno cites as typical of "late works": *The Lord of the Rings* "shows more traces of history than of growth". It does not appear as an organically conceived tale, but as a history or a tale whose different stages of development can still be perceived, and the impression the reader receives is not of one single story, but of many layers and fragments of stories: "a history of the Great War of the Ring [including] many glimpses of the yet more ancient history that preceded it" (*LotR* xiii). The history the novel is so concerned with on so many different levels (as shown above) also manifests itself in its form.

The Lord of the Rings's fictitious transmission history serves several purposes. For one, the whole critical apparatus accompanying *The Lord of the Rings* actually strengthens the impression, already given in the story itself, of the reality of the secondary world and the authenticity of the tale being told. However, the transmission history also neatly covers the traces of the real author – Tolkien himself. Adorno's question about Beethoven's music, "Is this supposed to sound as if it had not been composed?" ("Late Style II" 154), must thus remind one of Tolkien's strategies – for *The Lord of the Rings* is certainly supposed to read as if it had not been authored, at least not by any single person. Instead, it presents itself in a way as self-generated, as a multitude of already extant historical fragments found and collected together rather than a newly composed story. As already quoted above, Adorno states that "The force of subjectivity on late works is the irascible gesture with which it leaves them. It bursts them asunder, not in order to express itself but, expressionlessly, to cast off the illusion of art. Of the works it leaves only fragments behind" ("Late Style I" 125). *The Lord of the Rings* also wishes to "cast off the illusion of art", it poses as reality; in order to do so, the creative subject has to eliminate itself from the work. This however means that the disappearing authorial subject can leave behind only fragments, no complete narrative. In this sense then, too, *The Lord of the Rings* is a late work, and the concept of late style can be used to interpret its unusual form.

W.B. Yeats never truly abandoned conventional poetic form in favour of vers libre and the fragmentation found in works such as *The Waste Land* or *The Cantos*, a fragmentation reflected in the mass of poetic voices and apparent lack of a creative subjectivity, and thus akin to Tolkien's fragmented form. In Yeats's works, disintegration can be found on the level of poetic meaning and symbolism, and here, too, this can be attributed to the attempt to rid his works of a historically conditioned subjectivity that marks his entire oeuvre. This is evident in the Byzantium poems when the speaker desires to become a golden bird and "superhuman", and also in Yeats's earlier poetry in his use of "personae" or masks. However, these personae all "yearn for their own destruction"

(Emig, *Modernism* 49): for example, in "He mourns for the Change that has come upon him and his Beloved, and longs for the End of the World" (*Yeats's Poems* 95-96) the speaker concludes:

> I would that the Boar without bristles had come from the West
> And had rooted the sun and moon and stars out of the sky
> And lay in darkness, grunting, and turning to his rest.

As Emig points out, "This end of the world is clearly analogous to the end of poetic identity" (*Modernism* 49). As noted above, the end of poetic identity must also result in the end of the poem itself, as there can be no poetic utterance without identity. Poems such as "Byzantium", which attempt to present themselves as impersonal and self-generated, as "artifices of eternity" rather than the artifice of one particular historical person, must end in fragmentation and a lack of closure:

> Those images that yet
> Fresh images beget,
> That dolphin-torn, that gong-tormented sea.
> (*Yeats's Poems* 364)

The sheer amount of complex symbols and images used in the poem (dolphin, spirit, cathedral, bird, golden bough etc.) renders any coherent, unified poetic meaning impossible (I have yet to see an interpretation of "Byzantium" that can find such a meaning and prove it satisfactorily!); while Yeats himself saw Byzantium as "one single image", in their multiplicity the images actually fall back into single elements. The poem's complexity, purged of a fixed subjectivity that could confer meaning and unity on the poem, results in a fragmentation of meaning. Similarly, "He mourns the Change" uses such a multiplicity of symbols that the "clash of complexities of these symbols prevents the poem from establishing a clear message" (Emig, *Modernism* 48). If Yeats's poems are not truly fragmented in form, their meaning becomes increasingly fragmented as they are purged of creative subjectivity, and this clearly relates them to late style.

Tolkien also used personae, in fact one distinct persona: the editor-persona found in the Prologue and Appendices to *The Lord of the Rings* and *The Adventures of Tom Bombadil* (and, to a lesser degree and with different intent, in *Farmer Giles of Ham*). Besides masking personality, the persona makes us aware of another kind of tension in Tolkien's work. Several questions inevitably arise when reading the Prologue and the Appendices: Who is the "editor" of this story, and where and when is he writing? As already pointed out above, the editor appears to be mysteriously positioned somewhere between the primary world and Middle-earth, and it is strongly suggested that actually our world and Middle-earth are the same. Nonetheless, the enchanted and the disenchanted state of the two worlds places them in contrast to one another. This paradoxical state of primary and secondary worlds, both at odds with and connected to one another, reveals a tension between them – again, a tension that Tolkien never resolves. Tolkien's long narrative holds the two "opposites" of Primary and Secondary World, as Said says, "in tension, as equal forces straining in opposite directions", without ever resolving this tension. In fact, the entire structure of *The Lord of the Rings* is conditioned by this unresolved tension. For if it were to be resolved, then we would need either an explanation of the way Middle-earth changed into our present world – a gap which the present transmission history does not fill – or we would need a confession that Middle-earth actually does not exist, which would render the fragmented history provided totally unnecessary.

Again, this vexed relation between a mythic, prehistorical past and the actual present, between which a temporal continuity is simultaneously implied and denied, is also evident in works by Yeats, especially, as we have seen, in those that try to construct a coherent mythic past for a modern Ireland. To reconcile Mother Eire, Cathleen Ni Houlihan, Roisin Dubh and all the other mythic representations of Ireland with its historical actuality proved impossible, a failure evident in Yeats's last play *The Death of Cuchulain*. Yeats himself admits this in one of his last poems, "The Circus Animals' Desertion" (*Yeats's Poems* 471-472). Here the speaker laments "What can I but enumerate old themes?" These "themes" include the mythic Oisin, Countess Cathleen, and Cuchulain, out of whom Yeats tried to create a new Irish identity and failed. The speaker states "Players and painted stage took my love, / And not those things that they were emblems of" – he was so entranced by the myth he neglected reality. Now he sees the myths as "A mound of refuse or the sweepings of a street". Yet even in this poem the tension between mythic ideal and harsh realism is not resolved in favour of one or the other: after debunking all his symbols, Yeats resorts to one last one: his heart. Again, as in Tolkien, myth and historical actuality are held "in tension, as equal forces straining in opposite directions". Yeats does not succeed in truly turning the myth into history, but neither does he relinquish it entirely.

Said's statement that late works are characterised by a "particular melancholy associated with senescence, loss and death" has already been mentioned. When we relate these topics of age, loss, and death, constantly thematised in Yeats and Tolkien, back to the forms of their works, we can see that these forms are in fact conditioned by this loss. In Tolkien's case loss is in particular the loss of Middle-earth's culture as songs and stories are forgotten and fade away; in our time all that is left of these are the fragments that form the narrative. By the time the "edition" of the Red Book is made, all that is left of this "period of antiquity", as Tolkien calls it, is in fact the edition itself. *The Lord of the Rings* represents all that is left of Middle-earth in our modern day and age. In this, its fragmented and incomplete form, like Beethoven's polyphony, it "presents the lost totality of the alienated world" (Adorno, "Late Style II" 157). It is all that remains of a complete world that has given way to our modern and alienated one, in which, as Tolkien scoffs in "On Fairy-stories", motor-cars are perceived to be more alive than dragons and more real than horses: "How real, how startlingly alive is a factory chimney compared with an elm tree!" ("On Fairy-stories" 149). In this, too, *The Lord of the Rings* is late: as a text, it represents all that is left of Middle-earth's "lost totality". One might exclaim as with the speaker of T.S. Eliot's *The Waste Land*: "These fragments I have shored against my ruins." And once again, one of Adorno's statements on lateness comes to mind: "the work falls silent [...] turning its hollowness outwards" ("Late Style I" 126). In *The Lord of the Rings*, what ultimately remains is silence as the fragmented utterances of the work fade away. The fate of the late work is the same as what Arwen terms "the Doom of Men [...]: the loss and the silence" (*LotR* 1037).

This loss and silence is also evident in Yeats's poetry. While "The Happy Shepherd" mourns the loss of the Arcadian world, it still hopes that world can be recreated in the shepherd's songs and dreams, but as we have seen, "The Sad Shepherd" sees this song fade away into "inarticulate moan", ending in forgetting and closing off the poem itself. Later poems such as "Coole and Ballylee, 1931" also conclude with an envisaged end of poetry:

> We were the last romantics – chose for theme
> Traditional sanctity and loveliness;
> Whatever's written in what poet's name
> The book of the people; whatever most can bless
> The mind of man or elevate a rhyme;
> But all is changed, that high horse riderless,
> Though mounted in that high saddle Homer rode
> Where the swan drifts on the darkening flood.
> (*Yeats's Poems* 360)

In this, they are similar to Tolkien's work that mourns the passing of a culture, showing forth the "lost totality" of the world of the "last romantics"[43] that is now gone. "Nineteen Hundred and Nineteen", which lists the "Many ingenious things [that] are gone" functions as a kind of index whose form represents the loss sustained and thus "presents the lost totality of the alienated world". Lost totality is also evident in the disruption of the symbolic unity found in some earlier poems such as "The Wild Swans at Coole" (*Yeats's Poems* 233-234), which forms a counterpiece to "Coole and Ballylee, 1931". This poem's central image of the swan in the later poem becomes "Another emblem", one among many – and while the swans in "The Wild Swans" "drift on the still water", in "Coole and Ballylee" they fly away amid "thunder", disembodied as "stormy white", abandoning the poem. The poem reveals its inherent self-destruction when it says the white of the swan "can be murdered with a spot of ink": of course, this is exactly what the poem has done by eliminating the swan, thus "turning its hollowness outwards" (Adorno, "Late Style I" 126).

Thus the central concern of history in the works of Tolkien and Yeats, revealed in themes such as historical decline, death, time and escape from all these, can be related to the concept of late style. Late style can also reveal how history impacts on the forms of these works: the desire to present the work of art as self-generated and purged of a creative, historically conditioned subjectivity results in increasing fragmentation and, ultimately, silence; history's decline and the loss of totality is shown forth in formal loss of completeness and coherence. The self-destructive tendencies of the late work are evident in the self-reflexive manoeuverings of Tolkien's and Yeats's texts. Finally, the tensions between

---

43 This can be linked to Irish nationalism as shown in the poem "September 1913": "Romantic Ireland's dead and gone, / It's with O'Leary in the grave" (*Yeats's Poems* 210). The romantic idea of a unified Ireland has failed, leaving the poet to mourn a lost national totality.

myth and history, between the fantastic and the real found in both authors' works, make both Tolkien's and Yeats's art representative of lateness and thus of a modernist aesthetic.

Chapter Four

Language

Fantasy, Modernism and Language

Previous chapters have examined two central concerns of both fantasy and modernism, showing how the pressures of history and the experience of war shape and structure both literatures. However, it is the issue of language that is perhaps truly at the heart of modernist and fantastic writing, and that can deliver the greatest insight into what divides and – more strikingly – what unites modernism and fantasy.

It might seem a rather obvious statement that the fantastic worlds of fantasy texts exist only in words. Tzvetan Todorov elaborates on the subject:

> If the fantastic constantly makes use of rhetorical figures, it is because it originates in them. The supernatural is born of language, it is its consequence and its proof: not only do the devil and vampires exist only in words, but language alone enables us to conceive what is always absent: the supernatural. (*The Fantastic* 82)

It is thus language that allows the fantastic to come into being. Tolkien also points out that the origin of fantasy lies in "the fantastic device of human language" ("On Fairy-stories" 140):

> The human mind, endowed with the powers of generalisation and abstraction, sees not only *green-grass*, discriminating it from other objects (and finding it fair to look upon), but sees that it is *green* as well as being grass. [...] The mind that thought of *light, heavy, grey, yellow, still, swift*, also conceived of magic that would make heavy things light and able to fly, turn grey lead into yellow gold, and the still rock into swift water. If it could do the one, it could do the other; it inevitably did both. When we can take green from grass, blue from heaven, and red from blood, we already have an enchanter's power. (122)

It is thus no surprise that fantasy texts themselves show a high degree of language awareness – indeed, it has become something of a genre characteristic. Tolkien's own *The Lord of the Rings* leads the way here as in so many other things, the linguistic realism of Middle-earth being one of its most commonly remarked-upon features (at least eight languages are used in the epic). The philologist Tolkien found it impossible to create a secondary world without creating languages to go with it – indeed, in his case the languages actually preceded the world.[1] And since *The Lord of the Rings* just about every self-respecting fantasy author has come up with various languages with which to flesh out the reality of their secondary worlds (although none to my knowledge have constructed their languages in as much detail as Tolkien, whose "original use of language is perhaps the greatest factor which sets him apart from other writers of fantasy" (Smith 18). Linguistic diversity has become a key factor for the credibility of a secondary world. One example of a secondary language we shall examine more closely at a later point in this chapter is furnished by Tolkien's fellow Inkling C.S. Lewis, who created the language of "Old Solar" or Hressa-Hlab in his space trilogy, directly influenced by Tolkien.[2] A later example of fantasy fiction that makes use of secondary languages is Ursula Le Guin's *Earthsea* quintet, which features a variety of languages: "Hardic", "Kargish", and most importantly, "the Language of the Making".

Le Guin's "Language of the Making" is an original speech which first caused the world of Earthsea to come into being, much like the Biblical Word ("Let there be light!" Genesis 1:3) or the "Ëa!" of Tolkien's *The Silmarillion* (21). Earthsea's Song of Creation begins:

> Only in silence the word,
> only in dark the light,
> only in dying life:
> bright the hawk's flight
> On the empty sky.
>
> – *The Creation of Éa*
> (Le Guin, *Earthsea* 14)

This is a clearly self-reflexive stance: the novels, through their claim that Earthsea only came into being through language ("in silence the word"), emphasise that Earthsea does, of course, only exist in words – Ursula Le Guin's words, to be precise. In this way, fantasy texts subtly highlight their own constructed nature and their material. This notion that there is some "original" language

---

1 This is at least what Tolkien himself claims (cf. for example *Letters* 87, 375). Fimi's study *Tolkien, Race and Cultural History* shows that "language invention and myth-making did begin independently, but became interconnected very early in Tolkien's career as a writer" (66).
2 Although Lewis's *Out of the Silent Planet*, the first novel to introduce Old Solar, was published several years before *The Lord of the Rings*, Tolkien had been making up his languages for years and Lewis was acquainted with them.

that in some way offers a perfect reflection of reality and has power over it is encountered in numerous works of fantasy; Le Guin's hero-magician Ged, for example, explains:

> Once, in the beginning of time, when Segoy raised the isles of Earthsea from the ocean deeps, all things bore their own true names. And all the doing of magic, all wizardry, hangs still upon the knowledge, the relearning, the remembering – of that true and ancient language of the Making. [...] what a wizard spends his life at is finding out the names of things, and finding out how to find out the names of things. (Le Guin, *Earthsea* 267)

Magic, in Earthsea, consists of the "truth" of language. This idea of an inherent truth (and according power) of language we will encounter again in the novels of C.S. Lewis. It is also noteworthy that it is names that have power, and that everything has a "true" name – once again, a concept found over and over in fantasy.

Some of the very latest bestselling fantasy novels to take up this theme of a powerful originary language (drawing on both Tolkien and Le Guin) are Christopher Paolini's *Eragon* and its sequels *Eldest* and *Brisingr* (a final volume is to complete the tetralogy). After his first unconscious use of magic through the ancient language, the hero Eragon is told:

> "*Brisingr* is from an ancient language that all living things used to speak. [...] The language has a name for everything, if you can find it." "But what does that have to do with magic?" interrupted Eragon. "Everything! It is the basis for all power. The language describes the true nature of things, not the superficial aspects that everyone sees. For example, fire is called *brisingr*. Not only is that a name for fire, it is the name for fire. If you are strong enough, you can use *brisingr* to direct fire to do whatever you will." (Paolini, *Eragon* 140)

While Le Guin's *Earthsea* novels already stress the importance of the true naming of things, Eragon applies this concept to language itself when he asks:

> "Does this language have a name?" Brom laughed. "Yes, but no one knows it. It would be a word of incredible power, something by which you could control the entire language and those who use it. People have long searched for it, but no one has ever found it." (Paolini, *Eragon* 145)

In Paolini's novels the disastrous potential for abuse of this language becomes clear. Eragon, who is only just learning the ancient language, tries to bless a child in it but makes an error that turns his blessing into a curse:

"Do you remember how you worded this blessing?" "Aye." "Recite it for me." Eragon did so, and a look of pure horror engulfed Oromis. He exclaimed, "You used *skölir*! Are you sure? Wasn't it *sköliro*?" Eragon frowned. "No, *skölir*. Why shouldn't I have used it? *Skölir* means *shielded*. '...and may you be shielded from misfortune.' It was a good blessing." "That was not a blessing, but a curse." Oromis was more agitated than Eragon had ever seen him. "The suffix *o* forms the past tense of verbs ending with *r* and *i*. *Sköliro* means shielded, but *skölir* means shield. What you said was 'May luck and happiness follow you and may you be a *shield* from misfortune.' Instead of protecting this child from the vagaries of fate, you condemned her to be a sacrifice for others, to absorb their misery and suffering so that they might live in peace."
(Paolini, *Eldest* 294-295)

What is particularly interesting about this passage is that Eragon's failure lies not in simply using the wrong word, but in a *grammatical* error. Paolini's ancient language is not just a mystical correlative of the actual world in words, but is emphasised as a structure. Its power can be used only according to rules, not those of some magical law but the rules of language, grammar. The awareness of language, a characteristic found in the works of the Inklings, has by now become a tradition of the fantasy genre; fantasy literature is fundamentally self-reflexive.

The fact that fantasy's secondary worlds and their inhabitants exist only in words and that, in linguistic terms, there is no actual signified that corresponds to the signifier, makes fantasy a special kind of (literary) language. Rosemary Jackson states that fantasy "pushes towards an area of non-signification. It does this either by attempting to name 'the unnameable' [...] attempting to visualize the unseen, or by establishing a disjunction of word and meaning through a play on 'thingless names'" (41). When describing a fantastic secondary world, which only actually exists in the words that describe it, language becomes purely self-referential.[3] This is one of the ways in which "the fantastic represents an experience of limits" (Todorov 93) – because it exposes the very limits of language itself. This is the reason why language is repeatedly thematised in the fantastic texts themselves – because they are pushing at the boundaries of what is actually possible within that medium. In fantasy, the basic structure of language, that of the sign, starts to disintegrate, and the basic premise that

---

3 It is of course understood that there are limits as to how far a secondary world can depart from the primary. Tolkien for example writes: "Fantasy is made out of the Primary World, but a good craftsman loves his material, and has a knowledge and feeling for clay, stone and wood which only the art of making can give" ("On Fairy-stories" 147).

language and words must "mean" something or correlate to some external phenomenon is questioned. As Le Guin writes, "Fantasy [...] speaks the language of the night" (*The Language of the Night* 5); or, as Tolkien says: "Faërie cannot be caught in a net of words" ("On Fairy-stories" 114).

At the same time as fantasy exposes the limits of language, it brings the medium of its own construction into question. It is a literature that is not just self-referential, but that exposes the fragility of the structures it is founded upon. More often than not when language is thematised, its power is shown to fail, or languages are lost and forgotten. In the preceding chapters we have already seen how this works in Williams's Arthurian poems and in Tolkien's *The Lord of the Rings*. Williams's Logres is created through the word: "the word of the Emperor established a kingdom in Britain" ("Prelude" *TTL* 1), and it is repeatedly thematised how it is founded on language: "[Taliessin/Virgil] sought for the invention of the City by the phrase" ("Mount Badon" *TTL* 17). Yet Logres is lost, and this is due to (or reflected in) the loss of the power of language: there are only "mutes or rhetoricians instead of the sacred poets" ("The Prayers of the Pope" *RSS* 51), and Taliessin himself ends "[his] tongue tired of song, [his] brain fey" ("The Prayers of the Pope" *RSS* 56). Tolkien's *The Lord of the Rings* as the "Red Book" embodies the fragmentary remains (in language) of what remains of Middle-earth's entirety. In its incomplete state it testifies to the loss of language that it repeatedly makes its theme; but it also draws attention to its constructed state in other ways.

In Appendix F, "On Translation", the "editor" reveals that he has not only edited, but also translated the material from the Red Book:

> In presenting the matter of the Red Book, as a history for people of today to read, the whole of the linguistic setting has been translated as far as possible into terms of our own times. Only the languages alien to the Common Speech have been left in their original form; but these appear mainly in the names of persons and places. The Common Speech, as the language of the Hobbits and their narratives, has inevitably been turned into modern English. (*LotR* 1107)

In a certain sense, this "translation" strengthens the authenticity of *The Lord of the Rings* as a historical artefact. But when we learn that the familiar names of Sam and Merry (as just two examples of many) were actually the foreign-sounding

Banazîr and Kalimac, and the Shire was really Sûza (cf. *LotR* 1108-09), the secondary reality constructed in *The Lord of the Rings* is suddenly defamiliarised, the reader's response to it undercut. The editor-translator draws attention to the fact that language can both constitute reality, and let it collapse at the same time. It is a rather unsettling way to end a novel – to shock readers into realising that the reality they have let themselves be drawn into is constructed out of a medium that shifts and changes, and will not let itself be tied down. The works of C.S. Lewis show their awareness of the limits of language and its failure in other ways: in the space trilogy, it is made clear that language on Earth (the "Silent Planet") is "bent" as a result of the Fall, and in the apocalypse of Narnia the Talking Beasts' gift of speech is taken away from them again.

This emphasis of the Inklings' fantasy on language, an emphasis that simultaneously establishes and paradoxically questions its power at the same time, is shared by literary modernism. Modernism, moving on from the Aestheticist and Decadent movements that primarily emphasised language's surface, engaged in a quest for a new kind of language freed from outdated forms and conventions. Modernist literature, particularly poetry, attempted to create new relations of word and meaning; indeed some poetry, such as that of Gertrude Stein, defies the view of words as vehicles of meaning altogether, showing them to be tangible entities within themselves.

> A BOX.
>
> Out of kindness comes redness and out of rudeness comes rapid same question, out of an eye comes research, out of selection comes painful cattle. So then the order is that a white way of being round is something suggesting a pin and is it disappointing, it is not, it is so rudimentary to be analysed and see a fine substance strangely, it is so earnest to have a green point not to red but to point again. (Stein, *Tender Buttons* 1106)

A text such as this, taken from the "Objects" section of Stein's *Tender Buttons*, defies normal grammar and meaning, joining unexpected words together that make no sense in conventional terms (how can cattle be painful, and how can they come out of selection? And what on earth does all that have to do with a box?). It also points out some of the inconsistencies inherent in language: these sentences are all structurally, that is grammatically, correct, yet they are not "correct" on the level of meaning. This then leads one to ask how these different levels are interconnected, if conventions of what is right on the one level need not necessarily be so on the other.⁴ Can language really "mean" at all? Gilbert and Gubar (246) call Stein's language "fantastic", which might imply that it, like the language of fantasy, pushes towards non-signification.⁵

Movements such as Imagism and its more radical cousin Vorticism, both centrally influenced by Ezra Pound, rejected the ornamental in poetry and sought instead to condense language as far as possible. Thus in Pound's master-poem of Imagism already cited in Chapter One, "In a Station of the Metro", there truly is no word that could be left out or changed without altering the meaning of the text. Interestingly, this can be interpreted as "a self-destructive, an anti-poetic poetics" because "its restraint is directed against the poetic nature of language itself" (Emig, *Modernism* 107).⁶ The ideal behind this "direct treatment of the thing" is actually that of mathematics – Pound writes of images having "a variable significance like the signs a, b, x in algebra" (cf. Sanders 527). This quest for precision is also evident in the language philosophy of Russell and Wittgenstein, both of whom tried to systematise language according to mathematical and logical principles.

Other modern philosophers, most notably Bergson, saw reality and existence as flux. Modernist narrative techniques that attempt to incorporate this view of reality are interior monologue and stream of consciousness, which show how reality is constituted in and through the flow of an individual's thoughts. As these thoughts are expressed in language, these techniques show how reality itself is shaped through language and how language conditions the way external reality is perceived.

---

4 This is something picked up on by Bertrand Russell, who writes that "ordinary grammar and syntax is extraordinarily misleading. This is the case, e.g., as regards numbers; 'ten men' is grammatically the same form as 'white men', so that 10 might be thought to be an adjective qualifying 'men'" (*Introduction to Mathematical Philosophy* 205).
5 Gilbert and Gubar see this kind of writing as essentially feminine. I do not agree, as many male authors write in this manner as well (as is evident in this study). Besides, the view of masculine writing as "densest condensation, hard" (Gilbert and Gubar 261, citing Tennyson's *Idylls*) and, by contrast, feminine writing as flowing and subversive seems to me to reproduce the very gender stereotypes feminism aims to challenge. This is, however, not to discredit the important work of Gilbert and Gubar in returning women writers such as Stein to the modernist canon.
6 This kind of poetics is commented on by Roland Barthes, who cites "the essentialist ambitions of poetry, the conviction that it alone catches *the thing in itself*, inasmuch, precisely, as it wants to be an anti-language" (*Mythologies* 133).

> "It is time," said Rezia.
> The word "time" split its husk; poured its riches over him; and from his lips fell like shells, like shavings from a plane, without his making them, hard, white, imperishable, words, and flew to attach themselves to their places in an ode to Time; an immortal ode to Time. He sang. (Woolf, *Mrs Dalloway* 59)

In this passage the key word of Woolf's novel, "time", is not simply heard by Septimus; it produces reactions of a synaesthetic nature within his consciousness – he sees the words he speaks as "white" and "hard", and as flying away into a poem, the "ode to Time". Interestingly the words are "immortal", which would appear to testify to the power of language (at least in Septimus's mind).

Yet as with the Inklings, doubt of language's power was never far from modernism. The philosopher Bertrand Russell, already cited above, gave frustration with ordinary language as the reason behind his attempt to construct a new language based on pure logic:

> Since ordinary language has no words that naturally express exactly what we wish to express, it is necessary, so long as we adhere to ordinary language, to strain words into unusual meanings; and the reader is sure, after a time if not at first, to lapse into attaching the usual meanings to words, thus arriving at wrong notions as to what is intended to be said. (Russell, *Introduction to Mathematical Philosophy* 205)

Likewise, literary modernism itself grew out of dissatisfaction and frustration with earlier literary language. However, artists discovered that in trying to "make it new" (in Pound's famous phrase, cf. *Canto* 53) and drawing attention to their material (in this case, language), they also revealed the flaws inherent in it. Their paradoxical view of language at once asserted its centrality and pointed out its failure to actually provide meaning and coherence. Perhaps the bluntest expression of the feeling of the inadequacy of words can be found in T.S. Eliot's "The Love Song of J. Alfred Prufrock", where the speaker exclaims "It is impossible to say just what I mean!" (Eliot, *Collected Poems* 16). Later, Eliot was to describe writing poetry as

> [...] a raid on the inarticulate
> With shabby material always deteriorating
> In the general mess of imprecision of feeling,
> Undisciplined squads of emotion.
> ("East Coker" *Collected Poems* 203)

This is a typically modernist self-destructive tendency: by thematising the failure of language in a metapoetic text, the text itself is automatically brought into question. Unsurprisingly, Eliot was not the only one to express himself this way. The despair over language's failure to communicate adequately was for example also expressed by Hugo von Hofmannsthal in his Chandos letter. The fictional Chandos, in a letter to Francis Bacon, states: "Es ist mir völlig die Fähigkeit abhanden gekommen, über irgend etwas zusammenhängend zu denken oder zu sprechen"[7] (Hofmannsthal, "Ein Brief" volume 31, 48). He says that language is too abstract to describe life and reality: "[...] die abstrakten Wörter, deren sich doch die Zunge naturgemäß bedienen muß, um irgendein Urteil an den Tag zu geben, zerfielen mir im Mund wie modrige Pilze"[8] (48-49). He then goes on to describe his nightmare vision:

> Es zerfiel mir alles in Teile, die Teile wieder in Teile, und nichts mehr ließ sich mit einem Begriff umspannen. Die einzelnen Worte schwammen um mich; sie gerannen zu Augen, die mich anstarrten und in die ich wieder hineinstarren muß: Wirbel sind sie, in die hinabzusehen mich schwindelt, die sich unaufhaltsam drehen und durch die hindurch man ins Leere kommt.[9] (49)

The images here are very similar to those in Yeats's apocalyptic vision "The Second Coming": "Things fall apart; the centre cannot hold" (*Yeats's Poems* 294) ("Es zerfiel mir alles in Teile") – only that which is falling apart here are words, and it is words "turning in the widening gyre" (the gyre corresponding exactly to Hofmannsthal's "Wirbel"). Artistic (literary) creation is thus doomed to failure as its materials disintegrate, and the modernist work is often trapped within the paradox that literature no longer appears possible, but the artist is still driven to produce: "Modernism begins with the search for a Literature which is no longer possible" (Barthes, *Writing Degree Zero* 38). This is yet another example of modernism's inherent tension.

One result of this doubt of language is the precarious position in which it puts the artist and his or her authority. Many scholars have noted modern-

---

7 Translation: 'I have completely lost my ability to think or speak coherently about anything at all.'
8 Translation: 'The abstract words that the tongue has to use as a matter of course in order to voice any opinion fell apart in mouth like mouldy toadstools.'
9 Translation: 'Everything disintegrated into parts, and those parts again into parts, and nothing could be embraced by one simple term any longer. The separate words swam around me; they thickened, becoming eyes staring at me and that I had to stare back into; they are gyres, when I look down them I grow dizzy, they turn and turn ceaselessly, and passing through them there is only nothingness.'

ists' drive to establish absolute authority in their texts through making them as "objective" as possible, or/and creating mythic cosmic models that attempt to include all of the world, its history and literature within the work of art.[10] Great importance is attached to ideas of order (as opposed to the postmodern emphasis on play). These tendencies are particularly noticeable in the works of the so-called "Men of 1914", and are addressed in the theory of Pound, Eliot and Wyndham Lewis. This need for authority is fundamentally linked to the perceived failure of language – if language "worked" on its own, one would not need to recourse to myth and all-encompassing cosmic models in order to artificially control meaning.

In fantasy texts, it is perhaps also this fundamental doubt of language that creates the need for an all-powerful sub-creator. When W.H. Auden lists the "principal grievances" (*Secondary Worlds* 51) that drive an artist to create a secondary world, he acknowledges that one is a desire to be omniscient and in complete control; he does not mention a dissatisfaction with language, the very material used to establish that control. But as we have seen, a concern with language and particularly a desire to somehow re-create an originary (and thus authoritative and powerful) speech is of central importance to fantasy. And if dissatisfaction with the primary world leads to the creation of a secondary world, then surely it is a dissatisfaction with primary language that leads to the invention of secondary languages. The paradox again is that in order to establish the secondary world (the setting for the secondary languages) the supposedly insufficient primary tongue has to be used – Tolkien could not have written *The Lord of the Rings* in Elvish or Westron, it had to be "translated".

The ideas put forward here on modernism, fantasy and language will now be examined in greater detail in the cases of two specific authors. James Joyce is the most obvious modernist author to choose in this regard; he will be compared to the last of our three Inklings, C.S. Lewis.

---

10 For example, Maud Ellmann's *The Poetics of Impersonality* (Brighton: Harvester, 1987), and Peter Nicholls's *Modernisms. A Literary Guide* (Los Angeles: University of California Press, 1995), particularly Chapter 8, "Modernity and the 'The Men of 1914'" (165-92).

Worlds of Words: Joyce and Lewis

Although C.S. Lewis greatly admired Yeats, he never warmed to the one other Irish writer whose fame and influence could rival Yeats's: James Joyce.[11] He read *Ulysses*, but he disliked it, dismissing its style as *"steam* of consciousness" (Lewis, *The Dark Tower* 11). His main objection to Joyce's most famous work was that it was blatantly unrealistic:

> The disorganized consciousness which it regards as specially real is in fact highly artificial. It is discovered by introspection – that is, by artificially suspending all the normal and outgoing activities of the mind and then attending to what is left. In that residuum it discovers no concentrated will, no logical thought, no morals, no stable sentiments, and (in a word) no mental hierarchy. Of course not; for we have deliberately stopped all these things in order to introspect. (Lewis, *Preface to Paradise Lost* 153)

Joyce never had the chance to read this particular criticism as it was published a year after his death; whether he ever actually even heard of Lewis is doubtful. They never encountered one another in Ireland, Joyce permanently removing himself to the Continent by the time Lewis was seven; and Lewis (apart from a childhood holiday in Dieppe), never travelled outside Britain and Ireland until 1960. Looking at the works of both authors, one might at first glance – or even at a second – be hard pressed to find any resemblance between them. The works of Joyce examined here – *Dubliners*, *A Portrait of the Artist as a Young Man*, *Ulysses* and *Finnegan's Wake* – are all to a lesser or greater extent experimental texts, while Lewis's fiction – the space trilogy and the *Chronicles of Narnia* – remains rooted within the genres of science fiction and children's literature respectively (his last novel, *Till We Have Faces*, a retelling of the Cupid and Psyche myth, forms an exception). Yet it is possible to read Joyce and Lewis's works against one another: both authors share an interest in language and a delight in playing with it in myriad ways, as well as a typically modernist foregrounding of language tinged with doubt in its effectiveness.

---

11 Samuel Beckett is an exception of course, but he was of a later generation than Joyce, and Lewis appears not to have encountered his work. In terms of popularity if not prestige as a writer, it could probably be claimed that the only Irish writer to rival these three figures (except perhaps the ubiquitous Seamus Heaney) is actually Lewis himself. However, Lewis has yet to be claimed by Ireland as an "Irish" author. As Bresland notes: "it is ironic that one of the best selling Irish authors of all time has, until relatively recently, been somewhat neglected in his native land" (Bresland, *The Backward Glance* vii). This problem of national identity will be addressed at the end of the chapter.

One way of reading Joyce's works from *Dubliners* to *Finnegans Wake* is as progressing ever further along the road away from realist fiction towards the completely self-enclosed, purely self-referential text. All of these works, while their degree of linguistic self-awareness and the ways in which it is thematised vary, share an emphasis on language. Indeed, "Joyce's *oeuvre* is best seen as constantly trying to inform an evolutive linguistic poetics" (Milesi, "Introduction" 1). The short stories of *Dubliners* are naturalist fiction similar to that of Flaubert,[12] that "gives us Dublin exactly as it is" (Pound, *Literary Essays* 399), but they already display an intense awareness of language. The very first story, "The Sisters", uses a young boy as its narrator and shows how his knowledge and understanding of language shape his consciousness and thus the world presented to the reader in the story. The child is strangely fascinated by words – in particular by the key word of *Dubliners*, "paralysis":

> Every night as I gazed up at the window I said softly to myself the word paralysis. It had always sounded strangely in my ears, like the word gnomon in the Euclid and the word simony in the Catechism. But now it sounded to me like the name of some maleficent and sinful being. It filled me with fear, and yet I longed to be nearer to it and look upon its deadly work. (*Dubliners* 7)

The sound of the word paralysis is foregrounded, almost becoming more important than its actual meaning. The word also seems to possess some mysterious power in its own right, to be able to do "deadly work" (for the child, it is the *word* that does this, not the physical condition it refers to). Thus the word becomes more than a mere mirror of reality; it itself shapes reality around itself. Essentially, it becomes a magic word.[13]

The child's understanding is also limited by the language he hears. None of the adults want to explain the dead priest's mysterious crime to him, and the story is made up of a multitude of broken off utterances which the narrator struggles to make sense of: "I puzzled my head to extract meaning from his unfinished sentences" (*Dubliners* 9). The world portrayed in the text is incomplete, almost fragmented, and this is due to the fact it is constructed of fragmented sentences; the form of the text bears out its meaning. As readers,

---

[12] At least according to Ezra Pound (cf. *Literary Essays* 399).
[13] The third word, simony, has an explicitly magical context, as it refers to Simon Magus.

we follow the child's interpretative process, and become aware of how the way we perceive the world is conditioned by language.

This process is carried further in *A Portrait of the Artist as a Young Man*. Its famous opening passage shows how language, particularly storytelling and song, form young Stephen Dedalus's consciousness and his identity ("He was baby tuckoo" *Portrait* 3). Again, the sounds of words fascinate and they take on a life of their own beyond their meaning:

> He hid under the table. His mother said:
> —O, Stephen will apologise.
> Dante said:
> —O, if not, the eagles will come and pull out his eyes.
> > *Pull out his eyes,*
> > *Apologise,*
> > *Apologise,*
> > *Pull out his eyes.*
> (*Portrait* 4)

The impression given here is of words as tangible entities in their own right, rather than merely reflecting reality; indeed, "language overwhelms its rational communicative function: words are progressively emptied of their meaning through repetition, rhyming, and rhythmicization" (Attridge, *Joyce Effects* 69). Young Stephen is already trying to bring words into a certain aesthetic order (rhyme), but it is an order in which sound, not meaning, has primacy: "[Joyce's] conception of language might be termed *phonocentric*" (Yee 25).

Shortly afterwards, the young schoolboy Stephen displays further precocious awareness of language when he meditates on the colours of flowers:

> Lavender and cream and pink roses were beautiful to think of. Perhaps a wild rose might be like those colours and he remembered the song about the wild rose blossoms on the little green place. But you could not have a green rose. But perhaps somewhere in the world you could. (*Portrait* 9)

Stephen here realises something that is fundamental to literature of the fantastic: that words need not necessarily comply with reality, that they can actually create a reality of their own. Tolkien writes: "When we can take green from grass, blue from heaven, and red from blood, we have already an enchanter's power [...]. Anyone inheriting the fantastic device of human language can say *the green sun*" ("On Fairy-stories" 122; 140); one might as easily substitute

Stephen's "green rose" for "green sun". When young Stephen thinks "But you could not have a green rose. But perhaps somewhere in the world you could" he is thinking of where the necessary preconditions for a green rose might be fulfilled; ultimately, that place is in a secondary world of words, created by the writer: "To make a Secondary World inside which the green sun will be credible, commanding Secondary Belief, will probably require labour and thought, and will certainly demand a special skill, a kind of elvish craft" (Tolkien, "On Fairy-stories" 140). It is at this specific point that Joyce's language starts moving towards the cosmic models made of words that make up *Ulysses* and *Finnegans Wake*. It is also where it starts moving closer to the fantastic.

There are several passages in *Portrait* where the fantastic appears to intrude into the overt realism of its narrative, and each of these is linked in one way or another to language. I will examine two that I find especially interesting in more detail here. The first comes after Stephen, searching for his father's initials carved into a desk at his father's old college, instead reads carved in one of the desks the word "*foetus*". Foetus is "a wound more than a word [...]. Its sorcery arrests the narrative" (Maud Ellmann, "Polytropic Man" 95). The rupture produced by this word (again, significantly *a word* rather than an event) is expressed in a loss of both reality and language:

> The sunlight breaking suddenly on his sight turned the sky and clouds into a fantastic world of sombre masses with lakelike spaces of rosy light. His very brain was sick and powerless. He could scarcely interpret the letters of the signboards of the shops. By his monstrous way of life he seemed to have put himself beyond the limits of reality. Nothing moved him or spoke to him from the real world unless he heard in it an echo of the infuriated cries within him. He could respond to no earthly or human appeal [...] (*Portrait* 98)

Stephen is displaced from the "real world" into a "fantastic world" – he is in a place where he becomes acutely aware of (in Todorov's words) "the fragility of the limit between matter and mind" (Todorov 120). The result of this seems to be that language disappears: he can no longer read, he is cut off from communication. The world of the fantastic, in this case, would appear to be a world *beyond* language. It is a terrifying place that robs Stephen, who depends so strongly on words, of agency, making him "sick and powerless". However, this very loss of language is paradoxically produced by a word: the word *foetus*, which suggests that the fantastic world beyond language may also be the world of the womb before language – which makes it none the less terrifying for Stephen.[14]

Later in the novel, Stephen hears a long and vivid sermon about the terrors of hell, and this leads him to repent of his encounters with prostitutes and his hypocrisy. He has a monstrous vision of the place awaiting him in hell. This passage clearly plays upon the Waste Land motif which we have already examined in the second chapter of this study.

> A field of stiff weeds and thistles and tufted nettle-bunches. Thick among the tufts of rank stiff growth lay battered canisters and clots and coils of excrement. A faint marshlight struggled upwards from all the ordure through the bristling greygreen weeds. An evil smell, faint and foul as the light, curled upwards sluggishly out of the canisters and from the stale encrusted dung.
> Creatures were in the field; one, three, six: creatures were moving in the field, hither and thither. Goatish creatures with human faces, hornybrowed, lightly bearded and grey as indiarubber. The malice of evil glittered in their hard eyes, as they moved hither and thither, trailing their long tails behind them. A rictus of malignity lit up greyly their old bony faces. One was clasping about his ribs a torn flannel waistcoat, another complained monotonously as his beard stuck in the tufted weeds. Soft language issued from their spittleless lips as they swished in slow circles round and round the field, winding hither and thither through the weeds, dragging their long tails amid the rattling canisters. (*Portrait* 148-49)

This beautifully crafted passage forms a contrast with the previous episode, for Stephen's fantastic vision of hell contains language; the goat-like monsters that inhabit it can speak: "Soft language issued from their lips." The softness of their speech links them to his sin, lust: when he first goes with a prostitute, "her softly parting lips [...] pressed upon his brain as upon his lips as though they were the vehicle of a vague speech [...] softer than sound or odour" (*Portrait* 108). In contrast to the loss of language engendered by the foetal return to the womb, the fantastic waste land of lust is perceived by Stephen as possessing a language of its own.[15]

---

14 Maud Ellmann suggests in "Disremembering Dedalus" that the significance of the word *foetus* lies in the fact it "encroaches on the father's empire [...] A navel, where the mother's namelessness engraves itself upon the flesh before the father ever carved his signature" (96). The loss of language thus also entails a loss of (male) identity; Stephen has no name, he is not even the "baby tuckoo" from his father's story.
15 This idea also occurs in *Ulysses*. After Leopold Bloom has masturbated over Gerty MacDowell lifting her skirts on the beach, he reflects: "Still it was a kind of language between us" (370). Maud Ellmann examines the connection between language and lust further in her article "Disremembering Dedalus".

It is when Stephen starts to develop his artistic talent that language becomes truly constitutive of his world. Stephen finds it impossible to distinguish between emotions, sensations, and the poetic language he uses to express them; for him, the emotions are caused by words as much as events:

> *Darkness falls from the air.*
> A trembling joy, lambent as a faint light, played like a fairy host around him. But why? Her passage through the darkening air or the verse with its black vowels and its opening sound, rich and lutelike? (*Portrait* 253)

Again, the sound of the words is foregrounded rather than their meaning, emphasising the materiality of language. G.J. Watson (194) writes of "Stephen's immersion in his own verbal universe" and states that "Stephen may thus make a neat, self-enclosed – and hence safe – world for himself, and his love for, and power over, words may even lend his verbal universe an appealing intensity or beauty" (192). It almost goes without saying that through this foregrounding of language the novel draws attention to its own status as a "verbal universe".

The creation of a "verbal universe" goes further in *Ulysses* and is taken to an extreme in *Finnegans Wake*. As Katie Wales writes,

> Language for Joyce is not simply a transparent medium of reality but that reality itself. It is also its own world, consciously foregrounded by word-play, syntactic deviations, leitmotifs, symbolism and ambiguity. Those readers of *Ulysses* and *Finnegans Wake* who look for the "real world" beyond the complex words and structural technicalities of the texts will continually be thwarted. (*The Language of James Joyce* 67)

Ulysses itself puns on the connection between word and world when in Martha's letter to Bloom she misspells the one to produce the other: "I call you a naughty boy because I do not like that other world" (79).[16] It becomes impossible to tell which is which – are words made by the world or is the world made of words?

One of the most famous passages in *Ulysses* that thematises language is the "Oxen of the Sun" episode, in which Bloom visits the hospital where Mina Purefoy is in labour. The whole episode can be broken down into nine sections corresponding to the nine months of gestation of a human child, and each of

---

16 Rainer Emig writes that in doing this she "turns the textual realm of his erotic musings into a 'real' world" (Emig, *Ulysses* 24).

these sections represents one stage in the development of the English language. The sections also parody famous English literary works representative of these stages. For example when Bloom enters the hospital, the world portrayed seems to be that of Malory's *Morte D'Arthur*:[17]

> This meanwhile this good sister stood by the door and begged them at the reverence of Jesu our alther liege to leave their wassailing for there was one above quick with child a gentle dame, whose time hied fast. Sir Leopold heard on the upfloor cry on high and he wondered what cry that it was whether of child or woman and I marvel, said he, that it be not come or now. Meseems it dureth overlong. (*Ulysses* 385)

These passages simultaneously incorporate the literary canon and parody it; they show how language embodies history and culture and draw attention to its unfixed and changeable nature. The very strangeness of the ancient idioms in "Oxen" makes it hard for the reader to concentrate on anything but their form; the content conveyed appears secondary and it is well-nigh impossible to believe that "real(istic)" events are narrated thus. The world of language takes on myriad forms: the final section of "Oxen of the Sun" transforms into a babble of various contemporary dialects from Cockney ("Waiting, guvnor?" *Ulysses* 422) to Scots ("We're nae tha fou" *Ulysses* 424). This is part of the modernist paradox: while *Ulysses* overtly demonstrates that its universe is one of language, and that it as a novel embodies that very universe, it also draws attention to the fact that the medium of its construction, language, is unstable and liable to change and collapse at any given moment.

In *Finnegans Wake*, finally, Joyce writes "a transcription into miniaturized form of the whole western literary tradition" (Deane, "Introduction" vii). It is a work to which the label "cosmic model" can truly be applied, a work that attempts the impossible task of incorporating all of reality into itself and its language, and in doing so, pays the price of ultimately divorcing itself from that reality. The chaotic babble/Babel that constitutes *Finnegans Wake* represents Joyce's attempts to find "a language above all languages" (Joyce, cit. Ellmann, *James Joyce* 397) – a language referred to in the novel's pun "sprakin sea Djoytsch?" The common relationship between sound and meaning is disrupted (in a way similar to that of Gertrude Stein): Tolkien wrote of the *Wake* that "meaning

---

17 Cf. Harry Blamires, *The Bloomsday Book*. London: Routledge, 1988.

[...] is so clearly subordinate to sound. Listener nec[essarily] pays chief attention to the latter" (MS Tolkien 24, fol. 45). Tolkien also remarked that to read *Finnegans Wake* would require as much of "an ear and training to appreciate it [as] to listen to certain subordinated parts of orchestrated music" (MS Tolkien 24, fol. 45) – and we can note that Tolkien is actually describing the process of reading the book as *listening*.

Towards the end of writing it Joyce declared: "I have discovered I can do anything with language I want" (cit. Ellmann, *James Joyce* 702). In the *Wake*, there is no reality beyond language, nothing beyond the letters that make up the text of the world: "(Stoop) if you are abcedminded, to this claybook, what curios of signs (please stoop), in this allaphbed! Can you rede (since We and Thou had it out already) its world?" (*FW* 18). Characters are also no more than speech: "[HCE is] a onestone parable, a rude breathing on the void of to be, a venter hearing his own bauchspeech in backwords, or, more strictly, but tristurned initials, the cluekey to a worldroom beyond the roomwhorld" (*FW* 100). Ultimately, the subject of *Finnegans Wake*, while it is also a family saga and a monumental amalgamation of various myths and cultures, is of course language itself; as Samuel Beckett (14) states: "[Joyce's] writing is not *about* something; *it is that something itself.*" Joyce here "surrendered the 'ordinary' world, the world as represented by the great tradition of the realistic novel, for a world of capricious fantasy and inexhaustible word-play" (Deane, "Introduction" xlvii). With its circular (and thus theoretically neverending) form, its incessant play with words in "lashons of languages" (*FW* 29) and complete rejection of the conventions of plot and character, *Finnegans Wake* ultimately stands as a monument of its own magnificence, self-enclosed, purely language, nothing more, nothing less; a world of words.

C.S. Lewis's first novel, *Out of the Silent Planet*, already betrays its overriding concern with language (and its failure) in its title. Its protagonist, Elwin Ransom, is a philologist – a surprising choice of hero for a science fiction novel, and one that again gives a clue to the central role language will play in the text. The most important discovery Ransom makes when he is first transported to Malacandra, or Mars, is that of extraterrestrial language. When he encounters a *hross*, a member of one of the three intelligent species that live on Malacandra, he realises that it is trying to speak to him:

> The creature was *talking*. It had language. If you are not yourself a philologist, I am afraid that you must take on trust the prodigious emotional consequences of this realization in Ransom's mind. A new world he had already seen – but a new, an extra-terrestrial, a non-human language was a different matter. [...] The love of knowledge is a kind of madness. In the fraction of a second which it took Ransom to decide the creature was really talking, and while he still knew that he might be facing instant death, his imagination had leaped over every fear and hope and probability of his situation to follow the dazzling project of making a Malacandrian grammar. *An Introduction to the Malacandrian Language – The Lunar Verb – A Concise Martian-English Dictionary...* the titles flitted through his mind. And what might one not discover from the speech of a non-human race? The very form of language itself, the principle behind all possible languages, might fall into his hands. (*OSP* 62)[18]

This (pointedly comic) passage already hints at the true importance of Ransom's discovery: the language the *hross* is speaking in is "Old Solar" or *Hressa-Hlab*, which proves to be the original language of the solar system. Ransom later explains:

> I mean there was originally a common speech for all rational creatures inhabiting the planets of our system [...]. That original speech was lost on Thulcandra, our own world, when our whole tragedy took place. No human language now known in the world is descended from it. (*Perelandra* 20)

The loss of Old Solar upon Earth is linked to the Fall. Original Sin, falling off from God, has resulted in falling off from the original language – hence the Malacandrians' name for Earth: Thulcandra, the Silent Planet. While the further implications of this will be explored more fully at a later point in this chapter, it is already clear that Old Solar, as the language given to all intelligent species by God, must thus be endowed with a special power and truth – and an immediate relationship to the reality it is connected with. Lewis's space novels serve as a model for subsequent fantasy and science fiction texts that thematise a primary language and its ensuing loss (as we have already seen in the examples of Le Guin and Paolini). However, the paradox remains that the only language in which the originary, perfect language can be narrated remains the fallen, imperfect language. In the second novel of the trilogy, *Perelandra*, the narrator (a ficticious "Lewis") questions Ransom on his second space voyage to Venus, and touches on this issue:

---

18 This is a reference to philology of the 19th century, when it was thought that the attempted reconstructions of Indogermanic or Indo-European would eventually lead to the discovery of the tongue spoken in the Garden of Eden.

> I was questioning him on the subject – which he doesn't often allow – and had incautiously said, "Of course I realise it's all rather too vague for you to put into words," when he took me up rather sharply, for such a patient man, by saying, "On the contrary, it is words that are too vague. The reason why the thing can't be expressed is that it's too *definite* for language." (*Perelandra* 28)

Lewis's space romances establish an original language and contrast earthly language negatively with it; and as they are written in earthly language, they thus draw attention to their own imperfect state. Like many modernist texts, they posit a (past) perfection to which they aspire but which they can never attain.

While Lewis was obviously influenced by Tolkien's invented languages (indeed the whole idea to write *Out of the Silent Planet* was the result of a pact between the two[19]), he himself appears to have created Old Solar out of the sheer pleasure of playing with words:

> There is no conscious connection between any of the phonetic elements in my 'Old Solar' words and those of any actual language. I am always playing with syllables and fitting them together (purely by ear) to see if I can hatch up new words that please me. I want them to have an emotional, not intellectual, suggestiveness; the heaviness of *glund* for as huge a planet as Jupiter, the vibrating, tintillating quality of *viritrilbia* for the subtlety of Mercury, the liquidity […] of Maleldil. The only exception I am aware of is *hnau* which *may* (but I don't know) have been influenced by Greek *nous*. (Lewis, *Letters* 233-234)[20]

If Eliot could write that David Jones and Joyce had "the Celtic ear for the music of words" (Eliot, "Introduction" viii), it would appear that Lewis, too, possessed this ear.[21] An awareness of suggestive sounds is evident in the space trilogy – "Lewis", the narrator of Perelandra, declares:

---

19 Both writers were to produce a novel, Lewis on space travel and Tolkien on time travel. Lewis quickly completed his novel, which was *Out of the Silent Planet*; Tolkien started on *The Lost Road*, which represents his version of the Atlantis myth and contains the first seeds of the "straight road made bent" element of his mythology. He never completed it, but the fragments are now published as *The History of Middle-earth*, Vol. V (London: Unwin, 1987).
20 Lewis is here aspiring to the same ideal of "phonetic fitness" that characterises Tolkien's works. For a further exploration of this idea and a fascinating comparison of Tolkien's languages to the language invented by the Russian Futurists, Zaum, cf. Smith 99-106.
21 This fascination with sound and an emphasis on it, rather than any meaning attached to words, is evident in Lewis's poem "Narnian Suite" (*Poems* 6-7; Part 1: "March for Strings, Kettledrums, and Sixty-three Dwarfs"; Part 2: "March for Drum, Trumpet, and Twenty-one Giants") which actually moves very close to nonsense poetry. As Charles Huttar remarks, this is "a quasi-musical composition, the music being that of word sounds. Thus, there is less in the way of content and no thesis […] Lewis is […] fascinated by the onomatopoetic possibilities of language" ("A Lifelong Love Affair with Language" *Word and Story in C.S. Lewis* 89-90).

> Please understand that at ordinary times the idea of a "haunted house" means no more to me than it does to you. [...] It was just the *word* "haunted". "Haunted"…"haunting"…what a quality there is in that first syllable! Would not a child who had never heard the word before and did not know its meaning shudder at the mere sound if, as the day was closing in, it heard one of its elders say to another "This house is haunted"? (*Perelandra* 9-10)

This emphasis on the materiality of words is similar to the way they are perceived by Joyce's Stephen. The word "haunted" by virtue of its sound (not its meaning!) has the power to make its hearer shudder.

Thus we can see that Lewis's works, like Joyce's, draw overt attention to the medium of their construction and also to its instability. Lewis's texts are also hardly less intertextual than those of his fellow Irishman (except of course by their scale). Thrown into completely alien surroundings, it is his knowledge of literature that helps Ransom orient himself and give his presence on the strange planets meaning. As Rob Maslen (227-228) writes: "In wandering the landscapes of Mars and Venus [Ransom] is wandering the pages of the old books he (or rather Lewis) loves, come alive and bursting with energy." In *Perelandra*, Ransom is engaged in battle with the possessed human scientist Weston and finds himself "to his surprise – shouting a line out from *The Battle of Maldon*" (142): in hot pursuit of his enemy "he laughed aloud. 'My hounds are of the Spartan kind, so flew'd so sanded,' he roared" (145). While this scarcely compares with the complexity of an Ulyssean episode like "The Oxen of the Sun", it can be seen that both Lewis and Joyce take up the concept of a tradition of (English) literature in their works. This tradition is both upheld through these references and questioned at the same time; Joyce's "Oxen of the Sun" is openly a parody, and Lewis (who was always suspicious of what he called "highbrow" literature and the canon[22]) is similarly tongue-in-cheek when he writes:

> [Ransom] determined to give up guessing how the time was going. He beguiled himself by recapitulating the whole story of his adventure in Perelandra. He recited all that he could remember of the *Iliad*, the *Odyssey*, the *Æneid*, the *Chanson de Roland*, *Paradise Lost*, the *Kalevala*, the *Hunting of the Snark*, and a rhyme about Germanic sound-laws which he had composed as a freshman. (*Perelandra* 160)

---

22 Cf. his essay "High and Low Brows" (in *Rehabilitations* 95-116). Of course it can be argued that while Lewis disliked the (modernist) canon, he was quick enough to establish his own.

In reciting "the whole story of his adventure in Perelandra" alongside various epics, Ransom is putting his exploits on a par with those of Achilles and Odysseus/Ulysses; yet the inclusion in his list of Lewis Carroll's nonsense epic, "The Hunting of the Snark", at the same time debunks what could be seen as his claim to epic heroism. The inclusion of Carroll is also a nod towards the tradition of fantastic literature. However, in putting his own tale in this list, Ransom is also already fictionalising his story while it is still happening. This is one way in which the novels draw attention to their own fictional status – as Donald E. Glover (171) observes, "often the action of storytelling becomes the focus of a work and the symbolic centre of meaning."[23] The passages quoted here show how Ransom's world(s) is made up of language and literature, and how these are used to create the secondary reality of the novels.

The space romances differ somewhat from Lewis's other main body of work, the *Chronicles of Narnia*, in that they are still set within the primary universe. Narnia, by contrast, is a fully-fledged secondary world which can only be reached through magic, not by rockets.[24] As they are children's books, the Narnia tales do not offer as openly self-conscious an approach to language as the space trilogy. Yet in the *Chronicles*, too, we find language foregrounded in a number of ways. It may be significant that the approach to the magical wardrobe in *The Lion, the Witch and the Wardrobe* is through "a whole series of rooms that led into each other and were lined with books – most of them very old books and some bigger than the Bible in a church" (*LWW* 14). When Lucy first stumbles through the wardrobe into another world, she meets a mythical creature, the faun Mr. Tumnus. She realises that in his world she as a human is just as mythical as he is in hers when she sees the book "*Men, Monks and Gamekeepers;*

---

23 This can also be observed in the works of Tolkien and Williams. Williams's Taliessin makes a song of himself in the very first poem of *The Region of the Summer Stars*, "The Calling of Taliessin". And in *The Lord of the Rings* Sam says to Frodo: "Beren now, he never thought he was going to get that Silmaril from the Iron Crown in Thangorodrim, and yet he did, and that was a worse place and a blacker danger than ours. But that's a long tale, of course, and goes on past happiness and into grief and beyond it – and the Silmaril went on and came to Eärendil. And why, sir, I never thought of that before! We've got – you've got some of the light of it in that star-glass that the Lady gave you! Why, to think of it, we're in the same tale still! It's still going on. Don't the great tales ever end?" (696-697).
24 Lewis was never much interested in the mechanics of science fiction, and by the second volume of the space trilogy, *Perelandra*, he abandoned them completely: "I am inclined to think frankly supernatural methods are best. I took a hero to Mars in a space-ship, but when I knew better I had angels convey him to Venus" (Lewis, "On Science Fiction" *Other Worlds* 91).

A Study in Popular Legend or Is Man a Myth?" (*LWW* 22-23).²⁵ These are the subtle ways in which Lewis draws attention to the fact that fiction and reality are not easily divided, and that both are influenced by each other.

The main way in which language is emphasised in the *Chronicles* is through the speech of animals. In "On Fairy-stories", Tolkien cites "the desire to converse with other living things" as one of the central desires at the heart of fantasy; it is from this, he says, that the tradition of talking animals on fairy tales comes (152). In Tolkien's works, we encounter only very few such talking beasts, such as the great hound Huan who assists Beren and Lúthien on their quest for the Silmaril (cf. *Silmarillion* 194-225), but in Lewis's Narnia, the Talking Beasts, who are given speech at the creation of Narnia by Aslan, form a major part of its population alongside "mythical" creatures such as fauns, dryads and dwarves. Humans, by contrast, are rare – at the beginning of *The Lion* the White Witch at first thinks the boy Edmund is "a great overgrown dwarf that has cut off its beard" (*LWW* 41). The fact that in Narnia animals can speak immediately puts them in a very different relation to mankind than in the primary world. As Aslan says to Frank the Cabby, who is made the first King of Narnia, "[Remember] that they are not slaves like the dumb beasts of the world you were born in, but talking beasts and free subjects" (*TMN* 158). In this way language at once becomes the most significant factor in creating Narnia's otherness. It also affords a lot of comedy, especially when unwitting humans encounter talking beasts for the first time:

> Eustace burst out again. "Oh! Ugh! What on earth's that? Take it away, the horrid thing." He really had some excuse this time for feeling a little surprised. Something very curious indeed had come out of the cabin in the poop and was slowly approaching them. You might call it – and indeed it was – a Mouse. But then it was a Mouse on its hind legs and stood about two feet high. A thin band of gold passed round its head under one ear and over the other and in this was stuck a long crimson feather. [...] Its left paw rested on the hilt of a sword very nearly as long as its tail. Its balance, as it paced gravely along the swaying deck, was perfect, and its manners courtly. [...] Reepicheep [...] said in his shrill, piping voice: "My humble duty to your Majesty. And to King Edmund, too." (Here he bowed again.) "Nothing except your Majesties' presence was

---

25 I suspect this refers to Alice's encounter with the Unicorn in *Through the Looking-glass*: "'This is a child!' Haigha replied [...] 'I always thought they were fabulous monsters!' said the Unicorn. 'Is it alive?' [...] Alice could not help her lips curling up into a smile as she began: 'Do you know, I always thought Unicorns were fabulous monsters, too! I never saw one alive before!'" (Carroll 206).

lacking to this glorious venture." "Ugh, take it away," wailed Eustace. "I hate mice. And I never could bear performing animals. They're silly and vulgar and – and sentimental." "Am I to understand," said Reepicheep to Lucy after a long stare at Eustace, "that this singularly discourteous person is under your Majesty's protection? Because, if not –" (*VDT* 25-27).[26]

Another way in which language is foregrounded in the *Chronicles* is through magic. In *The Magician's Nephew* (chronologically the first of the *Chronicles* though the sixth in publication) the children Digory and Polly go to the world of Charn, where they find its last Queen Jadis (who later becomes the White Witch of Narnia). Jadis has destroyed every living thing in Charn through her deadliest magic – the "Deplorable Word":

> "That was the secret of secrets," said the Queen Jadis. "It had long been known to the great kings of our race that there was a word which, if spoken with the proper ceremonies, would destroy all living things except the one who spoke it. […] I did not use it until she forced me to it. […] I did not use my power till the last of my soldiers had fallen, and the accursed woman, my sister, at the head of her rebels was halfway up those great stairs that lead up from the city to the terrace. Then I waited till we were so close that we could see one another's faces. She flashed her horrible, wicked eyes upon me and said, 'Victory'. 'Yes,' said I, 'Victory, but not yours.' Then I spoke the Deplorable Word. A moment later I was the only living thing beneath the sun." (*TMN* 74-75)

Magical language is language that can directly influence its surroundings through its power. In Lewis's *Chronicles* it is only the characters with the greatest strength – Aslan and the Witch – that can do this. The Witch's Deplorable Word functions as a kind of linguistic atom bomb, wreaking absolute destruction. But Aslan has still greater power, the power to create through language (this will be the focus of one of the next sections). Thus it can be seen that even within the limits set by the genre of children's fiction Lewis succeeds in emphasising his material, language, in many different ways. It is perhaps the concluding passage of the final Narnia book, *The Last Battle*, that reveals best that Narnia is a world of words:

> And as [Aslan] spoke, He no longer looked to them like a lion; but the things that began to happen after that were so great and beautiful that I cannot write them. And for us this is the end of all the stories, and we can most truly say

---

26 Comic passages involving Reepicheep the Mouse and his speech abound: "'Silence!' thundered Caspian. 'I've been lessoned but I'll not be baited. Will no one silence that Mouse?' 'Your Majesty promised,' said Reepicheep, 'to be a good lord to the Talking Beasts of Narnia.' 'Talking Beasts, yes,' said Caspian. 'I said nothing about beasts that never stop talking.'" (*VDT* 248).

that they all lived happily ever after. But for them it was only the beginning of the real story. All their life in this world and all their adventures in Narnia had only been the cover and the title page: now at last they were beginning Chapter One of the Great Story which no one on earth has read: which goes on for ever: in which every chapter is better than the one before. (*TLB* 222)

In this passage, the conclusion to the seven *Chronicles* (when all the main characters of the novels – with the exception of Susan – have actually died), Lewis pictures all reality and even life after death as a story – as a book in fact, with a cover, title page and chapters.[27] As Lewis was a Christian writer, following a religion of the book, the centrality of the book in these final sentences is easily explained; it is interesting, however, that Lewis pictures Heaven as a neverending book. One might thus (rather naughtily) be tempted to see the (potentially) neverending *Finnegans Wake* as Lewis's version of Heaven![28] Death and heaven thus prove to be the ultimate validation of language, not its end, rather like in Eliot's "Little Gidding" where "the communication / Of the dead is tongued with fire beyond the language of the living" (Eliot, *Collected Poems* 215).

We have seen how both Lewis's and Joyce's works emphasise their textuality in various ways, and how language is foregrounded as both the central theme of their novels and the material of their construction. We shall now turn to a specific type of language – that of myth – and examine how myth is employed in Lewis's and Joyce's texts.

---

[27] Mallarmé's quote inevitably comes to mind: "Tout, au monde, existe pour aboutir à un livre" (Translation: 'Everything in the world exists to end up in a book'; Mallarmé in conversation with Jules Huret of *L'Echo de Paris* in 1891; cit. *Mallarmé*, ed. Anthony Hartley ix). Joyce incidentally commented upon this: "Contrairement à ce qu'affirmait Mallarmé, le monde n'existe pas pour aboutir à un livre, mais pour se transformer par le livre ou mieux sans le livre, en une pensée vivante et créatrice" (Translation: 'In contrast to what Mallarmé states, the world does not exist to end up in a book, but to transform itself through the book, or better, without the book, into a living and creative thought'; cit. Heath 131).

[28] Lewis was unable to dispense with language and literature even in his autobiographical works. In *A Grief Observed*, where he documents his emotional devastation and the failure of literature to comfort him after the death of his wife Joy, Lewis concludes with a quote from Dante. William Gray observes: "Life and death may be more real than novels, but this truth is conveyed to us in the artifice of a fictional text. It is typical of Lewis – that most intertextual of beings – to write a story about the uselessness of stories in the face of the reality of death, and to offer at the final moment of truth – a literary quotation!" (96).

Mythic Language

Myth is intrinsically connected to language. The general definition used earlier tells us a myth is "one story in a mythology – a system of hereditary stories of ancient origin once believed to be true by a particular cultural group, and which served to explain (in the terms of action of deities and other supernatural beings) why the world is as it is and things happen as they do" (Abrams 170). This shows that myth essentially is narrative; it is a story told in words. Furthermore, the work of Lévi-Strauss and Barthes (which we also have already encountered in previous chapters) demonstrates that "myth *is* language: to be known, myth has to be told; it is a part of human speech" (Lévi-Strauss 209). Myth functions as a world-formula in story: it is a narrative explanation of the world and reality. Thus, as explained earlier, it claims authority and aspires to universal significance, seeking to prove its validity for all times and places – in the language of *Finnegans Wake*, "Putting Allspace in a Notshall" (*FW* 455). However, in order to do this, it must exclude anything pointing beyond the myth itself from its picture of the world. Myth is thus always characterised by a tension between expansion and reduction – a tension that could be seen in Joyce's phrase that substitutes the negative "Notshall" (reminiscent of the prohibitions of the Decalogue) for the traditional "nutshell".

Earlier chapters have already shown the centrality of myth and mythic language for both modernism and fantasy (cf. Weinreich 43-61). We have seen how David Jones uses the Arthurian myth to structure and give meaning to the war experience, and how Charles Williams uses it to create the secondary world of Logres. We have also seen the importance of mythology for Tolkien and Yeats, and their endeavours to create national myths for their respective countries. In all these instances, the simultaneous expansion and exclusion typical of myth repeats itself in the literary work: for example, Yeats and Tolkien are forced to exclude large parts of their countries' histories in order to make their myths work, while these myths posit (and pose as) a unified past. Similarly, in all these cases the use of myth is bound up with language – language is the material that narrates the myth, power is attributed to the speech of mythic characters, and the structures of myth take hold of pre-existing literary material such as the *Mabinogion* (which is, of course, itself a myth) and use them to give meaning and authority to the new texts, while often depriving them of their own autonomous meaning and history. After all this, it will hardly come as a surprise that myth plays a central role in the works of Joyce and Lewis: this section aims to investigate how it is used and how its language structures these authors' texts.

Joyce's *Ulysses* is the most obvious place to start, as it already gives us the clue to its structuring myth in its title. Joyce parallels the wanderings of Bloom and Stephen through the Dublin of June 16th 1904 with the peregrinations of the hero of the *Odyssey*. It was in his essay on *Ulysses* that T.S. Eliot first defined the "mythical method" he saw as programmatic for modernism, and which has been quoted in earlier chapters. Eliot sees Joyce's use of the Odyssean myth as having "the importance of a scientific discovery" ("'Ulysses', Order and Myth" 177); in *Ulysses*, Joyce is "manipulating a continuous parallel between contemporaneity and antiquity" and thus creating "a way of controlling, of ordering, of giving a shape and significance to the immense panorama of futility and anarchy which is contemporary history" ("'Ulysses', Order and Myth" 177). According to Eliot, "Joyce is pursuing a method which others must pursue after him" ("'Ulysses', Order and Myth" 177). Thus, as we have seen, David Jones's *In Parenthesis* and Yeats's poetry can be seen to follow the "mythical method". Myth gives literature a form, a structure by which to orient itself at a time when, in the very act of discarding conventions, it seemed to have lost its direction. In the specific case of *Ulysses*, "the Homeric wanderings of Joyce's heroes [...] made possible a fairly sequential mode of writing" (Milesi, "Introduction" 3) in a novel that, with its confusing changes between various centres of consciousness and lack of a coherent plot, might otherwise have threatened to simply fall apart. The cyclical form typical of myth (cf. Blumenberg 114) is apparent in *Ulysses*, which traces one day from morning to night.

In *Ulysses*, Joyce's use of the myth is consciously ironic. In paralleling Bloom with Odysseus, Joyce is not claiming that Bloom is a hero of Homeric stature. His wanderings last one day, not ten years; he tricks mere drunks, not the Cyclops; he does not win the heart of the princess Nausicaa, but masturbates in isolation over the cripple Gerty MacDowell; and when he returns home, it is not to Penelope who remained faithful to him for over two decades, but to a wife who has let the rival suitor (Boylan) into the palace herself and slept with him. Bloom has no son, as his boy Rudy died when still a child; the place of Telemachus, Odysseus's son, is taken by Stephen, whose relationship to his own father is fraught. Both Joyce's Odysseus and Telemachus thus enter into a proxy father-son relationship doomed to remain unsatisfactory and unfulfilled – Stephen cannot become Bloom's heir, and Bloom cannot provide Stephen with the fatherly guidance and approval Simon Dedalus fails to give him. They ultimately "take leave, one of the other, in separation" (*Ulysses* 624). The cyclical form of myth evident in the novel can be seen on the one hand to endow Bloom's journeys with a kind of universal significance – he is, like Odysseus, Noman, but he also becomes Everyman: "What universal binomial denominations would be his as entity and nonentity? Assumed by any or known to none. Everyman and Noman" (*Ulysses* 648). On the other hand, the cycle also becomes emblematic of "stagnation, repetition, and [...] the mechanical structuring of life in an alienated reality" (Emig, *Ulysses* 10).

This failure of the modern counterpart of the Ulyssean myth indicates that the overall coherence supposedly provided by the "mythical method" may not be completely successful. In the novel, the focus shifts from Stephen to Bloom and from Bloom to Molly; there are other centres of consciousness in the novel too (the unidentified speaker in "Cyclops", or Gerty MacDowell in "Nausicaa"). All these have their own distinct voices – Molly's famous monologue characterised by an absence of punctuation which implies the unhindered and unstructured flow of thoughts ("no thats no way for him has he no manners nor no refinement nor no nothing in his nature slapping us behind like that on my bottom because I didnt call him Hugh the ignoramus that doesnt know poetry from a cabbage" 697),[29] Stephen's unsurprisingly showing poetic structures such as repetition, assonance and alliteration ("Day by day: night by night: lifted, flooded and let fall. Saint Ambrose heard it, sigh of leaves and waves, waiting, awaiting the fullness of their times" 55), and Bloom's using short, direct sentences often missing words ("Didn't look back when she was going down the strand. Wouldn't give that satisfaction. [...] Did she know

---

29 It has been pointed out that Molly's monologue is actually quite conventional once the missing punctuation has been restored (cf. Burgess 59); thus, the effect of "Penelope" "relies on the strategies and techniques of an activity that has nothing to do with the continuities of unexpressed thought: the activity of reading" (Attridge 99).

what I? Course." 369).³⁰ While this contributes to the overall "realism" of the text, it also breaks up narrative coherence, while at the same time the myth joining them all posits unification. The very different worlds of the characters' languages emphasise their separation as much as, if not more than, their failure to truly connect through action. The coherence conferred upon *Ulysses* through its master-myth is but a semblance, and this is borne out through the novel's language(s). According to Theodor Adorno, this is typical of modernist works, that insist on a wholeness that remains illusory: "Einheit ist Schein" (*Ästhetische Theorie* 455).³¹ Thus "Joyce's novel participates in a characteristically modernist endeavour. It acknowledges fragmentation in the reality it refers and relates to, but also wishes to perceive wholes, patterns and meanings" (Emig, *Ulysses* 2). Myth accordingly becomes the focal point of the typically modernist tension in *Ulysses*: it posits wholeness and significance, giving a kind of coherence to the novel's world(s) of words, but at the same time those words draw attention to the emptiness of its form.

Joyce himself was afterwards doubtful of the Ulyssean mythical method, and remarked that the form of *Ulysses* had been too strict (cf. Joyce, *Letters* I 204). His next and final work, *Finnegans Wake*, does not employ one single master-myth: instead, it uses a myriad of myths, from the founding myth of Western civilization, the Fall, and other Christian myths such as the Tower of Babel, to the Arthurian myth (especially that of "Sir Tristram, violer d'amores" *FW* 3), the *Bhaghavadgita*, the tales of the Arabian Nights ("this scherzarade of one's thousand one nightinesses" *FW* 51), and Irish mythology. These it fuses to one monumental whole: itself. One way of reading the *Wake* is thus to see it as the ultimate cosmic model: it tries to incorporate all myths, creating itself as a super-myth, as it were the "myth to end all myths". As Stephen Heath (142) writes: "The many stories of *Finnegans Wake* are one story, always the same; are so many versions of a kind of ur-narrative, permutations of a handful of agents and actions."

---

30 Cf. *Ulysses* (603): "What two temperaments did they [Bloom and Stephen] individually represent? The scientific. The artistic." This could mean that Bloom and Stephen are meant to represent (mythic) archetypes.
31 Translation: 'Unity is an illusion.'

> Yet it is but an old story, the tale of a Treestone with one Ysold, of a Mons held by tentpegs and his pal whatholoosed on the run, what Cadman could but Badman wouldn't, any Genoaman against any Venis, and why Kate takes charge of the waxworks. (*FW* 113)

Here it becomes evident that the way the previous myths (Tristan and Iseult), literature (Caedmon), and history (such as the Genoan war with Venice) are included suggests they are all only pointers towards the universal tale of *Finnegans Wake*, merely forming various aspects of the *Wake*'s monumental whole. In this way *Finnegans Wake* also becomes mythic in the Barthesian sense of the word, in that it takes a pre-existing system (earlier myths) and turns them from "meaning" into "form", into the structure of its own mega-myth. In Barthes's words, it steals their language to create its own. But of course the very fact that it displaces the primacy of these myths with its own suggests that its own authority might as easily be displaced. This is a fact that *Finnegans Wake* actually plays with quite openly. As with *Ulysses*, it is language itself that betrays the myth that seeks to appropriate it:

> Every person, place and thing in the chaosmos of Alle anyway connected with the gobblydumped turkery was moving and changing every part of the time: the travelling inkhorn (possibly pot), the hare and turtle pen and paper, the continually more and less intermisunderstanding minds of the anticollaborators, the as time went on as it will variously inflected, differently pronounced, otherwise spelled, changeably meaning vocable scriptsigns. (*FW* 118)

On the one hand, the changeability of language undermines the claim to immutable authority put forward by the myth. On the other, the range of the *Wake* itself could be seen to contain all possible variations: there is room in it for Tristram and Treestone, for the novel itself is "totalisating him" (29). Its language "Djyotsch", endlessly changing and shifting, able to accommodate everything and incorporate anything into itself, is the "language above all languages" and as such, it itself is the myth. Such is the universality of its language that an (admittedly obsessive) reader can (almost) find the title of C.S. Lewis's most popular novel in it: "the beauchamp, byward, bull and *lion, the white [witch], the wardrobe* and bloodied, so encouraging" (77; my emphases)!

A connection between myth and language is also central to C.S. Lewis's fiction. The way in which this connection is portrayed is strongly influenced by Lewis's friend and fellow Inkling Owen Barfield. In his book *Poetic Diction* (subtitled *A Study in Meaning*), Barfield sees myth as a stage in the development of language. At this stage, concrete and abstract meanings have not yet become separated; the absolutely material and absolutely abstract meanings we use now are merely branches of an older, unified meaning. Barfield's example is the Greek word πνευμα or the Latin *spiritus*, which have the triple English meanings *breath, wind,* and *spirit*.

> So far from the psychic meaning of "spiritus" having arisen because someone had the abstract idea, "principle of life..." and wanted a word for it, the abstract idea, "principle of life" is itself a *product* of the old concrete *meaning* "spiritus", which contained within itself the germs of both later significations. We must, therefore, imagine a time when "spiritus" or πνευμα, or older words from which these had descended, meant neither *breath,* nor *wind,* nor *spirit,* nor yet all three of these things, but when they simply had *their own old peculiar meaning,* which has since, in the course of the evolution of consciousness, crystallized into the three meanings specified. (Barfield 81)

At this stage of language and consciousness, "[c]onnections between discrete phenomena, connections which are now apprehended as metaphor, were once perceived as immediate realities" (Barfield 92). This implies that in the dawn of time, man saw the world and reality as a whole, and himself as part of this unity. Barfield calls this unity of language, meaning and reality "mythic" (cf. esp. Chapter IV "Meaning and Myth" 77-92).

This view of mythic language implies that instead of connections between words and objects (signifier and signified) being arbitrary constructions, there was once a primary unity of language, meaning and reality. This would make mythic language the expression of a primaeval reality, supporting the ancient view of myth as a true narrative.[32] Barfield (92) states: "Mythology is the ghost of concrete meaning. Connections between discrete phenomena, connections which are now apprehended as metaphor, were once perceived as immediate realities." This stands in marked contrast to theories such as Barthes's, which

---

32 Most original mythologies once held the position of religions and were thought true. That myth is the reflector of truth in spite of the mythologies themselves no longer being taken literally has been believed since the Renaissance, where it was seen as "an allegorical expression of religious, philosophical and scientific truths" (Meletinsky 3). For example, the Romantic philosopher Schelling called myth "a true universe in itself" (*Philosophie der Mythologie*, cit. Meletinsky 8). However, these definitions show that the concept of truth becomes irritatingly vague once the literal level of the myth is discarded, for if the truth supposedly expressed is not contained in the myth's literal meaning, this makes it virtually impossible to define.

claims that myth merely uses a semblance of truth achieved through distortion to hide its own motivation.

Lewis's own thoughts on myth can be related to Barfield's theory, and also show us how we are to interpret myth in works such as the space trilogy. His conversion to Christianity was partly the result of a long discussion with Tolkien about the life, death and resurrection of Christ as "true myth", myth become fact. All the old myths of dying and resurrected gods – Balder, Osiris, Adonis and the like – come true in the historical figure of Jesus. This however does not discredit the old myths, indeed it does quite the opposite: Christ is their ultimate verification. In Tolkien's words, "[t]he Evangelium has not abrogated legends; it has hallowed them" (Tolkien, "On Fairy-stories" 156). Lewis states in *Miracles*:

> My present view – which is tentative and liable to any amount of correction – would be that just as, on the factual side, a long preparation culminates in God's becoming incarnate as Man, so, on the documentary side, the truth first appears in mythical form and then by a long process of condensing or focusing finally becomes incarnate as History. This involves the belief that Myth in general is not merely misunderstood history (as Euhemerus thought) nor diabolical illusion (as some of the Fathers thought) nor priestly lying (as the philosophers of the Enlightenment thought) but, at its best, a real though unfocused gleam of divine truth falling on human imagination. (Lewis, *Miracles* 138)

This obviously carries implications for language. Influenced by Barfield's view of mythic language as expressing primary unities and truths, as well as by the traditions of nineteenth-century philology, Lewis believed in one original, true language that, from a Christian viewpoint, must also be prelapsarian. This explains why earthly mythology is a "ghost" – its abstract language is a shadow of the truth it carried before the Fall. While Lewis was aware of the structuralist view of myth and language, he did not agree with it:

> all our truth, or all but a few fragments, is won by metaphor. [...] if those original equations, between good and light, or evil and dark, between breath and soul and all the others, were from the beginning arbitrary and fanciful [as claimed by structuralism] then all our thinking is nonsensical. But we cannot, without contradiction, believe it to be nonsensical. And so, admittedly the view I have taken has metaphysical implications. But so has every other view. ("Bluspels and Flalansferes" *Rehabilitations* 158)

These thoughts on myth and its language play a prominent role in the space trilogy, where from being a mere vehicle of non-factual truth, myth actually "comes true": on the strange planets he visits, Elwin Ransom slowly discovers that old, mythical concepts of the universe are more real than their modern scientific counterparts, and that happenings described in terrestrial myth have actually really taken place in other worlds. Ransom is ultimately convinced of the reality of what passes on earth as classical mythology when he reaches Meldilorn, the dwelling-place of the Oyarsa (ruling spirit) of Malacandra. There he sees a depiction of the solar system which suggests the innate truth of classical mythology:

> The sun was there, unmistakably, at the centre of the disk: round this the concentric circles revolved. In the first and smallest of these was pictured a little ball, on which rode a winged figure something like Oyarsa, but holding what appeared to be a trumpet. In the next, a similar ball carried another of the flaming figures. This one, instead of the suggested face, had two bulges which after long inspection he decided were meant to be the udders or breasts of a female mammal. [...] The first ball was Mercury, the second Venus – 'And what an extraordinary coincidence,' thought Ransom, 'that their mythology, like ours, associated some idea of the female with Venus.' (*OSP* 129)

Ransom discovers that each of the planets is governed by an eldil, who corresponds to a god of classical mythology. The ancient terrestrial astrology that assigned the wandering stars to gods, far from being some pre-scientific delusion, was absolutely right. Throughout his exploits, Ransom has "the sensation not of following an adventure but of enacting a myth" (*Perelandra* 41). On Perelandra he finds a real garden of the Hesperides – complete with a tree bearing golden fruit and a dragon coiled round its stem (cf. *Perelandra* 39) – and on Malacandra meets the Sorns, "the original of the Cyclops, a giant in a cave and a shepherd" (*Perelandra* 39). Whereas Joyce realises the Cyclops as a drunk, bullying Irishman blinded by prejudice, ironising the myth, Lewis performs his myth-realisation by ennobling the Cyclops.[33]

---

[33] Besides forming one of the central differences between Lewis and Joyce, this is also what distinguishes Lewis's science fiction from its predecessors. Possibly because of its Christian bent, Lewis's fiction is determined to portray other worlds as better and more beautiful than the earth: "Before anything else [Ransom] learned that Malacandra was beautiful; and he reflected how odd it was that this possibility had never entered into his speculations about it. The same peculiar twist of imagination which led him to people the universe with monsters had somehow taught him to expect nothing on a strange planet except rocky desolation or else a network of nightmare machines. He could not say why, now that he came to think of it" (*OSP* 47).

In all three of Lewis's space romances a distinction is made between mythic, prelapsarian language and its fallen earthly counterpart. When Ransom thinks he can discover "the principle behind all languages" from the Hross's speech, this is not simply comic; Old Solar represents the original and unified language posited by Lewis and Barfield. Just as myth "comes true", this language manifests itself in the descent of Mercury (traditionally the mouthpiece of the gods). When he appears to Ransom and Merlin in *That Hideous Strength*, they find the power of language overwhelming:

> It was well that both men had some knowledge of poetry. The doubling, splitting, and recombining of thoughts which now went on in them would have been unendurable for one whom that art had not already instructed in the counterpoint of the mind, the mastery of doubled and trebled vision. For Ransom, whose study had been for many years in the realm of words, it was heavenly pleasure. He found himself sitting within the very heart of language, in the white-hot furnace of essential speech. All fact was broken, splashed into cataracts, caught, turned inside out, kneaded, and reborn as meaning. For the lord of Meaning himself, the herald, the messenger, the slayer of Argus, was with them: the angel that spins nearest the sun, Viritrilbia, whom men call Mercury and Thoth. (*THS* 199-200)

Mythic language is "essential speech". Here, language itself becomes not just "the predominant metaphor linking all three novels" (Wolfe 58) – it reveals itself as the real subject of the novel. The entire trilogy is, somewhat like *Finnegans Wake*, an epic and an amalgamation of myths; it is also a story about language.

One of the central points of focus in all three space novels is the discrepancy between the true speech Old Solar and the twisted language used by the scientists. This is first made explicit in the satirical judgement scene at the end of the first novel, where Ransom attempts to translate Weston's high-flown, abstract and ultimately meaningless propaganda into Old Solar:

> 'Life is greater than any system of morality; her claims are absolute. It is not by tribal taboos and copy-book maxims that she has pursued her relentless march from the amoeba to man and from man to civilization.' 'He says,' began Ransom, 'that living creatures are stronger than the question whether an act is bent or good – no, that cannot be right – he says it is better to be alive and bent than to be dead – no – he says, he says, I cannot say what he says, Oyarsa, in your language.' (*OSP* 158)

The speech (actually more like Orwellian "speak") of the scientists is actually a good example of what Barthes calls mythic language: language that poses as natural and self-evident while in fact being driven by an ulterior reason it attempts to hide. Thus Weston justifies his abduction of Ransom with the fact that such sacrifices are necessary for the development of the human race:

> As it is, I admit we have had to infringe your rights. My only defence is that small claims must give way to great. As far as we know, we are doing what has never been done in the history of man, perhaps never in the history of the universe. We have learned how to jump off the speck of matter on which our species began; infinity, and therefore perhaps eternity, is being put into the hands of the human race. You cannot be so small-minded as to think that the rights or the life of an individual or of a million individuals are of the slightest importance in comparison with this. (*OSP* 28-29)

This passage very obviously makes use of the ideology of progress – Weston appears to take it for granted that the survival and perfection of the human race is the ultimate goal which justifies any means in its pursuit. Ransom's protests that many humans and alien species will die in order for his dream of progress to come true are seen as "narrow and individualistic" (*OSP* 29), and "[d]efeatist trash" (*OSP* 163). Using high-flown rhetoric and lots of big words, Weston seeks to make his claims appear self-evident, while naturally it is his own dreams of power and imperialism that fuel them, totally excluding the voices of those to be "sacrificed". Ransom knows however that "nothing is great or small save by position" (*Perelandra* 99), and bursts Weston's bubble:

> I suppose all that stuff about infinity and eternity means you think you are justified in doing anything – absolutely anything – here and now, on the off chance that some creatures or other descended from man as we know him may crawl about a few centuries longer in some part of the universe. (*OSP* 29)

However, it also becomes clear when applying Barthes's theory to Lewis's novels as a whole that they themselves are mythic in the Barthesian sense of the word. In Lewis's novels – especially the space trilogy – pre-existing elements of the primary world such as classical mythology are incorporated into the secondary worlds with a second system of Christian meaning imposed upon them. In the space romances the gods Jupiter, Mars, Venus and others are made angels subject to Christ, robbed of their ancient identity – they become, in Barthes's words, "stolen language" (*Mythologies* 131), as to Lewis's mind classical mythology can only be meaningful as a pointer towards Christianity. While this might seem only mildly suspicious, Lewis was also almost blatant about the propagandistic effect he wished his novels to have: he wanted to evangelise his readers under the cover of a good story without their noticing: "any amount of theology can be smuggled into people's minds under the cover of romance without their knowing it" (*Other Worlds* 19). Leaving aside the question whether such evangelisation is ultimately good or bad, Lewis thus seeks to disguise his ultimate aim (to convert) behind the mask of entertainment, and such an attempt at disguise should be met with caution, whether or not the ultimate aim is approved of. Indeed the very form of the novel functions as a Barthesian primary mythic system, which is appropriated by Lewis's missionary ideology. Lynette Hunter sees this as typical of the fantasy genre, pointing out "the parallel between [fantasy novels'] stress on the 'natural', in other words unexamined, relationship that the book has to the topics they wish to valorise, and the way that self-enclosed worlds are created by the fantasy stance in the first place in its denial of persuasion and its implicit conveying of truth" (32). In Lewis's space novels, Christian values are presented uncritically, and the entire structure of the secondary worlds is presented as something self-evident and thus "truthful".

Furthermore, the incorporation of texts from the primary world such as the *Iliad* and *Odyssey* into the secondary worlds would also seem to make them appear meaningful only in relation to Ransom's quest on Perelandra. And in the second chapter of this study, we have seen how even the Second World War on Earth becomes but "our own little war here on earth" (*Perelandra* 19) in relation the greater War in Heaven. In the Narnia stories, Aslan's country incorporates both Narnia and the primary world: "That country and this country – all the real countries – are only spurs jutting out from the great mountains of Aslan" (*TLB* 220). Lewis tries to include the primary world and its reality into the cosmic models of his secondary worlds of words. In doing so, he tries to prove the validity of his myth: that all happenings in the primary world are to be related to the versions of the Christian gospel he puts forward in his texts. What relates his endeavour to modernism is the fact that this never quite works. We have already seen how the language he uses in his texts raises doubts about its validity while attempting to affirm its power, and how the literary texts he cites both establish his own as part of a tradition and question that tradition at the same time. Perhaps the conclusion of his last novel, *Till We Have Faces*, can stand as representative of his oeuvre in this respect. Its narrator Orual has attempted to come to terms with her sister Psyche's love for the god (Cupid) and her (Orual's) own destruction of their relationship, by writing her tale down. She dies before completing the scroll containing her final reconciliation to the existence of the god. In these final sentences, she writes that words are useless – although of course she is using words to make this very statement. The fact that her narrative breaks off as she dies and remains incomplete leaves the text hanging in between an affirmation and a rejection of language in an unresolved tension. A final note by her high priest concludes significantly with "we cannot read [the last words]."

> I ended my first book with the words No answer. I know now, Lord, why you utter no answer. You are yourself the answer. Before your face questions die away. What other answer would suffice? Only words, words; to be led out to battle against other words. Long did I hate you, long did I fear you. I might –
>
> (I, Arnom, priest of Aphrodite, saved this roll and put it in the temple. From the other markings after the word might, we think the Queen's head must have fallen forward on them as she died and we cannot read them. [...])
> (*TWHF* 319-320)

In this, Lewis's texts draw close to the positions we can find in Joyce's *Ulysses* and even *Finnegans Wake*, in which "realities and utopias are always textual" but also characterised by the awareness that "fictional universes are threatened by the unreliability of their material" (Emig, *Ulysses* 22).

> Does Joyce's text accept its status as a mere part of the universe of (here English) literature, or does it turn itself into an even larger structure that strives to dominate the forms and modes it employs? This is more than a question of style. It is a question of mastery and therefore related to the issues of power and authority [...]. (Emig, *Ulysses* 9)

These are questions that could be equally asked of Lewis's trilogy and *Chronicles*, and that will be addressed in the following section.

Language, Creation and Control

The language of myth is always linked to a claim to authority. This is never more so than with originary myths of creation, which explain how the world has come into being and thus why it is as it is. In fantasy, as we have seen, creation is inherently linked to language – it is words that bring fantastic worlds into being, both within the texts and in creating the texts themselves. In Lewis's space trilogy, we do not discover whether Old Solar is the language that actually created the universe when spoken by Maleldil, although it is the originary language originally given to all intelligent species by Maleldil and thus full of power. In *The Magician's Nephew* however we as readers experience the creation of Narnia. Transported through the Wood between the Worlds by their magic rings, Digory, Polly, Uncle Andrew, Jadis the Witch, the London Cabby and his horse find themselves in utter blackness which only starts to lift when a voice begins to sing. At first, "There were no words. There was scarcely even a tune" (*TMN* 114). As the new sun rises over Narnia, they see it is a lion – Aslan, of course – that is singing. Trees and bushes spring up, and in a scene obviously influenced by *Paradise Lost*, the earth begins to bubble and animals burst out of the ground.[34] Finally Aslan gathers a selection of the animals around himself and it is only then that instead of singing, he begins to speak:

> Then there came a swift flash like fire (but it burnt nobody) either from the sky or from the Lion itself, and every drop of blood tingled in the children's bodies, and the deepest, wildest voice they had ever heard was saying: "Narnia, Narnia, Narnia, awake. Love. Think. Speak. Be walking trees. Be talking beasts. Be divine waters." (*TMN* 133)

The trope of the world coming into being through song has a long history that is also connected to the idea of music as a reflector of the divine order (e.g. in the music of the spheres). It can also be found in Tolkien's *The Silmarillion* where the Music of the Ainur creates an abstract of the world that Ilúvatar gives actuality when he speaks "*Ëa!* Let these things be!" (21). Similarly, Aslan sings Narnia into existence, but significantly it is only his first words – and the Pentecostal "flash like fire" – that confer the gift of speech upon the chosen dumb beasts. Jadis may have had the power to destroy all life through her "Deplorable Word", but it is only Aslan who has the greater power to create life through his song and give it a voice through his word.

In this scenario, language is bestowed from above by a higher authority, and to possess language itself automatically gives authority. Thus the Talking Beasts are told: "The Dumb Beasts whom I have not chosen are yours also. Treat them gently and cherish them but do not go back to their ways lest you cease to be Talking Beasts" (*TMN* 135). A hierarchy is created, the beasts with language set

---

34 Cf. Milton, *Paradise Lost* Book VII, 449-474.

above those without. At the top of the hierarchy is Man; Aslan tells Frank the Cabby: "You shall rule and name all these creatures" (*TMN* 158). Like Adam, Frank is given the task of naming the beasts. It is this power of name-giving that sets him above the Talking Beasts as they are set above their dumb fellows. This relates to the idea, common in fantasy (and possessing magical and religious roots), that to know the true name of a thing is to possess power over it. This idea can also be found in the space romances: "This process of naming and knowing things in term of their names is central to the way in which Lewis treats language in his space novels" (Flieger, "The Sound of Silence" 43).[35] Similarly, in *That Hideous Strength* language is presented as a divine gift in the descent of Viritrilbia, when Ransom's followers suddenly find themselves

> talking loudly at once, each, not contentiously, but delightedly [...] plays upon words, certainly plays upon thoughts, paradoxes, fancies, anecdotes, theories laughingly advanced [...] such eloquence, such toppling structures of double meaning, such sky-rockets of metaphor and allusion. (*THS* 198-199)

This is comparable to the descent of the Holy Ghost upon the apostles at Pentecost, giving them the power to speak in tongues.

Thus we can see that the possession of language and power over it create a hierarchy and system of control within Lewis's novels. However, the question of control and authority is also one that conditions the structures of the texts themselves. We have already repeatedly seen that the sub-creator of a secondary world holds absolute power over that world: "What takes place and why is, necessarily, what he says it is" (Auden, "The Quest Hero" 50). To the extent that the fantastic secondary world attempts to incorporate the primary world, as Lewis's space romances and *Chronicles* do, it must also seek to extend the complete control of the sub-creator. This struggle for control is played out upon the level of language. Mythic language is one form of control, by which elements of the primary world such as literary texts can be used as alibis: the

---

[35] Name-giving is linked explicitly to fantastic creation in Michael Ende's classic *Die Unendliche Geschichte*; Bastian has to preserve Phantásien from ruin by giving its Childlike Empress a new name. This is explained in a song: "Die Adamssöhne, so nennt man mit Recht / die Bewohner des irdischen Ortes, / die Evastöchter, das Menschengeschlecht, / Blutsbrüder des wirklichen Wortes. / Sie haben seit Anbeginn / die Gabe Namen zu geben. / Sie brachten der Kindlichen Kaiserin / zu allen Zeiten das Leben." (Ende 109). Because humans (Ende uses Lewis's terms "Sons of Adam and Daughters of Eve") are "blood brothers of the True Word" they can give names ("From the beginning / they have had the gift of naming").

very fact that they appear seems to deny the authority of the secondary world, while actually the way they are incorporated subtly strengthens that authority. Also, the nature of fantastic language itself – the fact that it does make things new, that it creates things that do not actually exist, that its words are inherently lacking signs (signifiers without signifieds) – means that the sub-creator can wield absolute power of definition and control over meaning. Hunter comments on this in regard to Tolkien's *The Lord of the Rings*: "The potential critique of authority is undercut not only by the superficial glamouring references to kings and things, but also by the very structure of the language which defines its meaning, controls communications to its own ends and creates a totally self-enclosed world" (33). This can equally be applied to Lewis's *Chronicles* and the space trilogy.

With regard to this question of authority, it is also interesting to examine narratorial control. Lewis's *Chronicles* as children's stories appear relatively straightforward: they are told by a first-person narrator who occasionally intrudes into the tale to comment upon the action ("all the children thought – and I agree – that there's nothing to beat good freshwater fish" *LWW* 82) or to explain the unfamiliar happenings in terms readers will be able to relate to ("no dog, least of all a Talking Dog of Narnia, likes being called a 'Good Doggie, then'; any more than you would like being called 'My Little Man'" *TMN* 148). The narrator also appears to be omniscient in regard to Narnia; occasionally he (or she) appears to have derived this knowledge from what the characters of the novel have told him: "Lucy could only say, '[The song] would break your heart.' 'Why,' said I, 'was it so sad?' 'Sad!! No,' said Lucy" (*VDT* 251). Thus the voice of the narrator is friendly, creating identity between itself and its target audience, but through the omniscient stance it also carries authority; we are never led to question what it tells us.

The narratorial situation in the space trilogy is more complex. The first novel is told by a very unobtrusive first-person narrator, focusing upon Ransom. However, in the very final chapter this narrator suddenly pushes himself forward, stating: "At this point, if I were guided by purely literary considerations, my story would end, but it is time to remove the mask and to acquaint the reader with the real and practical purpose for which this book has been written" (*OSP* 177). He continues to tell of "Dr Ransom – and at this stage it will become obvious that this is not his real name", stating basically that the entire novel relates real happenings that are being told under cover of pseudonyms. The connection between the narrator (called "Lewis" by Ransom) and Ransom is an academic one: "I had corresponded with him on literary and philological subjects" (178). Lewis is clearly playing upon the fact that he himself is known as an academic and no attempt is made to disguise the actual author behind the novel by inventing a different identity for the narrator. Indeed, Lewis's identity appears to be exploited to give the entire narrative more credibility. Unsurprisingly, it is a question of language that brings "Lewis" and "Ransom" together: Lewis encounters the words *Oyarses* in the works of Bernardus Silvestris, and writes to Ransom asking whether he knows its meaning.

> The immediate result of this letter was an invitation to spend a weekend with Dr Ransom. He told me his whole story, and since then he and I have been almost continuously at work on the mystery. [...] It was Dr Ransom who first saw that our only chance was to publish in the form of fiction what would certainly not be listened to as fact. He even thought – greatly overrating my literary powers – that this might have the incidental advantage of reaching a wider public [...]. To my objection that if accepted as fiction, it would for that very reason be regarded as false, he replied that there would be indications enough in the narrative for the few reader – the very few – who *at present* were prepared to go into the matter. (*OSP* 178-180)

Thus *Out of the Silent Planet* establishes a strange mixture of fact and fiction; Lewis's own identity as an academic and writer is appropriated by the narrative. This could also be seen as a further control mechanism of the author: by including himself in his tale, he is giving it more authority.

This game is continued on into the second novel, which opens with Lewis travelling to meet Ransom at his home before Ransom sets off for Venus. However, when the narration turns to Ransom's adventures on Perelandra, Lewis's voice and direct commentary by the narrator gradually fade away. The entire frame is turned upon its head finally when Ransom is told by the Voice of Maleldil before his fight with the Un-man, "It is not for nothing that you are named Ransom" (*Perelandra* 134). Of course, we have been told in the first novel that the name "Ransom" is just a cover. But in the second book, the novel's entire theological symbolism and indeed the reason for Ransom's being chosen for the mission of saving Perelandra would collapse if his name were not his real one. Far from the name being discredited, we are actually given an etymology of "Ransom" to convince us of its reality:

> He had known for many years that his surname was derived not from *ransom* but from *Ranolf's son*. It would never have occurred to him thus to associate the two words. To connect the name Ransom with the act of ransoming would have been for him a mere pun. [...] he perceived that what was, to human philologists, a mere accidental resemblance of two sounds, was in truth no accident. [...] He had been forced out of the frame, caught up into the larger pattern. [...] Before his Mother had borne him, before his ancestors had been called Ransoms, before *ransom* had been the name for a payment that delivers, before the world was made, all these things had so stood together in eternity that the very significance of the pattern at this point lay in their coming together in just this fashion. [...] "My name also is Ransom," said the Voice. (*Perelandra* 135)

This of course throws the entire frame of the novel as well as the voice of "Lewis" into confusion – for if Ransom's name really *has* to be Ransom, then its entire disguise becomes pointless. Ultimately, the inner logic of Ransom's story proves stronger than the desire for the objectivity and heightened plausibility supposedly established through the frame. After this point in *Perelandra*, and on into in the third novel of the trilogy, "Lewis's" voice is silenced – the narration becomes entirely omniscient. Significantly, this occurs at the point where Ransom is "forced out of the frame", and this "forcing" occurs through language and the symbolism of names. At this point, it almost appears as if the narrator is acknowledging that he need not, after all, seek to control and "prove" the narrative through external devices: language itself possesses sufficient power to confer authority upon the story. The sham of the frame is dropped; the story itself becomes everything; the book is the world.

The symbolism of names is also of great importance in Joyce. For Stephen Dedalus, "his strange name seemed to him a prophecy" (*Portrait* 183); he is destined to be an artist by virtue of his name alone, which is that of the mythic "fabulous artificer" (183). As a boy, Stephen is repeatedly told "You have a queer name, Dedalus" (23); he becomes sensitive to the slightest hint of ridicule attached to it: "Was [the prefect] not listening to it the first time round or was it to make fun out of the name? The great men in the history had names like that and nobody made fun of them" (56-57). It is the singularity of his name that marks him out from his contemporaries and places him in the company (at least in his own mind) of the "great men". It is implied that this name also gives him his sensitivity to and power over words – a power shared to a certain extent by his father, whose stories actually open *Portrait* (we never see Stephen's mother, not a Dedalus from birth, telling him stories). It is the name of a creator – although it should not be forgotten that Daedalus's most important creation was actually the labyrinth containing the monstrous Minotaur.

However, names are not fixed. Stephen realises this early on when he muses that

> God was God's name just as his name was Stephen. Dieu was the French for God and that was God's name too; and when anyone prayed to God and said Dieu then God knew at once that it was a French person that was praying. But though there were different names for God in all the different languages still God remained always the same God and God's real name was God. (*Portrait* 13)

Stephen's own name undergoes several playful transformations in *Portrait* ("Bous Stephanoumenos! Bous Stephaneforos!" 182).[36] But it is in *Ulysses* and above all in the *Wake* that names change and shift. We have already seen that "Tristram" becomes also the (equally authentic) "Tristan" and (more absurd) "Treestone" – which incorporates completely different lexical meanings. The name is even transformed into an adjective (or possibly a participle) when HCE is described as "tristurned initials" (*FW* 100). Here "tristurned" carries the meanings of "tris" (*Lat.* thrice) and "turning" – the three letters of his name turned? Turned around three times? One letter at least is physically turned around twice in print (the E), and thus appears "tristurned" in three different positions. This use of the name Tristram to describe HCE is also a cloaked reference to his incestuous relationship with his daughter Issy (Iseult). But "Tristram" need not refer solely to the knight of Arthurian romance: "Or the birds start their treestirm shindy" (*FW* 621). Here the hero of Sterne's novel *Tristram Shandy*, in its own way as monumental and confusing a work as the *Wake*, also makes an appearance.

---

36 Incidentally, his Christian name "Stephen", that of the first martyr, means *sacrifice* and is thus not too distant from Lewis's *ransom*. God and his angels also have several different names in Lewis's trilogy, and Aslan also tells the children that in their world "I have another name. You must learn to know me by that name" (*VDT* 255).

The question of creation – particularly creation through language – is naturally a prominent one in *Finnegans Wake*, a novel obsessed with origins, beginnings and returns. ALP is repeatedly associated with the letters of the alphabet (her name starts with the first letter of the Roman alphabet, and is also close to the Greek *alpha* and the Hebrew *aleph*): "our turfbrown mummy is acoming, alpilla, beltilla, ciltilla, deltilla" (194). Thus she can be seen as "an originator of language" (Deane, "Introduction" xxxix), as it is from the alphabet that words are constructed. However, in the *Wake* – unlike Lewis's novels – there ultimately appears to be no true origin, as its cycle implies that any origin is in reality a return to a place or stage already known. Even ALP remembers someone (her mother? father? daughter? son?) "teaching me the perts of speech" (*FW* 620). If there is an origin, it is "The hundredlettered name again, last word of perfect language" (*FW* 424). But even that name appears in multiple variations throughout the *Wake*.

Literary creation and originality is thematised in the chapter of Shem the Penman, a character often associated with Joyce himself through name and profession ("Shem is as short for Shemus as Jem is joky for Jacob", *FW* 169: both Seamus and Jacob are different forms of the name James). Shem grows up, like Stephen Dedalus, already "playing with thistlewords" (*FW* 169), and his masterpiece is the "usylessly unreadable Blue Book of Eccles, *édition de ténèbres*" (*FW* 179). However, far from being an original genius, Shem is accused of being a plagiarist and forger: "Who can say how many pseudostylistic shamiana, how few or how many of the most venerated public impostures, how very many piously forged palimpsests slipped in the first place by this morbid process from his pelagiarist pen?" (*FW* 181-182). Shem's dwelling-place is the "Haunted Inkbottle" (*FW* 182), which would appear haunted by the fact that it can only repeat what has already been said, making a palimpsest of various layers of the past rather than something new.[37] But I remain skeptical about whether Shem is, as his brother Shaun the Post tries to convince his audience, truly a forger. If everything is merely a return to what has already been, truly original creation is impossible; what Shem, the "first till last alshemist" (*FW* 185), achieves however is to write "one continuous present tense integument

---

[37] In a way this can be seen as giving his texts validity and authority, placing them in a time-honoured tradition. We have seen how important the motif of the palimpsest is for David Jones.

slowly unfolded all marryvoising moodmoulded cyclewheeling history" (*FW* 185-186) – he writes the world. Thus he does in a way become the true creator. At the end of his chapter "He lifts the lifewand and the dumb speak" (*FW* 195): he possesses the power to give language, just like Aslan (his brother Shaun's "trifolium librotto, the authordux Book if Lief" (*FW* 425), by contrast is never actually "given to daylight" (*FW* 425)). Shem's power over language is portrayed as something magical as it is through a wand that he confers speech upon the speechless; his writing tool is a *"shillipen"* (*FW* 172), related to the Celtic wizard's *shillelagh* (magic rod or wand) – thus it is his pen that is his wand. Also he is linked to alchemy ("alshemist"), and his Blue Book of Eccles is an "édition de ténèbres", like a witch's Book of Shadows. Thus Shem's writing is a magical act, through which he creates the book of the world.[38]

The earlier *Portrait* gives a different picture of the origins of language, and how control is gradually assumed over language. As John Coyle (7) writes, "*A Portrait* begins with the frail babytalk of a character assailed by the language of others, and ends with the spectacle of his assumed mastery over language." Stephen begins appropriating the language of others very early – the song of the wild rose blossoms becomes his "*O, the green wothe botheth*" (*Portrait* 3). As yet however, his language makes no sense. During the course of the novel he is exposed to many different languages and influenced by them (particularly by the religious speech of the Jesuit brethren – it is not for nothing that the preacher's sermon forms the centrepiece of the novel), and towards its end he achieves enough linguistic autonomy to create his own verse. He also becomes aware of the power language has to mask and hide: in reply to his friend Davin's nationalist speeches he says: "I ask myself about you: *Is he as innocent as his speech?*" (*Portrait* 219). The conclusion of the novel sees the disappearance of any narrative mediation as Stephen's diary takes over the narration, giving us his words directly. This process of replacing the narrative voice is comparable to what Lewis does in his space trilogy: it shows us how (a certain kind of) language establishes its own logic and power.

---

[38] Although I have not the space to explore this further here, it is of course important that the material Shem writes on is "the only foolscap available, his own body" (*FW* 185). Cf. Maud Ellmann's "Disremembering Dedalus" for more on the importance of images of the body and its flows in connection with writing in the specific case of *Portrait*.

The question of narratorial control is a far more complicated one in Joyce than it is in Lewis.[39] Even in *Portrait*, it can be argued that "the whole idea of mastery of language has been turned inside-out by Joyce's exploitation of the narrative voice and perspective and of rhetorical effects" (Coyle 7). The shifting perspectives and styles of *Ulysses* undermine the notion of any single authoritative literary language. If the artist has, as Stephen theorises, become "invisible, refined out of existence, indifferent, paring his fingernails" (*Portrait* 233), this means refusing his readers the guidance of a narratorial voice, telling them which of the many voices to privilege and which are trustworthy. Nevertheless, the example of Shem the Penman from the *Wake* should make us wary of glibly announcing the death of the author and a free-for-all of voices and styles. The very way in which *Portrait*, *Ulysses* and the *Wake* call attention to their own status as literary works and their structural devices is a way in which the control of the author over his material is brought before our eyes: "I have discovered I can do anything with language I want" (cit. Ellmann, *James Joyce* 702). In fact, in *Finnegans Wake* Joyce's language pushes very close to the fantastic: in his strange neologisms that play on known words and their meanings but continually push beyond them, he is creating signifiers without a signified, just as fantastic language does. And thus he enters a realm which is, as we have seen, entirely dominated by the sub-creator: "Fantasy! Funtasy on fantasy, amnaes fintasies!" (*FW* 493).

Language and the Fall

In the Christian creation myth, the founding of the world and the creation of mankind is almost immediately followed by man's fall from grace. Adam's wife Eve is tempted by the serpent and disobeys the rule of God, eating an apple from the Tree of the Knowledge of Good and Evil. Adam follows suit, and consequently both are banished from Paradise and all their descendants are made subject to their first parents' Original Sin. The works of both Joyce and Lewis present accounts and retellings of the Fall. This section will examine how this is linked to language.

---

[39] This is not (or not simply) because Lewis was a less sophisticated writer than Joyce, and has much to do with the genre conventions both were writing within and against.

We have already seen that for many modernists, language was "held to be 'de-potentiated', 'de-substantiated', and hollowed-out'" (Sheppard 329), and artists began to doubt the very material they worked with. However, underlying their often desperate urge to create, the conviction can often be found that somewhere and somehow there must have been language equal to its task. This concept of an ideal primary language is not new – the Romantics also believed in an "*Ursprache*".[40] In modernism, this ideal language is usually linked to ancient cultures which have not yet declined like contemporary Western culture (this of course ties in with the picture of history as decline). In this case, its power can be retrieved by the rediscovery of these ancient cultures. It is this belief that fuels the "struggling pursuit of language culturally lost" (Sheppard 327) prominent in many modernist texts. The desire to recapture an authentic language related to either ancient history or the divine is also partly to be ascribed to the (male) modernists' desire for authority in their works. If their poetic or literary language can in some way reflect the authenticity of an ideal language, it must then automatically carry its own "paternal sanction" (Nicholls 167). This ideal language is also frequently linked to the supernatural or divine – often somewhat uneasily in an age which no longer could believe. Thus, in Hofmannsthal's Lord Chandos letter, Chandos states:

> die Sprache, in welcher nicht nur zu schreiben, sondern auch zu denken mir vielleicht gegeben wäre, [ist] weder die lateinische noch die englische noch die italienische und spanische [...], sondern eine Sprache, von deren Wörter mir auch nicht eines bekannt ist, eine Sprache, in welcher die stummen Dinge zu mir sprechen, und in welcher ich vielleicht einst im Grabe vor einem unbekannten Richter mich verantworten werde. (Hofmannsthal, "Ein Brief" 54)[41]

Chandos does not name God or any other divine power; instead he cites an "unknown judge" he will confront after death. His language is one "in which dumb things speak". This can be linked to the old idea that once mankind could commune with and understand all things. In traditional Western thought this time is set before the Fall, and it is Original Sin that takes away man's understanding of other creatures. The idea of a decline of language can thus be connected

---

40 Cf. for example August Wilhelm Schlegel, "Briefe über Poesie, Silbenmaß und Sprache" in *Kritische Schriften und Briefe*, volume I, ed. Edgar Lohner (Stuttgart: Kohlhammer, 1962) 141-180.
41 Translation: 'The language in which I could not only write, but also think, is not the Latin, nor the English, nor the Italian nor the Spanish, [...] but instead it is a language of which I know not a single word, a language in which the dumb things speak to me, and in which I will maybe have to justify myself in my grave, before a dumb judge.'

to a loss of immediate experience of the divine (in Barfield's terms, language becomes abstract rather than concrete). One modernist writer who thematises this is T.S. Eliot, for example in "Ash Wednesday" where he laments

> Where shall the word be found, where will the word
> Resound? Not here, there is not enough silence
> Not on the sea or on the islands, not
> On the mainland, in the desert or the rain land,
> For those who walk in darkness
> Both in the day time and in the night time
> The right time and the right place are not here
> No place of grace for those who avoid the face
> No time to rejoice for those who walk among noise and deny the voice
> (*Collected Poems* 102)

The Fall is brought up by Tolkien in connection with language in his theoretical essay "On Fairy-stories". He states that one of the central longings at the heart of fantastic sub-creation is

> the desire to converse with other living things. On this desire, as ancient as the Fall, is largely founded the talking of beasts and creatures in fairy-tales, and especially the magical understanding of their proper speech. This is the root, and not the "confusion" attributed to the minds of men in the unrecorded past, an alleged "absence of the sense of separation of ourselves from beasts". A vivid sense of that separation is very ancient; but also a sense that it was a severance: a strange fate and a guilt lies upon us. (152)

For Tolkien, fantasy becomes a way of recovering what the Fall has lost to man: the possibility of talking to animals, indeed the possibility of talking with all things (in his fiction, the Elves "wake up" the trees and teach them how to talk; cf. *LotR* 457). Lewis's fiction bears out this idea as well. In Malacandra, which is an unfallen world, Ransom thinks of the Hross as "an animal with everything an animal ought to have – glossy coat, liquid eye, sweet breath and whitest teeth – and added to all these, as though Paradise had never been lost and earliest dreams come true, the charm of speech and reason" (*OSP* 66). In Narnia the beasts are given speech by Aslan. But understanding is still not universal. Uncle Andrew, who has long practised evil magic and conducted animal experiments, is so blinded by his prejudice and fear that he refuses to believe Aslan and the animals can talk:

[...] when the sun rose and he saw that the singer was a lion ("*only* a lion", as he said to himself) he tried his hardest to make believe that it wasn't singing and never had been singing – only roaring as any lion might in a zoo in our own world. [...] The trouble about trying to make yourself stupider than you really are is that you very often succeed. Uncle Andrew did. He soon did hear nothing but roaring in Aslan's song. Soon he couldn't have heard anything else even if he had wanted to. (*TMN* 143-144)

Likewise, the Talking Beasts cannot understand him when he tries to say something to them – they only hear "a vague sizzling noise" (148). This leads to a hilarious discussion about whether he is really an animal or a tree, at the end of which he is planted in the ground and given a thorough watering. While this scene is comic, Lewis is making a serious point: Uncle Andrew, through an act of denial (by denying Aslan's song, he is denying his power), is cutting himself off from grace and thus from language and understanding. In effect, he is repeating the Fall and Adam and Eve's denial of God.

However, the Fall is not uniquely human in Lewis's world. When the animals are given speech, Aslan warns them: "Treat [the Dumb Beasts] gently and cherish them but do not go back to their ways lest you cease to be Talking Beasts. For out of them you were taken and into them you can return. Do not so" (*TMN* 135). This is an almost literal repetition of God's words to Adam after the Fall: "out of [the ground] wast thou taken; for dust thou art, and unto dust shalt thou return" (Genesis 3:19; AV). The fact Lewis takes this up again for his Talking Beasts seems to imply that for him, the Fall is something that is essentially tied to language rather than to humanity – and significantly that means that in Narnia, the Fall is not exclusively human. In *The Last Battle*, where Narnia comes to an end, one of the Talking Cats answers a challenge to look inside the stable in which "Tashlan" (a combination of the names Aslan and Tash, the god of the Calormenes) is dwelling. "Tashlan" is actually nothing but a donkey dressed up in a lion's skin, and the Cat should have nothing to fear; however, when he comes out of the stable something terrible has happened to him:

> "Now, Ginger," said the Captain. "Enough of that noise. Tell them what thou hast seen." "Aii – Aii – Aaow – Awah," screamed the Cat. "Art thou not called a *Talking* Beast?" said the Captain. "Then hold thy devilish noise and talk." What followed was rather horrible. Tirian felt quite certain (and so did the others) that the Cat was trying to say something: but nothing came out of its mouth except the ordinary, ugly cat-noises you might hear from any angry or frightened old Tom in a backyard in England. And the longer he caterwauled

> the less like a Talking Beast he looked. [...] "Look, look!" said the voice of the Boar. "It can't talk. It has forgotten how to talk! It has gone back to a dumb beast. Look at its face." Everyone saw that it was true. And then the greatest terror of all fell upon the Narnians. For every one of them had been taught – when it was only a chick or a puppy or a cub – how Aslan at the beginning of the world had turned the beasts of Narnia into Talking Beasts and warned them that if they weren't good they might one day be turned back again and be like the poor witless animals one meets in other countries. "And now it is coming upon us," they moaned. (*TLB* 110-113)

The Cat has been punished for his unbelief: speech is a gift that can be taken away again from the undeserving. Incidentally, the question of animal understanding is also raised in Joyce's *Ulysses*. Bloom thinks of the way Molly can understand animals: "songs without words. [...] Understand animals too that way. Solomon did. Gift of nature" (284). In regard to his cat, Bloom seems to think that it is humans who cannot understand animals rather than the other way around:

> – Milk for the pussens, he said.
> – Mrkgnao! The cat cried.
> They call them stupid. They understand what we say better than we understand them. She understands all she wants to. (*Ulysses* 57)

Bloom also, as Chandos hopes to, hears the "dumb things" speak to him:

> Sllt. The nethermost deck of the first machine jogged forwards its flyboard with sllt the first batch of quirefolded papers. Sllt. Almost human the way it sllt to call attention. Doing its level best to speak. That door to sllt creaking, asking to be shut. Everything speaks in its own way. Sllt. (*Ulysses* 123)

In *That Hideous Strength*, we also see speech is taken away as a punishment for sins. Shortly after Mercury has descended upon Ransom's company, giving them the gift of speaking in tongues, the wicked scientists of Belbury come together. Hidden in their midst however is the enchanter Merlin, significantly masquerading as an interpreter. Inspired by Mercury, he magically confuses the scientists' speech:

> The Deputy Director could not understand this, for to him his own voice seemed to be uttering the speech he had resolved to make. But the audience heard him saying, "Tidies and fulgemen – I sheel foor that we all – er – most steeply rebut the defensible, though, I trust, lavatory, aspasia which gleams to have selected our redeemed inspector this deceiving. It would – ah – be shark, very shark, from anyone's debenture [...]" (*THS* 220)

These passages turn positively Wakean in their confusion. Merlin looses "the curse of Babel" upon the scientists, crying out "*Qui Verbum Dei contempserunt, eis auferetur etiam verbum hominis*" (*THS* 224).[42] Here another biblical story about language is brought in: that of the Tower of Babel, where man attempts to reach the heavens through building a high tower (Genesis 11); God's way of foiling this and punishing the builders for their overambition is to confound their language, so they can no longer communicate. Here speech is confused as a punishment for sin, and can be seen as a consequence of the first Fall.[43] The parallel to Lewis's wicked scientists is self-evident, and they meet their end being devoured by the wild animals they had kept for purposes of vivisection – a less forgiving version of Uncle Andrew's fate.

Generally, the Christian Lewis seems to perceive the crisis of language as something linked to sin. In one of his poems, he writes that crisis has come about because "devils are unmaking language" ("Re-adjustment" *Poems* 102). In his adoption of Barfield's theory of a prelapsarian mythic language, he sees the loss of concrete meaning as an indication of a loss of spirituality; it is only God who can restore that directness of language: "Take not, oh Lord, our literal sense. Lord, in Thy great, / Unbroken speech our limping metaphor translate" ("Footnote to all Prayers" *Poems* 129). This division of concrete and abstract meaning can also be detected in Charles Williams's *Taliessin* poems:

> [...] his heart
> Beat lest dread or desolation wrecked his mind
> So that he fell from his kind, and the grand art failed –
> Control lost and all sense crossed;
> Or else he quit no more for a thrilling rhyme,
> Fulfilling a time of attention, but O pledged
> Beyond himself to an edged anguish dividing
> Word from thing and uniting thing to word –
> Each guiding and fighting the other.
> ("The Calling of Taliessin" *RSS* 9-10)

---

42 Translation: 'They that have despised the Word of God, from them shall the word of man also be taken away.'
43 The destruction of Babel can also be seen as jealousy on the part of God, who wishes to stop man from reaching his own celestial heights. It is also significant that one of the motivations of men to build the tower is to thus give themselves a name, and this is also something God prevents. Jacques Derrida discusses that "Babel" actually means "father-God", and that in destroying it, God is actually deconstructing himself. He also links this to a quote from *Finnegans Wake*, "and he war" (Derrida 244-253).

Taliessin is afraid of a "fall from kind" that will rob him of his poetic power; this power, for the time being, can overcome the division of word from thing and thing from word the Fall has brought about. Here, the Fall is not just given as the reason behind the failure of language; it also causes the loss of poetic control over language.

In James Joyce's *Finnegans Wake*, the Fall is presented in a different way, but here, too, it is connected to language. The Fall is the central narrative of the novel, just as it is that of Lewis's *Perelandra*: "The fall (bababadalgharaght-akamminarronnkonnbronntonnerronn-tuonnthunntrovarrhounawnskawn-toohoohoordenenthurnuk!) of a once wallstrait oldparr is retaled early in bed and later on life down through all christian minstrelsy" (*FW* 3). It is referred to again and again, and all the novel's action consists of various versions of the Fall – such as HCE's desire for his own daughter ("he who will be ultimendly respunchable for the hubbub caused in Edenborough" *FW* 29) and Shem's (self-chosen) exile from Ireland ("your birth-wrong was, to fall in with Plan" *FW* 190). As ALP concludes in her monologue: "It's something fails us. First we feel. Then we fall" (*FW* 627). The consequence is the Babel/Babble that the *Wake* plays on continuously:

> The babbelers with their thangas vain have been (confusium hold them!) they were and went; thigging thugs were and houhnhymn songtoms were and comely norgels were and pollyfool fiansees. [...] Who ails tongue coddeau, aspace of dumbillsilly? And they fell upong one another: and themselves have fallen. (*FW* 15)

The pun on Swift's houyhnhms, the wise and talking horses, brings in the question raised by Lewis of the speech of animals and its relation to the Fall. Another comic connection between the Fall and language is engineered through the nursery rhyme character Humpty Dumpty; in the *Wake*, the Fall is also taken to include the latter's fall off the wall: "The great fall of the offwall entailed at such short notice the pftjschute of Finnegan, erse solis man, that the humptyhillhead of humself prumptly sends an unquiring one well to the west in quest of his tumptytumtoes" (*FW* 3). In Lewis Carroll's *Through the Looking-glass*, Humpty Dumpty is associated with words as he explains the (apparently meaningless) song "Jabberwocky", and further proclaims: "When I use a word [...] it means just what I choose it to mean – neither more nor less"

(Carroll 193). When Alice ventures to doubt this, he replies: "The question is [...] which is to be master – that's all" (Carroll 193). In this way, Humpty Dumpty can also be connected to the issue of authority and language discussed in the previous section.

Shem makes the Fall the theme of his song. The song contains lines such as: "*By Nowwhere have Poorparents been sentenced to Worms, Blood and Thunder for Life / [...] Blamefool Gardener's bound to fall*" which tells of mankind's doom of death, and also seems to raise the theological debate of whether the Fall was inevitable: supposedly Man had free will and a choice whether to take the apple or not; but if God is all-knowing, then he knew man would fall, so why tempt him in the first place? Is Man thus really to blame for the Fall (a "blamefool Gardener")? "*Not yet have the Sachsen and Judder on the Mound of a Word made Warre*" brings in the issue of language, which in its fallen divided state causes strife. Humpty Dumpty and his wall make an appearance again with "*Broken Eggs will poursuive bitten Apples for where theirs is Will there's his Wall*" – "theirs is Will" referring again to the issue of free will. The song concludes "*Hirp! Hirp! For their missed Understandings! Chirps the Ballat of Perce-Oreille*" (*FW* 175). The "missed Understandings" are the consequence of the Fall; communication is lost. The "Ballat of Perce-Oreille" reminds me of Shakespeare's *Othello* (whose handkerchief and "greeneyed monster" are often referred to in the *Wake*) and Brabantio's claim that "words are words: I never yet did hear / That the bruised heart was pierced through the ear" (Act I, Scene 3, 219-220). Thus "Perce-Oreille" could be yet another reference to communication, the power of words to influence and to deceive. We can see just how intimately the Fall is connected to language in the *Wake*.

Shem's ballad also plays upon the idea of circularity that is so central to *Finnegans Wake* as a whole. "Not yet have…" implies that it is already certain this will, at a certain point, come to pass – or better, have come to pass. This happens over and over again, the same way as "Sir Tristram [...] has passencore rearrived from North Armorica" (*FW* 3). This means that the Fall is not something that happened at one specific point in time. It is something that is repeated over and over again, a "problem passion play of the millentury, running strong since creation" (*FW* 32). The consequences it has for language are also repeated over and over and endlessly varied. This is one reason why the hundred-letter word appears in different permutations throughout the novel – linked to the Fall, it will be rehearsed again in different versions of the same (linguistic) history. In his notes on *Work in Progress*, what was later to become the *Wake*, Joyce wrote of "Language destroyed every night & built up next day" (Joyce, *James Joyce Archive* Vol. 34, 140). Language is cyclically destroyed and rebuilt. The idea that the Fall did not only happen once is something we can find in Lewis's novels too; while he does not claim that it happened more than once in our own world (that would be blasphemy and render the coming of Christ useless), he repeats it in other worlds. Lewis also manages to envisage unfallen worlds: in some no temptation occurred (like Malacandra), and in some the Fall can be avoided and the course of history changed; thus on Perelandra Ransom manages to avert the Fall of that planet's Adam and Eve.

It has been claimed that "it is one of the [*Wake's*] implications that the myth of the Fall can be understood as a fall into language" (Deane, "Introduction" ix). In this case, language would be postlapsarian by nature – in contrast to Lewis and Barfield's theories that a perfect language did exist before the Fall, while postlapsarian language has "fallen" with humankind into crisis. The fact that the hundred-letter word of thunder appears for the first time after the first mention of the Fall confirms the link between the Fall and language, and thus the Fall possibly can be seen as the origin of language, with the hundred-letter word as its starting-point – an eruption of language, a linguistic Big Bang.[44] Thus one way of reading the nighttalk of the *Wake* is that "the secondary, postlapsarian nature of language might be the very thing the *Wake* seeks to overcome by replacing it with that putative directness of communication that preceded the Fall" (Deane, "Introduction" ix). The *Wake* is trying to render language unnecessary – but paradoxically *through* language. However, the word of thunder is also called "last word of perfect language" (*FW* 424). This could be taken to imply a view more like Lewis's, that there once was a perfect language that the Fall has confounded.

---

[44] In the work of Giambattista Vico, one of Joyce's major sources for the *Wake*, the Fall and language are connected through thunder: "primitive man, surprised in the sexual act by a clap of thunder, is stricken with fear and guilt at what he imagines is the angered voice of God. [...] Language arises when man attempts to reproduce the sound of thunder with his own vocal organs" (MacCabe, "Introduction" 34).

The ultimate conclusion drawn by this pessimistic view of language must be that it will fail altogether. This is what we find in Tolkien's works, that lament the inevitable "loss and [...] silence" (*LotR* 1037), and the poems of Eliot that invoke the "Lady of silences" and mourn "the word unheard, unspoken" ("Ash Wednesday" *Collected Poems* 97, 101). A similar interpretation could be given to the end of Lewis's *Till We Have Faces*, where the narrative breaks off and the last fact we are told is that Orual's words are so smudged we cannot read them. There appears to be no way out of the decline of language – unless, like Frodo (and Ransom), we travel beyond the world. In the conclusion to the space trilogy, there appears to be hope that Earth's status as the "Silent Planet", cut off from communication with the other worlds, might be changed by the fact that the gods descend upon it: "Perelandra is all about us, and Man is no longer isolated" (*THS* 248). However, Gregory Wolfe points out the ambiguity of this episode when he notes that "When the gods descend on St. Anne's, grace does not perfect or complete nature, but dominates and supplants it" (Wolfe 75). What will happen when they leave – taking Ransom with them? And would Ransom have to leave if the world were really set to rights?[45] Merlin and Mercury destroy the scientists' language, but no new tongue is given to those that speak a language that still remains cut off from Old Solar (for despite the descent of the gods, it is still the case that "no human language now known in the world is descended from [Old Solar]" *Perelandra* 20). Thus the conclusion of *That Hideous Strength* remains slightly unsatisfactory, as it employs a *deus ex machina* solution to the central conflict without truly following through the resolutions to their ultimate conclusion, which would have to be apocalyptic in form, "a new heaven and a new earth" (Revelations 21:1; AV). In Narnia, Lewis is more consequential in destroying Narnia completely to replace it with Aslan's country (the Great Story).[46]

---

45 This is exactly the same question that rises at the end of Tolkien's *The Lord of the Rings*, and that Tolkien's epic is more honest answering: there is no truly happy ending after conflicts of such magnitude, no reprieve from a history of terror within the circles of the world. It is of note that Frodo's journey to Valinor also represents a journey to the source of language, where Quenya is spoken in its uncorrupted form.

46 Another instance in Lewis's writing where the appearance of the divine among humans causes surprisingly ambiguous emotions is the long Arthurian poem "Launcelot", where the women of Camelot speak of the division the vision of the Holy Grail has brought to Arthur's court – a division again expressed through language: "What have they [the questing knights] eaten, or in what forgetful land / Were their adventures? Now they do not understand / Our speech. They talk to one another in a tongue / We do not know. [...] The Sangrail has betrayed us all" (Lewis, *Narrative Poems* 96).

Joyce's *Wake* solves the problem in a different way. The novel acknowledges the fall of language – it is something it can see no way past, as the world is a "static babel" (*FW* 499). While there are temporary silences in the *Wake* ("-Tit! What is the ti...? SILENCE." *FW* 501), the novel does not end in silence like Lewis's *Till We Have Faces*, or emphasise loss and silence like Tolkien's *The Lord of the Rings*. Instead, it emphasises the endless flux of language, a change that could be seen as a decline but that is not necessarily such. And if its last sentence is broken off, it is only to return to the beginning of the text. Thus *Finnegans Wake* embraces the fall of language.

Language, Identity and Exile

The previous chapter on history has already touched upon questions of nationalism, and we have seen just how problematic the concept of nationhood and nationalism was (and still is) for writers like Yeats and Tolkien, both writing at times of great change in their respective countries. Any evaluation of nationalism in modern(ist) literature will be difficult as modernism is frequently seen as a predominantly cosmopolitan, rather than national or local, movement. Many of its main figureheads have roots in different cultures and lived in different countries, making them difficult to categorise; writers such as the American expatriots Henry James, T.S. Eliot and Ezra Pound have been claimed equally by English and American literature, but they also lived in France and Italy besides England; Gertrude Stein lived most of her life in Paris; still others, such as Joseph Conrad and Vladimir Nabokov, became successful and highly regarded authors in English, a language not originally their own. As Peter Nicholls (166) points out, "None of the so-called 'Men of 1914' [...] was born in England, and their various contributions to a common modernism were thus highly sensitive to questions of exile and cultural displacement." Studies of James Joyce in particular cannot avoid the importance of his self-imposed exile for his writing, and it raises questions about how to interpret his work. Are we to see him as a cosmopolitan genius freeing himself from the shackles of provincial Dublin, or does the fact that he persists in writing about his city over thirty years after he left it signify that he is, after all, to be seen as a predominantly Irish and local writer? In more recent years, especially with the growth of Irish studies, much scholarship has been eager to reclaim Joyce as essentially Irish;[47] indeed, the "problems of isolation and marginalization, the same sense of being both inside and outside culture" (Castle 9) can be seen as typical of the Irish (colonial) situation.

This has been far less the case with C.S. Lewis, and it is for this reason that in this last section slightly more space will be devoted to Lewis, rather than repeating ideas and statements about Joyce's relationship to Ireland that have already been explored at length in the studies cited in the previous footnote. Several factors contribute to this neglect of Lewis. One of the most obvious is that he, unlike Joyce, scarcely thematised Ireland in his works (the unpublished "Belfast novel" is an exception), while England appears in many of them – not least in its mythologised form as "Logres" in *That Hideous Strength*. He references the English/British myth of Arthur in his works alongside classical mythology, but unlike Yeats whom he admired did not make use of Irish myth. Lewis also became famous as a scholar of English Literature at Oxford University (later a Professor of English at Cambridge), and thus a representative of English cultural traditions. Another obvious reason would seem to be that he did not actually live in Ireland after he left for university, and even before that had been schooled in England. However, it will be remarked that for writers like Joyce and Beckett non-residence in Ireland does not seem to have formed a problem for their being perceived as Irish. More crucial to this issue would appear to be the fact that Lewis was an Ulster Protestant, and the Irish nationalist movement, as we have already seen, sought to create a monolithic Irish identity that was "Celtic, Gaelic and Catholic" (O'Brien 29), excluding Protestants and those supposedly non-Celtic such as Lewis.[48] David Bleakley

---

47 Seamus Deane's "Joyce and Nationalism" (*New Perspectives*, 168-183) marked the beginning of this trend. More recent publications on Joyce and Ireland, which also draw heavily on postcolonial theory, are for example Emer Nolan's *James Joyce and Nationalism* (London: Routledge, 1995), G.J. Watson's *Irish Identity and the Literary Revival: Synge, Yeats, Joyce and O'Casey* (Washington, D.C.: Catholic University of America Press, 1994) and Derek Attridge and Marjorie Howes's *Semicolonial Joyce* (Cambridge: Cambridge University Press, 2000). None of these works deny the problems of "Irishing" a man who explicitly repudiated his home country in his works.

48 Lewis's family was actually originally from Wales (as his name reveals), and in later years Lewis was to state: "I'm more Welsh than anything" (cit. Sayer 21). Theoretically, he should thus be just as Celtic as the Catholic Irish. For a further discussion of the problematics inherent in calling Protestant Irish "Anglo-Irish", rather than Scots-Irish or Welsh-Irish (as their roots are just as likely to be), cf. Willy Maley's "Lost in the Hyphen of History: The Limits of Anglo-Irishness". This is related to the already

(19) suspects that "there were those in literary circles who sought to serve an exclusion order on a fellow countryman who did not conform to their all-too-narrow definition of Irishness." Hence the state that Seamus Heaney writes of in Lewis's centenary year 1998:

> As an undergraduate at Queen's University in the 1950s, I read C.S. Lewis's epoch making work, *The Allegory of Love*, and his volume in the *Cambridge History of English Literature* dealing with the prose and poetry of the sixteenth century. By then his name was enshrined, his voice authoritative, scholarly, unlocalized. It never occurred to us that he might have a biography, never mind one from Belfast. (cit. Bleakley 22)

Happily, narrow definitions of Irishness are being increasingly challenged today, and recent studies have pointed out the heterogeneous and hybrid nature of the Irish nation.[49] There should be room for C.S. Lewis in the Irish as well as the English canon.

It is not easy to come to fixed conclusions upon how Lewis himself felt about his nationality. He appears to have consistently regarded himself as Irish. We know that although he and his brother were sent to school in England in good colonial tradition, they experienced harsh bullying because of their Irishness (cf. W. Lewis, *The Lewis Papers* Vol. 3, 97, 146), and Lewis himself describes his first reaction to England in terms of horror: "The flats of Lancashire [...] were like the banks of the Styx. The strange English accents with which I was surrounded seemed like the voices of demons. [...] at that moment I conceived a hatred for England which took many years to heal" (*Surprised by Joy* 25-26). It is of note that it is not just the landscape, but the *speech* of the English that causes Lewis's feelings of strangeness. And later, when he was already at Oxford, he wrote to his friend Arthur Greeves: "I have no patriotic feeling for anything in England, [and] I begin to have a very warm feeling for Ireland in general. I mean the real Ireland of Patsy Macan [sic][50] etc, not so much our protestant north. Indeed, if I ever get interested in politics, I shall probably be a nationalist" (*They Stand Together* 195-196). When he first started to write seriously, he played with the idea of aligning himself with the Celtic Twilight

---

familiar Celtic / Saxon dialectic used to describe the Irish colonial situation – which is very similar to what we have already encountered in regard to Arthurian literature.
49 I particularly like Elizabeth Cullingford's *Ireland's Others: Gender and Ethnicity in Irish Popular Culture and Literature* (Cork: Cork University Press, 2001).
50 Lewis is referring to the hero Patsy MacCann of the Fenian James Stephens's novel *The Demi-Gods*.

School ("I think I shall try [the publisher] Maunsel, those Dublin people, and so tack myself definitely onto the Irish school" *They Stand Together* 195) but in the end rejected the idea; as he wrote to Greeves, in "the Irish school you might get into a sort of little by-way of the intellectual world, off the main track and lose yourself there" (*They Stand Together* 229). Lewis was obviously concerned about sacrificing universal appeal for local and limited success, and this according to Bresland (60) is "at the heart of why Lewis has been considered an English, rather than an Irish, writer."[51] However, later still, Lewis was to rail bitterly about "the Parisian riff-raff of denationalised Irishmen and Americans who have perhaps given Western Europe her death-wound" (cit. Ricks 198). Although his main focus of attack is T.S. Eliot, the phrase "Parisian denationalised Irishmen" without a doubt refers to Joyce. Here the "nationalist" Lewis openly condemns giving up one's nationality and living in exile. The problem of course is that this is in effect exactly what he himself has done: "For what was Lewis but that doubly denationalized Irishman, the Ulsterman who lives in England?" (Ricks 198). Lewis would have been aware that under Irish nationalist terms he himself, as an Protestant Ulsterman, would already be regarded as a kind of (unwanted) exile in the place of his birth – he suffers from already being born an exile. Lewis's contradictory and in part hateful comments show just how fraught the question of Irishness and national identity was for him. As Ricks (198) notes, "Lewis's rhetoric is madly unmisgiving, whereas Eliot's art is lucidly fraught, yet both begin in pain at foreignness and at denationized disintegration."

It is thus not surprising that the theme of exile and desire to belong should figure prominently in Lewis's work. From Ransom, who sighs: "I'd give anything I possess [...] just to look down one of those gorges again and see the blue, blue water winding in and out of the woods. Or to be up on top – to see a Sorn go gliding along the slopes. [...] It is hardly ever out of my mind" (*Perelandra* 17), to the Pevensie children who beg Aslan not to send them back to their own world (cf. *VDT* 255, *TLB* 221), to the Fox (a slave in exile) and Psyche (who

---

51 This stands in contrast to the idea put forward by Eliot, that writers like Yeats "in becoming more Irish [...] became more universal" (Eliot, "Yeats" *Selected Prose* 252). But of course Yeats's art could not be contained by the Irish school; this is probably the reason why Lewis continued to admire him after he had lost interest in the Celtic twilight. Lewis also wrote of the Irish school as a "cult" (*They Stand Together* 229) – a view apparently shared by Joyce, who in the *Wake* refers to the school as the "cultic twalette" (*FW* 344).

is sacrificed by her family to the god, cast out of his palace for unbelief, and "wanders over the earth, weeping, weeping, always weeping" *TWHF* 154), his characters are driven by a longing for a place they cannot stay or belong to, or have never even known. However, many of Lewis's works are also filled with an almost obsessive Englishness, from the micro-level of the "pint of bitter" that Ransom orders as his first act on returning from Malacandra (*OSP* 177) to the grand idea of a mythic Logres with Ransom as the re-incarnated Pendragon as its head.[52] This is one instance of how England or the cultural idea of England can also become an object of desire to the Irish writer, whose work "reveal[s] a cultural desire for Englishness, [...] a self-dividing doubleness that is at the very heart of an Irish culture long dominated by the hegemony of English discourse and desire" (Cheng 258). This has also been noted in Joyce's *Ulysses*, particularly in the Circe episode (cf. Gibson).[53] Interestingly this is also one of the episodes in *Ulysses* that moves closest to the fantastic, culminating in Bloom's vision of his dead son Rudy as "*a fairy boy of eleven, a changeling, kidnapped, dressed in an Eton suit with glass shoes and a little bronze helmet*" (*Ulysses* 532).

For all of the Inklings, exile and foreignness play a dominant role. Tolkien's Smith is told in Faëry, "You do not belong here. Go away and never return!" (*Smith of Wootton Major* 21). In his *The Silmarillion*, the Noldor elves leave Valinor and go into exile in Middle-earth after Fëanor's oath to regain the Silmarils. They live there over a thousand years but never forget the Undying Lands: "We still remember, we who dwell / In this far land beneath the trees / Thy starlight on the Western Seas" (*LotR* 78). Even the elves born in Middle-earth are in a sense already born as exiles, and in the end long to return to their long home in Valinor. Some – like Arwen – give up the chance of taking the ship to Valinor for love of mortals and the mortal world. Yet Arwen's fate, in the end, is all the more bitter: she cannot go to Valinor after Aragorn's death, but she can also no longer stay among mortals. The fact that she chooses to live out the rest of her days in deserted Lórien shows that she has actually become

---

52 Interestingly, Lewis identifies "Logres" with England rather than Britain, in marked contrast to David Jones for example. Britain appears to take on connotations of evil: "But in every age [the Pendragons] and the little Logres which gathered round them have been the fingers which gave the tiny shove or the almost imperceptible pull, to prod England out of the drunken sleep or to draw her back from the final outrage into which Britain tempted her" (*THS* 241).
53 Elizabeth Cullingford explores Irish desire for Englishness more thoroughly in *Ireland's Others*, particularly Part One, "Acting the Englishman" (13-95).

doubly an exile from both kindreds. The line of Númenorean Kings is also a line of exiles, refugees from the isle of Númenor destroyed through the folly of its rulers (in the Appendices to *The Lord of the Rings* their kingdoms are actually called "The Realms in Exile", cf. *LotR* 1014). Frodo too of course becomes an exile in his home of the Shire, which he leaves for Valinor (with Arwen's token that he may travel there in her stead). Interestingly, in the Appendices we discover that actually *none* of the hobbits of the Fellowship find their long home in the Shire: Merry and Pippin in their last years travel to Gondor "and passed what short years were left to them in that realm, until they died and were laid in Rath Dínen among the great of Gondor" (*LotR* 1072), and Sam ultimately follows Frodo over the sea (cf. *LotR* 1072). We can thus conclude that it is not just Frodo, but also the other three hobbits of the Fellowship that have, through their quest, become exiles in their own home. Taliessin, the protagonist of Williams's cycles, by virtue of his strange birth and his calling as a poet, is neither "flesh nor fish" whose "true region is the summer stars" ("The Calling of Taliessin" *RSS* 7). It is repeatedly emphasised that Taliessin is not truly of this world, and after the disaster of Camlaan he appears to lose what mortal cloak he had and returns to his origins: "that which was once Taliessin rides to the barrows of Wales / up the vales of the Wye" ("Taliessin at Lancelot's Mass" *TTL* 91). This foreignness and sense of not belonging is a central feature of modern fantasy. Lucie Armitt writes in her study *Theorising the Fantastic*: "If fantasy is about being absent from home [...], then the inhabitant of the fantastic is always the stranger" (8). Or, as Ursula Le Guin puts it: "the point of Elfland is that you are not at home there. It's not Poughkeepsie. It's different" ("From Elfland to Poughkeepsie" *The Language of the Night* 71).

One reason that exile features so prominently in the works of these writers, and in the works of Lewis also, is their Christianity. According to the Christian worldview, all humanity is exiled from Paradise on account of the Fall. Earth is not our true home – heaven is. Thus a fundamental longing for an unknown home and a sense of foreignness must be essential to human existence, as is written in Psalm 39 (which also is used for the burial services): "Hear my prayer, O Lord [...] For I am a stranger with thee: and a sojourner, as all my fathers were." This is the reason why the characters in Lewis's novels feel they have come home when they enter unfallen Malacandra or Perelandra, or Aslan's country (which represents, of course, heaven). A sense of recognition overcomes all who pass through the stable door: "It reminds me of somewhere but I can't give it a name. Could it be somewhere we once stayed for a holiday when we were very, very small?" says Peter (*TLB* 203); Jewel the Unicorn shortly after realises "I have come home at last! This is my real country! I belong here. This is the land I have been looking for all my life, though I never knew it till now. The reason we loved the old Narnia is that it sometimes looked a little like this" (*TLB* 207).

Ransom, after his journeys to Malacandra and Perelandra, can also no longer feel at home on earth: "I am homesick for my old Malacandrian valley when I think of [the Hrossa's songs]", he writes to Lewis, but immediately conceding "yet God knows when I heard it there I was homesick enough for the Earth" (*OSP* 181). Ransom is in the position that he is foreign in the strange worlds he travels to, but that through the experiences he has there he becomes even more of a stranger in his own world; this is expressed symbolically by the fact that he becomes very ill after being wounded by the Un-man on Perelandra and cannot be cured on Earth, and in the end must be taken back to Perelandra to become whole. Like Arwen, he has become a double exile.

So what does this sense of exile, "this desire for our own far-off country" as Lewis puts it (*Weight of Glory* 4), have to do with the issue of language? Obviously exile accounts for changes in language – it is responsible for the sundering of the elven tongues in Middle-earth, and for the falling-off from *Hressa-Hlab* in Thulcandra. But exile and the desire for an (unknown) home also complement, on a thematic level, the pattern of lack and desire that is crucial to fantastic language. Rosemary Jackson (3) writes that fantasy is essentially "a literature of desire, which seeks that which is experienced as absence and loss." This absence and loss manifests itself on a thematic level as the absence and loss of a home and a mother tongue. But fantastic language is, as we have seen, characterised by a push "towards an area of non-signification" (Jackson 41), and in this way it is constantly pushing towards an absence, towards the non-signified. Thus the loss and desire connected with the topic of exile are already inherent in the structure of fantastic language itself.

It is difficult to draw fixed conclusions upon how much C.S. Lewis's Irish legacy influences the topics of exile we find in his work, simply because of the fact that their real-world starting-point is (with the exception of *Till We Have Faces*) always England. Critics have – not surprisingly, given the desire for England that manifests itself in his works – tended to read Narnia as an idealised England,[54] but in fact an equally good case could be made for it being an idealised Ireland. Lewis talks of the view he enjoyed from his boyhood home:

> From our front door we looked down over wide fields to Belfast Lough and across it to the long mountain line of the Antrim shore [...] Behind the house, greener, lower, and nearer than the Antrim mountains, were the Holywood Hills, but [...] The north-western prospect was what mattered at first; the interminable summer sunsets behind the blue ridges, and the rooks flying home. (*Surprised by Joy* 15)

It is hard not to interpret the descriptions of Narnia – "those hills [...] the nice woody ones and the blue ones behind" (*TLB* 204) – as versions of the landscapes Lewis loved as a child and still held dearer than any others in his adult years, when he wrote "none loves the hills of Down (or Donegal) better than I" (to Arthur Greeves; *They Stand Together* 196).[55] Lewis also specifically attributed the Mourne mountains with awakening "strange longing, that discontent" – the desire that characterises fantasy – and calls them "source of my dreams perhaps even to this day" (W. Lewis, *The Lewis Papers* Vol. 11, 253). Yet Bresland (59) is correct when he points out that "the warm feelings Jack had for Ireland are for an Ireland of the imagination and not one that reflects the realities of the violent events that led to the formation of the Irish Free State."[56] He also notes, significantly, that it was actually exile from Ireland that brought on these feelings: "The repressive reality of being an Irishman at home in Belfast compared

---

54 Cf. Roger Sale, "England's Parnassus: C.S. Lewis, Charles Williams and J.R.R. Tolkien" *Hudson Review* 17 (Summer 1964). 203-225.
55 David Bleakley, a Northern Irish student of Lewis's at Oxford, tells the following anecdote. Lewis demanded that Bleakley define heaven for him. Bleakley (53) writes: "I tried – he soon interrupted my theological meanderings. 'My friend, you're far too complicated; an honest Ulsterman should know better. Heaven is Oxford lifted and placed in the middle of the County Down."
56 This does not mean Lewis was unaware or dismissive of the conflict. He particularly loathed those he called "the offenders on our own side": the Orangemen and the Black and Tans, whom he compared to "Hiroshima...the Gestapo...Russian slave camps" (Lewis, *Compelling Reason* 177). This is all the more striking (or perhaps not, given Lewis's difficult relationship with his father) as his father was a loyal member of the Belfast Orange Lodge, VII (cf. Bresland 59). For example, he wrote to his friend, the Catholic priest Don Giovanni Calabria: "I am crossing over to Ireland: my birthplace and dearest refuge so far as charm of landscape goes, and temperate climate, although most dreadful because of the strife, hatred and often civil war between dissenting faiths" (*A Study in Friendship* 83).

to being the romantic Irishman in exile in Oxford, produced a highly coloured sense of Irishness" (Bresland 58). Exile from home becomes the prerequisite for artistic imagination and creation. And perhaps it is the very reticence with which Lewis addresses Ireland in his fiction, preferring to displace it into a fantastic secondary world, that can be read alongside his often contradictory statements on the Irish situation as "testify[ing] to the uncertain, divided consciousness of the colonial subject" (Attridge and Howes, "Introduction" 2).

An imagined Ireland is also the key to Joyce's self-chosen exile. It was only when he was not surrounded by Ireland's repressive realities that he felt free to imagine it in his writings; thus his exile became his inspiration. Like Lewis, in an undergraduate essay he rejected the Celtic twilight for "its isolation from (the more exciting) European traditions and (prophetically) for its subservience to nationalism" (Wales 27),[57] although unlike Lewis he did not espouse a romantic view of the country he left. Stephen Dedalus's Luciferian "I will not serve" (*Portrait* 260) repeats Joyce's own refusal to be appropriated by the Irish nationalist cause, which is represented in *Portrait* by Stephen's friend Davin. This conflict between nationalism and free artistic expression is represented through language issues. It is Stephen's awareness of language that makes him suspicious of Davin's simplistic rhetoric of ideals ("I ask myself about you: *Is he as innocent as his speech?*" *Portrait* 219). And while Stephen is painfully aware that in using English, he is using a tongue not his own, but that of the colonisers ("[The dean's] language, so familiar and so foreign, will always be for me an acquired speech" *Portrait* 205), he also refuses to learn Irish Gaelic, the speech associated with the nationalist movement.[58] Stephen appears to reject both languages available to him. It is no surprise, then, that "silence" is one of the arms famously numbered among his weapons in his bid for freedom:

> You have asked what I would do and what I would not do. I will tell you what I will do and what I will not do. I will not serve that in which I no longer believe whether it call itself my home, my fatherland or my church: I will try to express myself in some mode of life or art as freely as I can and as wholly as I can, using for my defence the only arms I allow myself to use – silence, exile, and cunning. (*Portrait* 268-269)

---

57 The essay is titled "The Day of the Rabblement" and is from 1901. Cf. Wales 27.
58 Stephen's reservations about English are echoed by Joyce during the writing of *Finnegans Wake*: "I cannot express myself in English without enclosing myself in a tradition" (cit. R. Ellmann, *James Joyce* 397).

Silence does not appear as an admission of the failure of language; instead, it appears as a refusal to be used by it. It becomes a further way in which Stephen can assert control over language. This language dilemma also appears in Lewis's *Till We Have Faces*, where Orual writes down her tale in Greek but stubbornly keeps "all the names of people and places in our own language" (*TWHF* 12).

It becomes evident that the language question, for Joyce, is always also a question of politics and history: "Joyce's handling of political matters is always mediated by his strong interest in, and immense skill with, language: the two domains are, finally, inseparable in his work" (Attridge and Howes, "Introduction" 3). Silence, the failure of language and the search for a super-language are intrinsically connected, as Stephen states, with exile and the search for an identity that does not conform to the absolute definitions of nationalism. It is not by chance that the three main voices of *Ulysses* – Stephen, Bloom and Molly – are all in one way or another exiles: Stephen has left Ireland for Paris and returns only unwillingly; Bloom, as a Jew (albeit christened), can never conform to the monolithic Irish, Celtic and Catholic identity; Molly was born in Gibraltar and only came to Ireland after marrying Bloom. This enables Joyce to give a far more differentiated picture of what constitutes "Irishness". Traditionally, the Jews have been seen as a nomadic nation with no home, exiled from their promised land in Egypt and Babylon for their faithlessness in Biblical times, occupied by the Romans, driven out from Israel again after the fall of the Roman Empire, persecuted and unwanted throughout the world. Through taking a Jew as his main protagonist Joyce is able to voice issues of marginality and exile, showing sympathy for the oppressed colonial position of Ireland which parallels the Jewish situation, while revealing its inherent bigotry.

> – Persecution, says [Bloom], all the history of the world is full of it. Perpetuating national hatred among nations.
> – But do you know what a nation means? Says John Wyse.
> – Yes, says Bloom.
> – What is it? Says John Wyse.
> – A nation? Says Bloom. A nation is the same people living in the same place.
> – By God, then, says Ned, laughing, if that's so I'm a nation for I'm living in the same place for the past five years.
> So of course everyone had a laugh at Bloom and says he, trying to muck out of it
> – Or also living in different places.
> – That covers my case, says Joe.
> – What is your nation if I may ask, says the citizen.

> – Ireland, says Bloom. I was born here. Ireland. [...] And I belong to a race too, says Bloom, that is hated and persecuted. Also now. This very moment. This very instant. (*Ulysses* 329-331)

Jews are unwanted in Ireland ("Saint Patrick would want to land again at Ballykinlar and convert us, says the citizen, after allowing things like that to contaminate our shores" 336), because they supposedly do not belong there and this makes them incapable of patriotic feelings. Yet parallels are drawn between the Irish situation and the Jewish:

> – And after all, says John Wyse, why can't a jew love his country like the next fellow?
> – Why not? Says J.J., when he's quite sure which country it is. [...]
> – That's the new Messiah for Ireland! says the citizen. Island of saints and sages!
> – Well, they're still waiting for their redeemer, says Martin. For that matter so are we. (*Ulysses* 336)

It is pure irony that Joyce has one of his characters state that "Bloom gave the idea for Sinn Fein to Griffith to put in his paper" (*Ulysses* 334).[59]

In the *Wake's* language, which is both English and more than English, a multicultural Babel which includes Irish Gaelic and Hebrew, Joyce seems to have overcome Stephen's stubborn refusal to use either English or Gaelic in creating his own language, one which possibly can overcome the trap of nationalism. But we have already noticed the similarity of the language of *Finnegans Wake* to the language of the fantastic, and thus it must also embody that lack of the signified which lends itself so well to the topics of exile and desire.

So is there a way out of the language of exile and lack? Joyce does not, as does Yeats at first, deny the fragmentation inherent in Irish culture by seeking to

---

59 A further, more subtle way in which Joyce may be playing on the difficulties of Bloom's identity is through his use of Mozart's operas in the text. Bloom often thinks of phrases from operas such as *Don Giovanni*: "Doing her hair, humming: *voglio e non vorrei*. No: *vorrei e non*" (*Ulysses* 95). These passages bring another dimension of meaning to the text – if Molly hums Zerbinetta's answer to Giovanni's seduction, "I would like to and yet I would not like to", it could hint at her own infidelity. But significantly, it is only the operas with libretti by Lorenzo da Ponte that are quoted, and as the music is not reproduced in the text, it is only da Ponte's words that appear (although the reader immediately thinks of Mozart's music and da Ponte probably does not come to mind at first). However, da Ponte's situation was actually somewhat similar to Bloom's; he was an Italian Jew baptised at the age of 14, who actually became a Catholic priest but fell into ways of vice in Venice, was banished, and came to the Viennese court an exile seeking to earn his way as a poet. Later he again fell from favour, emigrated to London, and from thence finally to New York. In using da Ponte's words, I think Joyce may be adding yet another dimension to the theme of (Jewish) exile and homelessness – characteristically through the medium of language.

return to a mythic past. Nor does he subscribe to a false image of a unified Irish identity, instead he insists on the right to cultural difference. Nonetheless, as we have seen, his works attempt to achieve wholeness and unity. But this can only be reached upon the level of form through the superimposition of mythic structures, while the language of the works betrays their incompleteness and show exactly how deep the sense of exile runs. If Molly ends *Ulysses* with an affirmative "Yes" (704), it is because she is thinking of Gibraltar, not of Ireland. The same can be said for Lewis's works. Like Joyce, he rejects a nationalist monolithic Irish identity – possibly because he knew he could never have been part of it in the first place. And although Lewis does not address the Irish situation in his works, the prominence of displacement and exile found in their themes and language itself can be traced to his own experiences as an Irishman. In this sense, for Lewis as well as Joyce, "[Irish] incompleteness was the very ground of his art" (Deane, "Joyce and Nationalism" 173). This incompleteness is not to be overcome, for as Lewis insists in his theories, fantastic desire is in itself desirable precisely because it can never be appeased (cf. "On Three Ways of Writing for Children" 65). Lack is constitutive of fantastic language. Both Lewis's and Joyce's works thus remain characterised by exile; they enter into a typically modernist tension in which exile is lamented but becomes the very matter out of which their works are created.

Conclusion

Modernist Fantasy, Fantastic Modernism

This study has, true to its title, attempted to locate aspects of modernism in the works of Lewis, Tolkien and Williams. But it has in almost equal measure attempted to locate aspects of the fantastic in the works of Jones, Yeats and Joyce. As I stated in the Introduction, it has not been my aim to recast the Inklings as secret modernists, nor the modernists as fantasy writers, but to re-examine the relationship between these two literatures in such a way that they might be read profitably side by side. An exact and rigid definition of this relationship is, to my mind, undesirable, as it is precisely (negative) definitions of it that have up till now kept critics from looking for interrelations. Thus at the end of this study, rather than deliver a set of fixed conclusions, I want to take up again some terms and concepts that have appeared in the course of this work but that have not really been explored. These terms once again exemplify the problems inherent in attempting to categorise fantasy and modernism. Besides recapitulating the most important aspects already covered, they can give us further pointers towards how their relationship can be examined and which paths further studies on fantasy and modernism might take.

A term frequently linked to fantasy in recent years, and which also plays a role in this study, is that of "magic realism". Originally applied to a school of painting in the Twenties (and thus contemporary with modernism), the term is now taken to describe a type of writing which "interweave[s], in an ever-shifting pattern, a sharply etched realism in representing ordinary events and descriptive details together with fantastic and dreamlike elements, as well as with materials derived from myth and fairy-tales" (Abrams 196). Generally, this is seen as a post-Second World War development and expressive of postmodernism, which is characterised (among many things) by the attempt to show that reality itself is a construct, and that hence any form of realism must also be a construct. The texts of magic realism are often openly metafictional, involving the reader in the process of inventing the tale, or collaborating in constructing an artificial story. The use of myths and fairy-tales in magic realist fiction also gestures towards the role that both play in creating our consciousness, and magic realism often employs mythic archetypes overtly to create patterns in its fiction.

Many of these features are also, as we have seen, prevalent in fantasy literature: the use of myth, the linguistic self-awareness, the departure from "realism". There are, however, also some differences. Magic realism is much closer to – or indeed exemplifies – Todorov's category of the fantastic, demonstrating the fragility of the (artificially constructed) limits between the natural and the supernatural. Texts are in most cases also set in the primary world, relying on the supposed intrusion of the supernatural and mythic into that world for their special effect. For example, in Salman Rushdie's *Midnight's Children* the narrator Saleem, growing up in Mumbai, bashes his huge nose in a bicycle accident, clearing it of snot – and suddenly becomes able to hear the thoughts of people around him – his large nose acting as a kind of magic "All-India Radio" (Rushdie 166).[1]

Genre fantasy, on the other hand, seeks to create a coherent secondary world in which natural and supernatural are both the norm. Its effect is not dependent on surprise, like Rushdie's text, but on the convincing thoroughness with which the secondary world is constructed and its magic made plausible. Nonetheless, the demarcations between primary and secondary world cannot always be drawn easily (as we have already seen for Williams's Logres and Tolkien's Middle-earth).

If one gives credence to this connection between fantasy and magic realism (and as both are forms of fantastic literature, there definitely is a connection), it follows that fantasy can also be related to postmodernism in the same way magic realism can. Indeed, this might seem a more credible claim than that it is related to modernism, given fantasy's (apparent) rejection of an elitist culture, and its associations with the New Age and Green movements.[2] However, the very act of creating a world that lays claim to coherence and wholeness, that presents an (albeit artificial) unity, is far more of a modernist endeavour. Of

---

1 On the other hand, the Houri episode in *Midnight's Children* could be seen as a departure into an alternate reality similar to a secondary world (this is complicated by the fact that this alternate reality is supposedly the Muslim heaven). Rushdie's collection for children, *Haroun and the Sea of Stories*, also takes its protagonist off on a series of voyages into fantastic worlds (the worlds of stories).
2 Cf. Roberts 8-10; Curry 59-97; Rosebury 193-220.

course the rise in the popularity of fantasy can be dated (mainly) to the success of *The Lord of the Rings*, published in the Fifties; hence most well-known fantasy was written during the era of postmodernism, not that of modernism. But certain traits characteristic of fantasy as a genre – the construction of secondary worlds that function like cosmic models, and the attempt to preserve the creator's authority within the work of art – place these texts much closer to the ideology of modernism than that of their postmodern contemporaries. The works of Lewis, Tolkien and Williams, all of whom can be seen as *Übervater* of contemporary fantasy, were written for the greater part during the heyday of modernism (and I hope this study has been able show convincingly that their works are influenced by this fact); perhaps it is no surprise that fantasy works that follow their example closely should adopt some of their more modernist aspects.

If fantasy is (to a certain extent) thus modernist, one must surely also ask the opposite question: is modernism fantastic? "Fantastic" is a term applied as little to modernist literature as "modernist" is to fantasy. Yet this study has attempted to show that in all of the modernist works examined, there are episodes that could be termed fantastic – from the unicorns and the *Mists of Avalon*-like Queen of the Woods in Jones's *In Parenthesis*, to Eliot's Sea-Bell from *Four Quartets*, to Yeats's mythic ghosts in *The Dreaming of the Bones*, to the goat-like beasts of sin that torment Stephen Dedalus in *A Portrait of the Artist*, to the apparition of the fairy Rudy to his father Bloom in *Ulysses*. Similarly, the cosmic models of modernism seek to create an all-encompassing reality within the work of art that draw close to the secondary worlds of fantasy. In *Gothic Modernisms*, a rare example of criticism connecting modernism and the fantastic, Andrew Smith and Jeff Wallace write: "British literary modernism is indebted to an innovative, anti-realist tradition inaugurated in the popular fiction of the *fin de siècle* – Gothic horror, sensation fiction, science fiction" ("Introduction" 2). We have already encountered the claim that fantasy and science fiction are descended from the Gothic (cf. Roberts 8); if modernism is also, then modernism and fantasy cannot be entirely unrelated as has been hitherto assumed.

This connection with the Gothic adds another dimension to some of the shared themes already examined. For example, Smith and Wallace write that "In both modernist and popular discourse, the body can seem to promise authentic personal identity, yet is ghosted by a sense of something potentially alien and strange" (Smith and Wallace, "Introduction" 3). We have seen how bodies figure in the poetry of Williams and Jones, as both corresponding to divine order and, in the form of dismembered corpses and zombie figures, making a mockery of that order. Neither Taliesin nor Dai Greatcoat seem at the end of the respective cycles to be in possession of a proper body, their identity is lost. Even more "alien" are of course the strange races that populate Middle-earth and Malacandra, reflective perhaps of "[a]nxieties about the physical health of the collective body – human species, race, nation-state, culture" (Smith and Wallace, "Introduction" 3). These anxieties are evident in both fantasy and the modernist fiction we have examined, that both in their own ways mourn the loss of culture and are obsessed with the past (this, again, is typically modernist – postmodern fiction tends to revel in the freedom found in the loss of a collective cultural inheritance). The prominence of war can be attributed not just to the proximity of the texts examined to the World Wars, but to the issues connected to it: again, the loss of culture, the loss of (national) identity in the face of a hostile power, and ultimately the destruction of the human race altogether.

Particularly the issues of nationalism (and connected to it, of course, race) have become evident in the course of the study. I have found it especially striking that in all three main chapters of this study the issue of Celticism has arisen, branching off from the leading question about the relationship between fantasy and modernism. All the writers examined, both modernists and Inklings, are concerned with national identity, and for most of them this identity is somehow constructed along the traditional Celtic/Saxon binary – and their constructions reveal how fraught this dialectic actually is. David Jones places a Celtic (or Welsh) Britain against the invading Saxon, while Williams fuses Celtic and English elements that oppose an oriental Muslim force. For both these writers, religion plays an important role in their binaries: Christianity stands in opposition to heathenry. Yeats is concerned with an Irish Celtic identity that stands in opposition to English/British/Saxon tyranny, while Tolkien, the lover of Anglo-Saxon, puts Englishness against Norman colonial forces (the Saxons were, after all, the first victims of Norman colonial expansion, not the Irish). For both Joyce and Lewis, their search for a national Irish identity that could include their own versions of Irishness, inclusive of but not exclusively Celtic, is reflected in the prominence of exile in their works. While the present study does not have the scope to pursue this connection to Celticism further, some fruitful crossovers have been found between Irish or Celtic studies and the works of Tolkien;[3] these could perhaps be applied to fantasy studies more generally.

Another aspect connected to Celticism that could well be fruitfully pursued in both modernist and fantasy works is their relationship to colonialism or postcolonialism. Once again, this is something the present study could not include. The relationships of at least Yeats and Joyce to colonialism (or "Semicolonialism") have already been explored in criticism; David Jones, the Welshman born in London, who could not speak Welsh but created a distinctly Welsh atmosphere in his works, would also profit from a postcolonial reading. That Tolkien's works can be interpreted as postcolonial and that Lewis's works are conditioned by his situation as a colonised Irishman has been touched upon; the way Williams's texts deal with the construction of an "Empire" and its fall could also be analysed with the help of postcolonial theory. This might be another way in which the connections between modernism and (the Inklings') fantasy could be explored further.

Incidentally, postcolonialism brings us back to magic realism, a genre often associated with the fiction written in the former British colonies. In a way, it represents their adapting aspects of the British literary tradition and making them their own. Thus, their efforts mirror what modernists and Inklings were trying to do – namely take the old and make it new. To a certain extent, this "making it new" involves for all three literatures the employment of the fantastic. This dominance of the fantastic throughout these various literary epochs and genres would seem to bear out Tom Shippey's claim that "[t]he dominant literary mode of the twentieth century has been the fantastic" (Shippey, *Author* vii).

Perhaps the main characteristic shared by the Inklings' fantasy and literary modernism which distinguishes both from postmodern genres such as magic realism is the tension that runs through their thematic concerns as well as their

---

3 Cf. Burns (2005) and Fimi (2009).

structure. On the surface, features such as self-awareness and an emphasis on the material of their construction are shared by postmodernism. However, as we have seen, modernist works as well as those of Tolkien, Lewis and Williams seek to create an authority that counters the subversion created by this self-awareness. Thus they remain caught in constant tension. They both condemn war and are dependent upon it for the structure it gives their work; they seek to replace history by myth, and succeed in only undermining the narratives of both; they make language and its failure their subject and thus demonstrate this failure in their own texts – while asserting the absolute power of the creator at the same time. It is this tension inherent in the central subjects of war, myth and history, and language that conditions the fantastic breaking through into modernist works. It is tension that is the single most important aspect of modernism in the works of Lewis, Tolkien and Williams – and it is the most important fantastic aspect in works of modernism.

List of Works Cited

ABRAMS, M.H. *A Glossary of Literary Terms.* Orlando: Harcourt Brace College, 1999.

ACKROYD, Peter. *Ezra Pound.* London: Thames & Hudson, 1980.

ADORNO, Theodor W. *Minima Moralia: Reflexionen aus dem beschädigten Leben.* Frankfurt a.M.: Suhrkamp, 1969.

— *Ästhetische Theorie.* Frankfurt a.M.: Suhrkamp, 1970.

— "The Late Style (I)." In *Beethoven. The Philosophy of Music.* Edited by Rolf TIEDEMANN, translated by Edmund JEPHCOTT. Cambridge: Polity Press, 1998, 123-137.

— "The Late Style (II)." In *Beethoven. The Philosophy of Music.* Edited by Rolf TIEDEMANN, translated by Edmund JEPHCOTT. Cambridge: Polity Press, 1998, 154-161.

ARMITT, Lucie. *Theorising the Fantastic.* London: Arnold, 1996.

ARNOLD, Matthew. *On the Study of Celtic Literature.* London: Smith, Elder and Co., 1867.

ASHENDEN, Gavin. *Charles Williams: Alchemy and Integration.* Kent, Ohio: Kent State UP, 2008.

ATTRIDGE, Derek. *Joyce Effects.* Cambridge: Cambridge University Press, 2000.

— and Marjorie HOWES. "Introduction." In *Semicolonial Joyce.* Edited by Derek ATTRIDGE and Marjorie HOWES Cambridge: Cambridge University Press, 2000, 1-20.

— and Marjorie HOWES (eds.). *Semicolonial Joyce.* Cambridge: Cambridge University Press, 2000.

AUDEN, Wynstan H. *Secondary Worlds.* New York: Random House, 1968.

— "The Quest Hero." In *Tolkien and the Critics.* Edited by Neil D. ISAACS and Rose A. ZIMBARDO. Notre Dame: University of Notre Dame Press, 1968, 40-61.

— "At the End of the Quest, Victory." In *The Tolkien Scrapbook.* Edited by Alida BECKER. Philadelphia: Running Press, 1978, 44-48.

— *The Ascent of F6: A Tragedy in Two Acts.* Reprint. London: Faber, 1986.

"On *In Parentheses*, On *The Anathemata*." In *David Jones: Man and Poet*. Edited by John MATTHIAS. Orono, Maine: National Poetry Foundation, 1989, 43-50.

BARFIELD, Owen. *Poetic Diction: A Study in Meaning*. New York: McGraw-Hill, 1964.

BARTHES, Roland. *Writing Degree Zero*. Translated by Annette LAVERS and Colin SMITH. New York: Hill and Wang, 1968.

Mythologies. Translated by Jonathan CAPE. London: Vintage, 1993.

BASNEY, Lionel. "Myth, History and Time." In *Understanding The Lord of the Rings: The Best of Tolkien Criticism*. Edited by Neil D. ISAACS and Rose A. ZIMBARDO. Boston: Houghton Mifflin, 2004, 183-194.

BAUDRILLARD, Jean. *Fatal Strategies*. Edited by J. FLEMING, translated by P. BEITCHMAN and W.C.J. NIESLUCHOWSKI. London: Pluto Press, 1999.

Selected Writings. Edited by Mark POSTER. Cambridge: Polity, 2001.

BECKETT, Samuel. *Our Exagmination Round His Factification For Incamination of Work in Progress*. Paris: Shakespeare & Co., 1929.

BELL, Michael. "The Metaphysics of Modernism." In *The Cambridge Companion to Modernism*. Edited by Michael LEVENSON. Cambridge: Cambridge University Press, 1999, 9-32.

BENJAMIN, Walter. *Angelus Novus*. Frankfurt a.M.: Suhrkamp, 1968.

BERGONZI, Bernard. *The Myth of Modernism and Twentieth Century Literature*. Brighton: Harvester, 1986.

Heroes' Twilight: A Study of the Literature of the Great War. Manchester: Carcanet, 1996.

BERMAN, Art. *Preface to Modernism*. Urbana: University of Illinois Press, 1994.

BLAKENEY WILLIAMS, Louise. *Modernism and the Ideology of History: Literature, Politics, and the Past*. Cambridge: Cambridge University Press, 2002.

BLAMIRES, David. *David Jones: Artist and Writer*. Manchester: Manchester University Press, 1971.

BLAMIRES, Harry. *The Bloomsday Book*. London: Routledge, 1988.

BLEAKLEY, David. *C.S. Lewis at Home in Ireland*. Bangor, Co. Down: Strandtown, 1998.

BLISSETT, William. "The Welsh Thing in Here." In *David Jones: Artist and Poet*. Edited by Paul HILLS. Aldershot: Scolar Press, 101-121.

BLOOM, Harold (ed.). *Classic Fantasy Writers*. New York: Chelsea House, 1994.

BLUMENBERG, Hans. *Arbeit am Mythos*. Frankfurt a. M.: Suhrkamp, 1979.

BOOTH, Allyson. *Postcards from the Trenches*. Oxford: Oxford University Press, 1996.

BRADBURY, Michael and James MCFARLANE (eds.). *Modernism. A Guide to European Literature and Culture 1890-1930*. London: Penguin, 1991.

BRADLEY, Marion Zimmer. *The Mists of Avalon*. New York: Random House, 2001.

BRESLAND, Ronald W. *The Backward Glance: C.S. Lewis and Ireland*. Belfast: Queen's University Press, 1999.

BROOKE-ROSE, Christine. *A Rhetoric of the Unreal: Studies in Narrative and Structure, Especially of the Fantastic*. Cambridge: Cambridge University Press, 1981.

BURGESS, Anthony. *Joysprick. An Introduction to the Language of James Joyce*. London: Andre Deutsch, 1973.

BURNS, Marjorie. *Perilous Realms: Celtic and Norse in Tolkien's Middle-earth*. Toronto: University of Toronto Press, 2005.

CARPENTER, Humphrey. *J.R.R. Tolkien: A Biography*. London: HarperCollins, 1977.

W.H. Auden: A Biography. London: George Allen & Unwin, 1981.

The Inklings. London: HarperCollins, 1997.

CARROLL, Lewis. *The Philosopher's Alice: Alice's Adventures in Wonderland and Through the Looking-glass*. Edited by Peter HEATH. London: Academy Editions, 1974.

CASTLE, Gregory. *Modernism and the Celtic Revival*. Cambridge: Cambridge University Press, 2001.

CAVALIERO, Glen. *Charles Williams: Poet of Theology*. Grand Rapids, Michigan: Eerdmans, 1983.

CHANCE, Jane. *The Lord of the Rings: The Mythology of Power*. New York: Twayne, 1992.

CHENG, Vincent J. "Authenticity and Identity: Catching the Irish Spirit." In *Semicolonial Joyce*. Edited by Derek ATTRIDGE and Marjorie HOWES, Cambridge: Cambridge University Press, 2000, 240-261.

CHESTERTON, Gilbert K. "Fairy Tales." In Gilbert K. CHESTERTON. *All Things Considered*. London: Everyman, n.d., 253-258.

CORCORAN, Neil. "Spilled Bitterness: *In Parenthesis* in History." In *David Jones: Man and Poet*. Edited by John MATTHIAS. Orono, Maine: National Poetry Foundation, University of Maine, 1986, 209-226.

CORNWELL, Neil. *The Literary Fantastic*. Hemel Hempstead: Harvester, 1990.

COYLE, John. "Introduction." In *The Icon Critical Guide to James Joyce's A Portrait of the Artist as a Young Man and Ulysses*. Edited by John COYLE. Cambridge: Icon, 1997, 5-8.

— (ed.). *The Icon Critical Guide to James Joyce's A Portrait of the Artist as a Young Man and Ulysses*. Cambridge: Icon, 1997.

CROFT, Janet Brennan. *War and the Works of J.R.R. Tolkien*. Westport, Connecticut: Praeger, 2004.

CULLINGFORD, Elizabeth. *Yeats, Ireland and Fascism*. London: Macmillan, 1981.

— *Gender and History in Yeats's Love Poetry*. Cambridge: Cambridge University Press, 1993.

— *Ireland's Others*. Cork: Cork University Press, 2001.

CURRY, Patrick. *Defending Middle-earth. Tolkien: Myth and Modernity*. London: HarperCollins, 1997.

DEANE, Seamus. "Joyce and Nationalism." In *James Joyce: New Perspectives*. Edited by Colin MACCABE. Bloomington: University of Indiana Press, 1982, 168-183.

— "Introduction." In James JOYCE. *Finnegans Wake*. London: Penguin, 1992, vii-xlx.

DE MAN, Paul. *Blindness and Insight*. Minneapolis: University of Minnesota Press, 1983.

DECOSTE, Damon Marcel. "'Do you remember tomorrow?' Modernism and its Second War in Malcolm Lowry's *Under the Volcano*." *Modern Fiction Studies* 44.3 (Fall 1998), 767-791.

DERRIDA, Jacques. *A Derrida Reader*. Edited by Peggy KAMUF. New York: Harvester Wheatsheaf, 1991.

DILWORTH, Thomas. *The Shape of Meaning in the Poetry of David Jones*. Toronto: University of Toronto Press, 1988.

DODDS, David Llewellyn, (ed.). *Charles Williams (Arthurian Poets)*. Woodbridge: D.S. Brewer, 1991.

DUNSANY, Lord. *The King of Elfland's Daughter*. London: Gollancz, 2001.

— *Don Rodriguez: Chronicles of the Shadow Valley*. Holicong, Pennsylvania: Wildside, 2002.

EAGLETON, Terry. *Literary Theory*. Oxford: Blackwell, 1986.

Heathcliff and the Great Hunger: Studies in Irish Culture. London: Verso, 1995.

and Fredric JAMESON and Edward W. SAID. *Nationalism, Colonialism, and Literature*. Minneapolis: University of Minnesota Press, 1990.

EDDISON, E.R. *The Worm Ouroboros*. London: Gollancz, 2000.

ELIOT, T.S. *Collected Poems 1909-1962*. London: Faber, 1963.

"A Note of Introduction." In David JONES. *In Parenthesis*. London: Faber, 1963, vii-viii.

Selected Prose of T.S. Eliot. Edited by Frank KERMODE. London: Faber, 1975.

ELLMANN, Maud. "Polytropic Man." In *James Joyce: New Perspectives*. Edited by Colin MACCABE. Bloomington: Indiana, 1982, 73-104.

The Poetics of Impersonality. Brighton: Harvester, 1987.

"Disremembering Dedalus." In *The Icon Critical Guide to James Joyce's A Portrait of the Artist as a Young Man and Ulysses*. Edited by John COYLE. Cambridge: Icon, 1997, 87-125.

ELLMANN, Richard. *James Joyce*. Oxford: Oxford Universiy Press, 1982.

Yeats: The Man and the Masks. Harmondsworth: Penguin, 1987.

EMIG, Rainer. *Modernism in Poetry*. London: Longman, 1995.

Krieg als Metapher im 20. Jahrhundert. Darmstadt: Wissenschaftliche Buchgesellschaft, 2001.

Ulysses: New Casebooks. Basingstoke: Palgrave, 2004.

ENDE, Michael. *Die Unendliche Geschichte*. Stuttgart: Thienemann, 1979.

ESTY, Jed. *A Shrinking Island: Modernism and National Culture in England*. Princeton: Princeton University Press, 2005.

FALLON, Peter and Derek MAHON (eds.). *The Penguin Book of Contemporary Irish Poetry*. London: Penguin, 1990.

FIMI, Dimitra. *Tolkien, Race and Cultural History: From Faeries to Hobbits*. Basingstoke: Palgrave, 2009.

FLIEGER, Verlyn. "The Sound of Silence." In *Word and Story in C.S. Lewis*. Edited by Peter J. SCHAKEL and Charles A. HUTTAR. Columbia: University of Missouri Press, 1991, 42-57.

A Question of Time: J.R.R. Tolkien's Road to Faërie. Kent, Ohio: Kent State University Press, 1997.

FORSTER, E.M. *Howard's End*. London: Penguin, 1989.

FRIEDMAN, Barton. "Fabricating History: Narrative Strategy in *The Lord of the Rings*." *Clio* 2 (1973), 123-144.

Adventures in the Deeps of the Mind: The Cuchulain Cycle of W.B. Yeats. Princeton: Princeton University Press, 1977.

FUSSELL, Paul. *The Great War and Modern Memory*. London: Oxford University Press, 1975.

GARNER, Alan. *Elidor*. London: Collins, 1965.

GARTH, John. *Tolkien and the Great War*. Boston: Houghton Mifflin, 2003.

GIBSON, Andrew. "'Strangers in My House, Bad Manners to Them!': England in 'Circe'." *European Joyce Studies*. Amsterdam: Rodopi, 1994, 179-221.

GIKANDI, Simon. *Reading Chinua Achebe: Language and Ideology in Fiction*. Portsmouth, New Hampshire: Heinemann, 1991.

GILBERT, Sandra and Susan GUBAR. *The War of the Words: The Place of the Woman Writer in the Twentieth Century*. Volume I. New Haven: Yale University Press, 1988.

GILCHRIST, K.J. *A Morning After War: C.S. Lewis and World War I*. New York: Peter Lang, 2005.

GLOVER, Donald. "Bent Language in Perelandra: The Storyteller's Temptation." In *Word and Story in C.S. Lewis*. Edited by Peter J. SCHAKEL and Charles A. HUTTAR. Columbia: University of Missouri Press, 1991, 171-181.

GOETSCH, Paul. "The Fantastic in Poetry of the First World War." In *War and the Construction of Cultural Identities in Britain*. Edited by Barbara KORTE and Ralf SCHNEIDER. Amsterdam: Rodopi, 2002, 125-141.

GOLDMAN, Jane. *Modernism, 1910-1945. Image to Apocalypse*. Basingstoke: Palgrave, 2004.

GRAVES, Robert. *The White Goddess: A Historical Grammar of Poetical Myth*. London: Faber, 1961.

GRAY, William. *C.S. Lewis*. Plymouth: Northcote House, 1998.

GREEN, Roger Lancelyn and Walter HOOPER. *C.S. Lewis: A Biography*. Glasgow: Collins, 1974.

HADFIELD, A.M. *Charles Williams: An Exploration of his Life and Work*. New York: Oxford University Press, 1983.

HAGUE, René. *Dai Greatcoat*. London: Faber, 1980.

HAMMOND, Wayne G. and Christina SCULL. *J.R.R. Tolkien: Artist and Illustrator*. London: HarperCollins, 1995.

HAPGOOD, Lynn and Nancy L. PAXTON (eds.). *Outside Modernism*. Basingstoke: Palgrave, 2000.

HARDY, Thomas. *Tess of the D'Urbervilles*. London: Macmillan, 1961.

HEATH, Stephen. "Joyce in Language." In *James Joyce: New Perspectives*. Edited by Colin MACCABE. Bloomington: Indiana, 1982, 129-150.

HILEY, Margaret. "(Sub)Creation and the Written Word in Michael Ende's *Neverending Story* and Cornelia Funke's *Inkheart*." In *Towards or Back to Human Values? Spiritual and Moral Dimensions of Contemporary Fantasy*. Edited by Marek OZIEWICZ and Justyna DESZCZ-TRYHUBCZAK. Newcastle upon Tyne: Cambridge Scholars Press, 2006, 121-134.

"Tolkien and 'Late Style'." In *Tolkien and Modernity 2*. Edited by Thomas HONEGGER and Frank WEINREICH. Zurich and Berne: Walking Tree Publishers, 2006, 53-73.

HILLS, Paul (ed.). *David Jones: Artist and Poet*. Aldershot: Scolar Press, 1997.

HOFMANNSTHAL, Hugo von. *Sämtliche Werke: Kritische Studienausgabe*. Edited by Rudolf HIRSCH et al. Frankfurt a.M.: Fischer, 1991.

HONEGGER, Thomas. "The Rohirrim: "Anglo-Saxons on Horseback?" An Inquiry into Tolkien's Use of Sources." In *Tolkien and the Study of his Sources*. Edited by Jason FISHER. McFarland, 2011, 116-132.

HOWES, Marjorie. *Yeats's Nations: Gender, Class and Irishness*. Cambridge: Cambridge University Press, 1996.

HULME, Peter. "Including America." *ARIEL* 26.1 (January 1995), 117-123.

HUME, Kathryn. *Fantasy and Mimesis: Responses to Reality in Western Literature*. London: Methuen, 1984.

HUNTER, Lynette. *Modern Allegory and Fantasy*. London: Macmillan, 1989.

ISAACS, Neil D. and Rose A. ZIMBARDO (eds.). *Tolkien and the Critics*. Notre Dame: University of Notre Dame Press, 1968.

Tolkien: New Critical Perspectives. Lexington: University of Kentucky Press, 1981.

JACKSON, Rosemary. *Fantasy: The Literature of Subversion*. London: Methuen, 1981.

JAMES, Henry. *Letters*. Volume II. Edited by Percy LUBBOCK. New York: Scribner, 1920.

JANDL, Ernst. *Gesammelte Werke*. Volume I. Edited by Klaus SIBLEWSKI. Darmstadt: Luchterhand, 1985.

JONES, David. *Epoch and Artist*. London: Faber, 1959.

In Parenthesis. London: Faber, 1963.

The Dying Gaul and Other Writings. London: Faber, 1978.

The Roman Quarry. London: Faber, 1981.

JOYCE, James. *Ulysses*. London: Penguin, 1939.

A Portrait of the Artist as a Young Man. London: Penguin, 1992.

Finnegans Wake. London: Penguin, 1992.

Dubliners. London: Penguin, 1996.

Letters. Volume I. Edited by Stuart GILBERT. London: Faber, 1957.

The James Joyce Archive. Edited by Michael GRODEN, Hans Walter GABLER, David HAYMAN, A. Walton LITZ and Danis ROSE with John O'HANLON, 63 volumes. New York: Garland, 1977-79.

KAZIN, Alfred. *Bright Book of Life. American Novelists and Storytellers from Hemingway to Mailer*. London: Secker and Warburg, 1974.

KEARNEY, Richard. "Myth and Terror." In *Yeats's Political Identities*. Edited by Jonathan ALLISON. Ann Arbor: University of Michigan Press, 1996, 165-179.

KIBBLE, Matthew. "The 'Still-Born Generation': Decadence and the Great War in H.D.'s Fiction." *Modern Fiction Studies* 44.3 (Fall 1998), 540-567.

KIBERD, Declan. *Inventing Ireland*. Cambridge, Massachusetts: Harvard University Press, 1996.

KIRSCHNER, Paul. "Yeats and Time." In *Between Time and Eternity*. Edited by Paul KIRSCHNER and Alexander STILLMARK. Amsterdam: Rodopi, 1992, 1-20.

and Alexander STILLMARK (eds.). *Between Time and Eternity: Nine Essays on W.B. Yeats and his Contemporaries, Hofmannsthal and Blok*. Amsterdam: Rodopi, 1992.

KOLOCOTRONI, Vassiliki, Jane GOLDMAN, and Olga TAXIDOU (eds.). *Modernism: An Anthology of Sources and Documents*. Edinburgh: Edinburgh University Press, 1998.

KRANZ, Gisbert. *Die Arthur-Gedichte von Charles Williams: Einführung, Übersetung, Kommentar, Konkordanz*. Frankfurt a.M.: Peter Lang, 1991.

LASSNER, Phyllis. "'Camp Follower of Catastrophe': Martha Gellhorn's World War II Challenge to the Modernist War." *Modern Fiction Studies* 44.3 (Fall 1998), 792-812.

LE GUIN, Ursula K. *The Language of the Night: Essays on Fantasy and Science Fiction*. London: The Women's Press, 1989.

The Earthsea Quartet. London: Penguin, 1993.

Rocannon's World: Worlds of Exile and Illusion. New York: Tom Doherty Associates, 1994.

LEHAN, Richard. "James Joyce: The Limits of Modernism and the Realms of the Literary Text." In *Ulysses: New Casebooks*. Edited by Rainer EMIG. Basingstoke: Plagrave, 2004, 30-48.

LEVENSON, Michael. *A Genealogy of Modernism*. Cambridge: Cambridge University Press, 1984.

(ed.). *The Cambridge Companion to Modernism*. Cambridge: Cambridge University Press, 1999.

LÉVI-STRAUSS, Claude. *Structural Anthropology*. Translated by Claire JACOBSEN and Brooke GRUNDFEST SCHOEPF. New York: Basic Books, 1963.

LEWIS, C.S. *Rehabilitations*. London: Oxford University Press, 1939.

A Preface to 'Paradise Lost'. Oxford: Oxford University Press, 1942.

Essays Presented to Charles Williams. Oxford: Oxford University Press, 1947.

Out of the Silent Planet. London: Pan, 1952.

Voyage to Venus (Perelandra). London: Pan, 1953.

That Hideous Strength. London: Pan, 1955.

The Pilgrim's Regress: An Allegorical Apology for Christianity, Reason and Romanticism. Grand Rapids, Michigan: Eerdmans, 1958.

They Asked for a Paper: Papers and Addresses. London: Geoffrey Bles, 1962.

Poems. Edited by Walter HOOPER. London: Geoffrey Bles, 1964.

The Weight of Glory and Other Addresses. Grand Rapids, Michigan: Eerdmans, 1965.

Letters of C.S. Lewis. Edited by W.H. LEWIS. London: Geoffrey Bles, 1966.

Of Other Worlds. Edited by Walter HOOPER. London: Harvest, 1966.

Narrative Poems. Edited by Walter HOOPER. London: Geoffrey Bles, 1969.

Surprised By Joy. Glasgow: Collins, 1977.

The Dark Tower and Other Stories. Edited by Walter HOOPER. London: Collins, 1977.

Till We Have Faces. Glasgow: Collins, 1978.

They Stand Together: The Letters of C.S. Lewis to Arthur Greaves (1914-1963). Edited by Walter HOOPER. New York: Macmillan, 1979.

A Study in Friendship: Letters, C.S. Lewis and Don Giovanni Calabria. Edited by Martin MOYNIHAN. Glasgow: Collins, 1989.

Compelling Reason. London: Fount, 1996.

The Lion, the Witch and the Wardrobe. London: Collins, 1998.

The Voyage of the Dawn Treader. London: Collins, 1998.

The Magician's Nephew. London: Collins, 1998.

The Last Battle. London: Collins, 1998.

Lewis, Warren. *The Lewis Papers.* Volumes 1-11. Private typescript, 1933.

LEWIS, Wyndham. "A Later Arm than Barbarity." *Outlook* 24 (5 Sept 1914).

LEWTY, Simon. "The Palimpsest." In *David Jones: Artist and Poet.* Edited by Paul HILLS. Aldershot: Scolar Press, 1997, 54-65.

LONGENBACH, James. *Modernist Poetics of History.* Princeton: Princeton University Press, 1973.

MACCABE, Colin. "An Introduction to *Finnegans Wake.*" In *James Joyce: New Perspectives.* Edited by Colin MACCABE. Bloomington: University of Indiana Press, 1982, 29-44.

(ed.). *James Joyce: New Perspectives.* Bloomington: Indiana University Press, 1982.

MACDIARMID, Hugh. *Lucky Poet: A Self-Study in Literature and Political Ideas.* Berkeley: University of California Press, 1972.

Complete Poems. Volumes I & II. Edited by Michael GRIEVE and W.R. AITKEN. Manchester: Carcanet, 1993.

MACDONALD, George. *George Macdonald: An Anthology.* London: Geoffrey Bles, 1946.

The Light Princess and Other Tales. London: Gollancz, 1973.

MALLARMÉ, Stéphane. *Mallarmé.* Edited by Anthony HARTLEY. London: Penguin, 1965.

MALEY, Willy. "Lost in the Hyphen of History: The Limits of Anglo-Irishness." *Irish Review* 20 (1997), 23-29.

MALORY, Sir Thomas. *Le Morte Darthur*. Volumes I & II. Edited by Janet COWEN. London: Penguin, 1969.

MANLOVE, Colin. *The Impulse of Fantasy Literature*. London: Macmillan, 1983.

MASLEN, Robert W. "Towards an Iconography of the Future: C.S. Lewis and the Scientific Humanists." *Inklings* 18 (2000), 222-249.

MAY, Keith M. *Nietzsche and Modern Literature: Themes in Yeats, Rilke, Mann and Lawrence*. Basingstoke: Macmillan, 1988.

MEDCALF, Stephen. "The Athanasian Principle in Williams's Use of Images." In *The Rhetoric of Vision*. Edited by Charles A. HUTTAR and Peter J. SCHAKEL. Lewisburg: Bucknell University Press, 1996, 27-43.

MELETINSKY, Eleazar. *The Poetics of Myth*. Translated by Guy LANOUE and Alexandre SADETSKY. London: Routledge, 1998.

MICHALSON, Karen. *Victorian Fantasy Literature: Literary Battles with Church and Empire*. Lampeter: Edwin Mellen, 1990.

MILESI, Laurent, "Introduction: Language(s) with a Difference." In *James Joyce and the Difference of Language*. Edited by Laurent MILESI. Cambridge: Cambridge University Press, 2003, 1-27.

— (ed.). *James Joyce and the Difference of Language*. Cambridge: Cambridge University Press, 2003.

MILTON, John. *Paradise Lost*. London: Penguin, 1968.

MOORMAN, Charles. *The Celtic Literature of Defeat*. Lampeter: Edwin Mellen, 1993.

MORRIS, William. *The Wood Beyond the World*. New York: Dover, 1972.

MURRAY, Atholl C.C. *Mediaevalism in the Works of David Jones and Charles Williams: A Study in Literary Tradition*. M.Litt. Thesis, University of Glasgow, 1970.

MYERS, Doris T. *C.S. Lewis in Context*. Kent, Ohio: Kent State University Press, 1994.

NICHOLLS, Peter. *Modernisms: A Literary Guide*. Los Angeles: University of California Press, 1995.

NIETZSCHE, Friedrich. *Götzendämmerung*. Stuttgart: Kröner, 1964.

— *Vom Nutzen und Nachteil der Historie für das Leben*. Basel: Diogenes, 1984.

— *Die Geburt der Tragödie aus dem Geiste der Musik*. Frankfurt a.M.: Insel, 1987.

NOLAN, Emer. *James Joyce and Nationalism*. London: Routledge, 1995.

Norris, Margot. "Modernisms and Modern Wars." *Modern Fiction Studies* 44.3 (Fall 1998), 505-509.

North, Michael. *The Political Aesthetic of Yeats, Eliot, and Pound*. Cambridge: Cambridge University Press, 1991.

O'Brien, Eugene. *The Question of Irish Identity in the Writings of William Butler Yeats and James Joyce*. Lewiston: Mellen, 1998.

Owen, Wilfred. *The Complete Poems and Fragments*. Edited by Jon Stallworthy. Oxford: Oxford University Press, 1983.

Pacey, Philip. *Hugh MacDiarmid and David Jones: Celtic Wonder-Voyagers*. Preston: Akros, 1977.

Paolini, Christopher. *Eragon*. London: Corgi, 2005.

Eldest. London: Doubleday, 2005.

Piette, Adam. *Imagination at War: British Fiction and Poetry 1939-1945*. London: Papermac, 1995.

Plain, Gill. *Women's Fiction of the Second World War*. New York: St. Martin's, 1996.

Plato. *Symposion*. Edited by Barbara Zehnpfennig. Hamburg: Meiner, 2000.

Pound, Ezra. *The Literary Essays of Ezra Pound*. Edited by T.S. Eliot. London: Faber, 1954.

The Cantos of Ezra Pound. London: Faber, 1960.

Selected Poems. London: Faber, 1975.

Prickett, Stephen. *Victorian Fantasy*. Hassocks: Harvester Press, 1979.

Raitt, Suzanne and Trudi Tate. *Women's Fiction and the Great War*. Oxford: Clarendon, 1997.

Rainey, Lawrence. "The Cultural Economy of Modernism." In *The Cambridge Companion to Modernism*. Edited by Michael Levenson. Cambridge: Cambridge University Press, 1999, 33-69.

Remarque, Erich Maria. *Im Westen Nichts Neues*. Edited by Brian Murdoch. London: Methuen, 1984.

Ricks, Christopher. *T.S. Eliot and Prejudice*. London: Faber, 1988.

Ridler, Anne. "Introduction to *The Image of the City and Other Essays*." Oxford: Oxford University Press, 1958, i-lxxii.

Roberts, Adam. *Silk and Potatoes: Postwar Arthurian Fantasy*. Amsterdam: Rodopi, 1997.

ROSEBURY, Brian. *Tolkien: A Critical Assessment.* Basingstoke: Palgrave, 1992.

Tolkien: A Cultural Phenomenon. Basingstoke: Palgrave, 2003.

RUSHDIE, Salman. *Midnight's Children.* London: Pan, 1981.

RUSSELL, Bertrand. *Introduction to Mathematical Philosophy.* New York: Simon and Schuster, n.d.

SAID, Edward. "Yeats and Decolonization." In *Nationalism, Colonialism, and Literature.* Edited by Terry EAGLETON, Fredric JAMESON, and Edward W. SAID. Minneapolis: University of Minnesota Press, 1990, 69-95.

"Thoughts on Late Style." *LRB* 26.15 (2004), 3-7.

SALE, Roger. "England's Parnassus: C.S. Lewis, Charles Williams and J.R.R. Tolkien." *Hudson Review* 17 (Summer 1964), 203-225.

Modern Heroism: Essays on D.H. Lawrence, William Empson, and J.R.R. Tolkien. Berkeley: University of California Press, 1973.

SANDERS, Andrew. *Short History of English Literature.* Oxford: Oxford University Press, 2004.

SAYER, George. *Jack: C.S. Lewis and his Times.* London: Macmillan, 1988.

SCHAKEL, Peter J. and Charles A. HUTTAR (eds.). *Word and Story in C.S. Lewis.* Columbia: University of Missouri Press, 1991.

SCHLEGEL, August. *Kritische Schriften und Briefe.* Volume I. Edited by Edgar LOHNER. Stuttgart: Kohlhammer, 1962.

SCHNEIDER, Angelika. *A Mesh of Chords. Sprache und Stil in der Artusdichtung Charles Williams'.* Ph.D. Diss. Universität Köln, 1984.

SENIOR, W.A. "Loss Eternal in Tolkien's Middle-earth." In *J.R.R. Tolkien and His Literary Responses.* Edited by George CLARK and Daniel TIMMONS. Westport: Greenwood Press, 2000, 173-182.

SEYMOUR-JONES, Carole. *Painted Shadow: A Life of Vivienne Eliot.* London: Robinson, 2001.

SHAKESPEARE, William. *Othello.* Edited by E.A.J. HONIGMANN. London: Arden, 1997.

SHELLEY, Percy Bysshe. *Critical Prose.* Edited by Bruce M. MCELDERRY, Jr. Lincoln: University of Nebraska Press, 1967.

SHEPPARD, Richard. "The Crisis of Language." In *Modernism. A Guide to European Literature and Culture 1890-1930.* Edited by Michael BRADBURY and James McFARLANE. London: Penguin, 1991, 323-336.

SHIPPEY, Tom A. *The Road to Middle-earth.* London: HarperCollins, 1992.

"Tolkien as a Post-War Writer." In *Scholarship and Fantasy: The Tolkien Phenomenon*. Edited by Keith J. BATTARBEE. Finland: University of Turku Press, 1993, 217-236.

J.R.R. Tolkien: Author of the Century. London: HarperCollins, 2000.

SHOWALTER, Elaine. *Sexual Anarchy: Gender and Culture at the Fin de Siecle*. London: Bloomsbury, 1991.

SIMONSON, Martin. *The Lord of the Rings and Western Narrative Tradition*. Zurich and Jena: Walking Tree Publishers, 2008.

SMITH, Andrew and Jeff WALLACE. "Introduction: Gothic Modernisms: History, Culture and Aesthetics." In *Gothic Modernisms*. Edited by Andrew SMITH and Jeff WALLACE. Basingstoke: Palgrave, 2001, 1-10.

(eds.). *Gothic Modernisms*. Basingstoke: Palgrave, 2001.

SMITH, Ross. *Inside Language. Linguistic and Aesthetic Theory in Tolkien*. Zurich and Jena: Walking Tree Publishers, 2007.

STEIN, Gertrude. "Tender Buttons." In *The Norton Anthology of American Literature* II. Edited by Nina BAYM. New York: Norton, 1998, 1105-1115.

SURETTE, Leon. *The Birth of Modernism: Ezra Pound, T.S. Eliot, W.B. Yeats and the Occult*. Montreal: McGill & Queen's University Press, 1993.

TODOROV, Tzvetan. *The Fantastic*. Translated by Richard HOWARD. New York: Cornell University Press, 1975.

TOLKIEN, J.R.R. *Notes on Finnegans Wake* (unpublished manuscript). Bodleian Library, MS Tolkien 24, fols. 44-45.

The Adventures of Tom Bombadil. London: George Allen & Unwin, 1962.

The Silmarillion. London: George Allen & Unwin, 1979.

The Letters of J.R.R. Tolkien. Edited by Humphrey CARPENTER. London: George Allen & Unwin, 1981.

Farmer Giles of Ham. London: George Allen & Unwin, 1983.

Smith of Wootton Major and Leaf by Niggle. London: George Allen & Unwin, 1983.

The Lost Road and Other Writings. (The History of Middle-earth volume V.) London: HarperCollins, 1987.

"On Fairy-Stories." In *The Monsters and the Critics and Other Essays*. London: HarperCollins, 1990, 109-161.

Sauron Defeated. (The History of Middle-earth volume IX.) London: HarperCollins, 1992.

The Hobbit. London: HarperCollins, 1996.

The Lord of the Rings. London: HarperCollins, 1997.

TURNER, Jenny. "Reasons for Liking Tolkien." *London Review of Books* 23.22 (2001), 15-24.

WALES, Katie. *The Language of James Joyce*. Basingstoke: Macmillan, 1992.

WALSH, Chad. *The Literary Legacy of C.S. Lewis*. New York: Harcourt Brace, 1979.

WATSON, G.J. *Irish Identity and the Literary Revival: Synge, Yeats, Joyce and O'Casey*. Washington, D.C.: Catholic University of America Press, 1994.

WEINREICH, Frank. *Fantasy. Einführung*. Essen: Oldib, 2007.

WHITAKER, Thomas. *Swan and Shadow: Yeats's Dialogue with History*. Chapel Hill: University of North Carolina Press, 1964.

WHITTINGHAM, Elizabeth. *The Evolution of Tolkien's Mythology: A Study of the History of Middle-earth*. Jefferson, North Carolina: McFarland, 2008.

WILLIAMS, Charles. *Divorce*. London: Oxford University Press, 1920.

War in Heaven. London: Gollancz, 1930.

The Greater Trumps. London: Gollancz, 1932.

Taliessin through Logres. Oxford: Oxford University Press, 1938.

The Descent of the Dove. London: Longmans, 1939.

All Hallow's Eve. London: Faber, 1945.

Arthurian Torso. Oxford: Oxford University Press, 1948.

The Region of the Summer Stars. Oxford: Oxford University Press, 1950.

The Image of the City and Other Essays. Oxford: Oxford University Press, 1958.

Collected Plays. London: Oxford University Press, 1963.

Descent into Hell. Grand Rapids, Michigan: Eerdmans, 1999.

WILLIAMS, Gwyn. *The Burning Tree*. London: Faber, 1956.

WILLIAMS, Louise Blakeney: see BLAKENEY WILLIAMS

WOLFE, Gregory. "Essential Speech." In *Word and Story in C.S. Lewis*. Edited by Peter J. SCHAKEL and Charles A. HUTTAR. Columbia: University of Missouri Press, 1991, 58-75.

WOOLF, Virginia. *Mrs Dalloway*. Oxford: Oxford University Press, 2000.

YEATS, W.B. *Essays and Introductions*. Basingstoke: Palgrave Macmillan, 1961.

Selected Plays. Edited by A. Norman JEFFARES. Basingstoke: Macmillan, 1964.

Uncollected Prose. Volume II. Edited by John P. FRAYNE and Colton JOHNSON. London: Macmillan, 1975.

A Vision. Basingstoke: Macmillan, 1981.

Yeats's Poems. Edited by A. Norman JEFFARES. Basingstoke: Macmillan, 1989.

YEE, Cordell D. K. *The Word According to James Joyce*. Lewisburg: Bucknell University Press, 1997.

Index

A
A Question of Time 40-41
A Vision 111-113
Adorno, Theodor 100-101, 142-145, 147-148, 150-151, 181
Adventures of Tom Bombadil, The 106, 136-137, 146, 148
aestheticist movement 24, 158
All Hallows' Eve 12, 50, 82
Armitt, Lucie 32, 213
Arthurian myth, a myth of failure 53-54
Arthurian poetry/poems 24-25, 27, 29-30, 52-59, 64-65, 72-76, 79-82
Arthurian Torso 50, 52, 54, 66, 79
artist, as historian 98
Ascent of F6 44
Ästhetische Theorie 181
Auden, W.H. 11, 13-14, 18-19, 21-22, 44, 51-52, 103-104, 162, 191
Author of the Century 225

B
Barfield, Owen 182-184, 186, 200
Barthes, Roland 108-109, 161, 182-184, 187-188
Beckett, Samuel 62
Beethoven, Ludwig van 143
Beethoven. The Philosophy of Music (Late Style I, II) 143-145, 147, 150-151
Bell, Michael 110
Benjamin, Walter 99
Beowulf 19, 127
Bergonzi, Bernard 9, 57, 84, 97, 100
Bergson, Henri-Louis 159
Berman, Art 100
Bhaghavadgita 181
Blumenberg, Hans 109, 111-112
Blunden, Edmund 33
Brisingr 155
Byzantium poems 139, 141, 147

C

C.S. Lewis in Context 3
Cantos of Ezra Pound, The 22, 26, 83, 97, 110, 112, 117, 147, 161
Carlyle, Thomas 112-113
Carroll, Lewis 20, 174, 204-205
Cavafy, Constantine P. 143
Chapell, William 71
Chaucer, Geoffrey 18
Chesterton, G.K. 40
Chronicles of Narnia 25, 27-29, 43-44, 135, 174-177, 189-192, 200-202
Cocktail Party, The 13
Coleridge, Samuel Taylor 18
Collected Poems (T.S. Eliot) 25, 30, 68, 90, 101, 134, 137-138, 142, 160, 177, 200, 207
Complete Poems (MacDiarmid) 63-64
Croft, Janet Brennan 44-45, 50

D

Dante 3, 9, 17, 24, 52, 69
Darwin, Charles 21
de Man, Paul 97-98
Death of Cuchulain, The 122-123, 149
decadent movement, see aestheticist movement
DeCoste, D.M. 101, 113
Descent Into Hell 13, 30
Descent of the Dove, The 13-14
Dickens, Charles 20
Die Geburt der Tragödie aus dem Geiste der Musik 107-108
Divorce 49
Don Rodriguez: Chronicles of Shadow Valley 41-42
Dryden, John 18
Dubliners 163-164,
Dumas, Alexandre 112-113
Dying Gaul, The 61

E

Earthsea 154-155
Eddings, David 21
Eddison, E.R. 14, 41
Eldest 155-156
Eliador 75

Index   249

Eliot, T.S. 3, 9, 11-16, 22-24, 26-27, 30, 33-35, 51, 53, 55, 66, 68-69, 71, 90, 97-98, 101, 109-110, 117, 128, 134, 137-138, 161-162, 172, 179, 200, 208, 211, 221, 223
Ellmann, Maud 34, 162, 166-170, 197-198
Ellmann, Richard 123, 198
Emig, Rainer 32, 36-39, 56-57, 61, 71, 83, 93-94, 110, 141-142, 144, 147-148, 180, 189
Epoch and Artist 51, 53-54, 62
Eragon 155
Esty, Jed 128-129
Ezekiel (Bible) 78

F
fantasy
    and gothic 223-224
    and modernism 1, 4
    war a central topic 42-43
Farmer Giles of Ham 148
Faulkner, William 22
Fimi, Dimitra 126, 129
Finnegans Wake 18, 82, 163-164, 168-170, 178-179, 181-182, 189, 195-198, 204-206, 218
Flaubert, Gustave 164
Flieger, Verlyn 40-41, 191
Flint, F.S. 9
Ford, Ford Madox 84
Forster, E.M. 125, 128
Four Quartets 25, 35, 90, 134, 138, 223
Frazer, James George 21
Fusell, Paul 39, 45, 57, 70-71, 76, 83-84

G
Garner, Alan 75
Garth, John 48
Gaudier-Brzeska, Henri 34
Gibbon, Edward 52
Gododdin 58, 63, 89
Goetsch, Paul 40
Gothic Modernisms 223
Great Divorce, The 50
Great War and Modern Memory, The 39, 45
Greater Trumps, The 30

Grecan myths 111, 113-114
Greeves, Arthur 15-16, 47, 211

H
Haggard, Rider 20
Hardy, Thomas 144
Hegel, G.W.F 100
history, central position in modernism 98, 107
Hobbit, The 85, 103-104, 129, 145-146
Hofmannsthal, Hugo von 161, 199
Hopkins, Gerard Manley 12
Hugh Selwyn Mauberley 8, 29, 33, 35, 62, 71, 100, 106
Hume, Kathryn 25-26

I
Iliad 173, 188
Im Westen nichts Neues 77
imaginary world, see secondary world
Imagism 26
    imagist movement 27
    imagist poetry 9
In Parenthesis 29, 37, 40, 51-52, 55-60, 63, 66-67, 69-78, 82, 88-90, 93-95, 223
Inklings 2-4, 12, 20, 30, 41, 85
    and war 41, 44-45
Inklings, The 2, 49-50
intertextuality 23-24, 32
Introduction to Mathematical Philosophy 159-160
Irving, Washington 135

J
Jackson, Rosemary 214
James Joyce: New Perspectives 169-170
James, Henry 14, 33, 208
Jandl, Ernst 36
John Hopkins Guide to Literary Theory and Criticism 3
Johnson, Samuel 18
Jones, David 1-2, 5, 29, 37, 40, 48, 51-67, 69-78, 82, 85, 88-90, 93-95, 126, 172, 178, 221, 224-225
Joyce, James 1-2, 5, 9, 11, 18, 22, 27, 30, 51, 62, 68-69, 82-83, 86, 88, 97, 109-110, 133, 162-170, 172-173, 177-182, 194-198, 202, 204-206, 208-209, 212, 215-219, 221, 224-225

K

Kavanagh, Patrick 62, 128
Kazin, Alfred 33
Kilby, Clyde 2
King of Elfland's Daughter, The 138
Kipling, Rudyard 20
Klee, Paul 100
Krieg als Metapher im 20. Jahrhundert 36-39, 56-57, 61, 71, 93-94

L

Lampedusa, Giuseppe Tomasi di 143
language 9-10, 24-26, 88-91
    and reality 171-172, 186
    issue at the heart of modernist ad fantastic writing 153
    limits of 157-158
    tool of creation 153-156, 196
Language of James Joyce, The 168
Language of the Night, The 157, 213
late style 142-145, 147-148, 150-151
Lawrence, D.H. 11, 14, 68
Le Guin, Ursula 154-155, 157, 213
Le Morte Darthur, (Le) Morte d'Arthur 62, 70, 74, 169
Lear, Edward 20
Letters of C.S. Lewis 2
Lévi-Strauss, Claude 108
Leviticus (Bible) 84
Lewis in Context 2
Lewis Papers, The 210, 215
Lewis, C.S. 1, 3-5, 12, 14-18, 20-21, 24-31, 39, 43-50, 60, 65-66, 79, 82, 85, 134-135, 154, 162-163, 170-177, 182-194, 196, 200-203, 207-217, 219, 221, 223-226
    and war 29
Lewis, Warren 210
Lewis, Wyndham 97, 99, 162
Lindsay, David 21
Literary Essays of Ezra Pound, The 11, 164
Logres 27, 52-53, 55-57, 61, 63, 65-66, 72-74, 76, 79-81, 86, 88-92, 178, 209, 212, 222
Lord Dunsany (Edward John Morton Drax Plunkett) 21, 41-42, 138
Lord of the Rings and Western Narrative Tradition, The 3
Lord of the Rings, The 1, 21, 23, 26, 29-30, 43-44, 47, 50, 61, 67-68, 70, 85, 103-107, 114-117, 125, 129-132, 134-135, 140-141, 145-150, 153-154, 157-158, 162, 192, 200, 207-208, 212-213, 223
loss 31-32

M

Mabinogion 52, 58-59, 178
MacDiarmid, Hugh 63-64
MacDonald, George 15, 20
magic realism 221-222
Malory, Thomas 52, 54, 62, 70, 169
Michalson, Karen 20
Middle-earth 23-25, 28, 31, 43, 48, 56, 71, 85, 115-117, 149, 222
    its linguistic realism 153-154
Midnight's Children 222
Milton, John 52, 190
Modern Heroism: Essays on D.H. Lawrence, William Empson, and J.R.R. Tolkien 68
modernism 2
    and language 158-159
    and the fantastic 32
    and war 7-8, 36-38, 56-57
    classical/high modernism 7-8
    international movement 11
    power and authority 23
Modernism in Poetry 9, 22-23, 32, 83, 110, 112, 141-142, 144, 147-148, 159
Moorman, Charles W. 62, 64
Mordor 68
More, Paul Elmer 16
Morris, William 3, 20
Mrs Dalloway 8, 33, 160
Murder in the Cathedral 13
myth 27-28
    and meaning 109-110
    and war 55
    central to modernism and fantasy (with history) 107
Myth of Modernism, The 9, 97

N

Narrative Poems 207
Nesbit, Edith 20
Nicholls, Peter 162, 199, 208
Nietzsche, Friedrich 21, 98-99, 101, 107-110, 114, 140
North, Michael 118

O

O'Brien, Flann 5, 209
O'Neill, Eugene 27
Odyssey 173, 179, 188, 200

On Fairy Stories 18, 25, 42, 48, 107, 133-135, 150, 153, 156, 165-166, 175, 184
Once and Future King, The 66, 85
Orwell, George 41, 186
Othello 205
Ovid 100
Owen, Wilfred 33, 83
Oxford Book of Modern Verse 12
Oxford Companion to English Literature, The 3

P

Paolini, Christopher 155-156
Parade's End 84
Paradise Lost 190
Peake, Mervyn 5
Perelandra (space trilogy) 25, 43-44, 60, 163, 170-174, 185-188, 192-194, 200, 202-203, 207, 209, 211-214
Piette, Adam 71, 75
Pilgrim's Regress, The 16
Poems (C.S. Lewis) 14, 172, 203
Poems (W. Owen) 83
Poetic Diction 182-183
Portrait of the Artist as a Young Man, A 30, 88, 163, 165-168, 194-195, 197-198, 215
Pound, Ezra 3, 7, 9-11, 14, 17, 22, 26, 28-29, 33, 35, 62, 71, 83, 97-98, 100, 106, 110-112, 117, 159, 161-162, 164, 208
Preface to Paradise Lost (C.S. Lewis) 15, 17

Q

quest 26

R

Region of the Summer Stars, The 50, 59, 72-76, 80-82, 87-89, 203-204
Rehabilitations 184
Remarque, Erich Maria 77, 82
Renaissance 24
Ricks, Christopher 211
Rip van Winkle 135
Road to Middle-earth, The 125-127
Rosebury, Brian 3, 49
Rushdie, Salman 222
Russell, Bertrand 159-160

S

Sacred Emily 8
Said, Edward 143-145
Sale, Roger 68
Sassoon, Siegfried 33
Sauron Defeated 23
secondary world 22-23, 28
    as linguistic construction 25
Secondary Worlds 19, 23, 162
Selected Poems (Pound) 8, 10, 35, 98, 100
Selected Prose (Eliot) 9
Shakespaere, William 205
Shelley, Mary 20
Shippey, Tom 3, 24, 41, 125-127, 225
Silmarillion, The 26, 29, 43, 85, 104-106, 114, 154, 175, 190, 212
Simonson, Martin 3
Smith of Wootton Major 212
Spirits in Bondage 46
Stead, William Force 15-16
Stein, Gertrude 11, 17, 34, 158, 208
Sterne, Laurence 195
sub-creation 22-23
supernatural 153
Surprised by Joy 210, 215

T

Taliessin through Logres 12, 27, 52-56, 59, 65, 72-76, 79-81, 86-92, 117, 157
Taliessin/Taliesin 12, 30, 53, 58-61, 65-66, 72-73, 79-81, 86-92, 224
Tender Buttons 158
Tess of the d'Urbervilles 144
Theorising the Fantastic 213
They Stand Together 15-16, 211, 215
Thomas Cranmer of Canterbury 13
Through the Looking-glass 204-205
Till We Have Faces 28, 163, 188-189, 207-208, 212, 215-216
Time Machine, The 134
Todorov, Tzvetan 40, 67, 153, 156, 166, 222
Tolkien, J.R.R. 1, 3-5, 12, 17-31, 39, 40-42, 47-48, 50, 56, 61, 67-68, 70-71, 79-80, 85, 103-107, 114-118, 125-138, 140-142, 144-153, 156-158, 162, 165-166, 169-170, 172, 174, 178, 184, 190, 192, 200, 207-208, 212-213, 221-223, 225-226
    and war 29-30
Tolkien and the Great War 48
Tolkien: A Critical Assessment 49

Tolkien: A Cultural Phenomenon 3
Tolkien: Author of the Century 3, 41, 225
Tristram Shandy 195

U

Ulysses 9, 26, 30, 69, 83, 97, 109-110, 133, 163, 168-169, 179-182, 189, 195, 198, 202, 212, 217-219
Ulysses: New Casebooks 180, 189
Uncollected Prose (W.B. Yeats) 120

V

Victorian (era) 20
Victorian Fantasy 20-21
Victorian Fantasy Literature 20
Vom Nutzen und Nachteil der Historie für das Leben 110, 114
Vonnegut, Kurt 41
Vorticism 26, 159

W

Wales, Katie 168
War and the Works of J.R.R. Tolkien 44
War in Heaven 30
war, as topic 33, 35-36
Waste Land, The 16, 23, 26, 33, 51, 53, 68-69, 71, 101, 117, 147
Watson, G.J. 168
Waves, The 26
Weight of Glory and Other Addresses, The 214
Wells, H.G. 24, 134
White, T.H. 41, 66, 85
Whitman, Walt 112-113
Williams, and war 29-30
Williams, Charles 1, 3-5, 12-13, 17, 20-21, 24-31, 39, 49-67, 72-76, 79-81, 86-92, 94-95, 117, 157, 174, 178, 203-204, 221-224, 226
Woolf, Virginia 3, 8-9, 11, 22, 33, 128, 144, 160
Wordsworth, William 52
world of letters 19-20
World War I 8, 29-30, 33-34, 40, 44-49, 51, 55, 58, 90
World War II 35, 43-44, 49-50
Worm Ouroboros, The 14, 41

Y

Yeats, W.B. 1-2, 5, 11-12, 15-16, 27, 31, 62, 98-99, 101-103, 106-107, 110-112, 117-124, 128, 132, 134-136, 144-145, 147-152, 163, 178, 208, 221, 224-225

Yeats's Poems 102, 107, 111, 113-114, 119-121, 123-124, 134-140, 145, 148-149, 151, 161

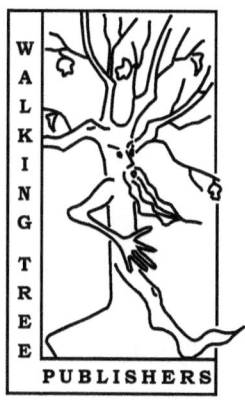

Walking Tree Publishers

Walking Tree Publishers was founded in 1997 as a forum for publication of material (books, videos, CDs, etc.) related to Tolkien and Middle-earth studies. Manuscripts and project proposals can be submitted to the board of editors (please include an SAE):

Walking Tree Publishers
CH-3052 Zollikofen
Switzerland
e-mail: info@walking-tree.org
http://www.walking-tree.org

Cormarë Series

The *Cormarë Series* has been the first series of studies dedicated exclusively to the exploration of Tolkien's work. Its focus is on papers and studies from a wide range of scholarly approaches. The series comprises monographs, thematic collections of essays, conference volumes, and reprints of important yet no longer (easily) accessible papers by leading scholars in the field. Manuscripts and project proposals are evaluated by members of an independent board of advisors who support the series editors in their endeavour to provide the readers with qualitatively superior yet accessible studies on Tolkien and his work.

News from the Shire and Beyond. Studies on Tolkien
Peter Buchs and Thomas Honegger (eds.), Zurich and Berne 2004, Reprint, First edition 1997 (Cormarë Series 1), ISBN 978-3-9521424-5-5

Root and Branch. Approaches Towards Understanding Tolkien
Thomas Honegger (ed.), Zurich and Berne 2005, Reprint, First edition 1999 (Cormarë Series 2), ISBN 978-3-905703-01-6

Richard Sturch, *Four Christian Fantasists. A Study of the Fantastic Writings of George MacDonald, Charles Williams, C.S. Lewis and J.R.R. Tolkien*
Zurich and Berne 2007, Reprint, First edition 2001 (Cormarë Series 3), ISBN 978-3-905703-04-7

Tolkien in Translation
Thomas Honegger (ed.), Zurich and Jena 2011, Reprint, First edition 2003 (Cormarë Series 4), ISBN 978-3-905703-15-3

Mark T. Hooker, *Tolkien Through Russian Eyes*
Zurich and Berne 2003 (Cormarë Series 5), ISBN 978-3-9521424-7-9

Translating Tolkien: Text and Film
Thomas Honegger (ed.), Zurich and Jena 2011, Reprint, First edition 2004 (Cormarë Series 6), ISBN 978-3-905703-16-0

Christopher Garbowski, *Recovery and Transcendence for the Contemporary Mythmaker. The Spiritual Dimension in the Works of J.R.R. Tolkien*
Zurich and Berne 2004, Reprint, First Edition by Marie Curie Sklodowska, University Press, Lublin 2000, (Cormarë Series 7), ISBN 978-3-9521424-8-6

Reconsidering Tolkien
Thomas Honegger (ed.), Zurich and Berne 2005 (Cormarë Series 8),
ISBN 978-3-905703-00-9

Tolkien and Modernity 1
Frank Weinreich and Thomas Honegger (eds.), Zurich and Berne 2006 (Cormarë Series 9), ISBN 978-3-905703-02-3

Tolkien and Modernity 2
Thomas Honegger and Frank Weinreich (eds.), Zurich and Berne 2006 (Cormarë Series 10), ISBN 978-3-905703-03-0

Tom Shippey, *Roots and Branches. Selected Papers on Tolkien by Tom Shippey*
Zurich and Berne 2007 (Cormarë Series 11), ISBN 978-3-905703-05-4

Ross Smith, *Inside Language. Linguistic and Aesthetic Theory in Tolkien*
Zurich and Berne 2007 (Cormarë Series 12), ISBN 978-3-905703-06-1

How We Became Middle-earth. A Collection of Essays on The Lord of the Rings
Adam Lam and Nataliya Oryshchuk (eds.), Zurich and Berne 2007 (Cormarë Series 13), ISBN 978-3-905703-07-8

Myth and Magic. Art According to the Inklings
Eduardo Segura and Thomas Honegger (eds.), Zurich and Berne 2007 (Cormarë Series 14), ISBN 978-3-905703-08-5

The Silmarillion - Thirty Years On
Allan Turner (ed.), Zurich and Berne 2007 (Cormarë Series 15),
ISBN 978-3-905703-10-8

Martin Simonson, *The Lord of the Rings and the Western Narrative Tradition*
Zurich and Jena 2008 (Cormarë Series 16), ISBN 978-3-905703-09-2

Tolkien's Shorter Works. Proceedings of the 4th Seminar of the Deutsche Tolkien Gesellschaft & Walking Tree Publishers Decennial Conference
Margaret Hiley and Frank Weinreich (eds.), Zurich and Jena 2008 (Cormarë Series 17), ISBN 978-3-905703-11-5

Tolkien's The Lord of the Rings: Sources of Inspiration
Stratford Caldecott and Thomas Honegger (eds.), Zurich and Jena 2008 (Cormarë Series 18), ISBN 978-3-905703-12-2

J.S. Ryan, *Tolkien's View: Windows into his World*
Zurich and Jena 2009 (Cormarë Series 19), ISBN 978-3-905703-13-9

Music in Middle-earth
Heidi Steimel and Friedhelm Schneidewind (eds.), Zurich and Jena 2010 (Cormarë Series 20), ISBN 978-3-905703-14-6

Liam Campbell, *The Ecological Augury in the Works of JRR Tolkien*
Zurich and Jena 2011 (Cormarë Series 21), ISBN 978-3-905703-18-4

Margaret Hiley, *The Loss and the Silence. Aspects of Modernism in the Works of C.S. Lewis, J.R.R. Tolkien and Charles Williams*
Zurich and Jena 2011 (Cormarë Series 22), ISBN 978-3-905703-19-1

J.S. Ryan, *In the Nameless Wood* (working title)
Zurich and Jena, forthcoming

Rainer Nagel, *Hobbit Place-names. A Linguistic Excursion through the Shire*
Zurich and Jena, forthcoming

The Broken Scythe. Death and Immortality in the Works of J.R.R. Tolkien
Roberto Arduini and Claudio Antonio Testi (eds.), Zurich and Jena, forthcoming

Christopher MacLachlan, *Tolkien and Wagner: The Ring and Der Ring*
Zurich and Jena, forthcoming

Renée Vink, *Wagner and Tolkien*
Zurich and Jena, forthcoming

Constructions of Authorship in and around the Works of J.R.R. Tolkien
Judith Klinger (ed.), Zurich and Jena, forthcoming

Tolkien's Poetry
Julian Morton Eilmann and Allan Turner (eds.), Zurich and Jena, forthcoming

Beowulf and the Dragon

The original Old English text of the 'Dragon Episode' of *Beowulf* is set in an authentic font and printed and bound in hardback creating a high quality art book. The text is illustrated by Anke Eissmann and accompanied by John Porter's translation. The introduction is by Tom Shippey. Limited first edition of 500 copies. 84 pages. Selected pages can be previewed on: www.walking-tree.org/beowulf
Beowulf and the Dragon
Zurich and Jena 2009, ISBN 978-3-905703-17-7

Tales of Yore Series

The *Tales of Yore Series* grew out of the desire to share Kay Woollard's whimsical stories and drawings with a wider audience. The series aims at providing a platform for qualitatively superior fiction with a clear link to Tolkien's world.

Kay Woollard, *The Terror of Tatty Walk. A Frightener*
CD and Booklet, Zurich and Berne 2000, ISBN 978-3-9521424-2-4

Kay Woollard, *Wilmot's Very Strange Stone or What came of building "snobbits"*
CD and booklet, Zurich and Berne 2001, ISBN 978-3-9521424-4-8

www.ingramcontent.com/pod-product-compliance
Lightning Source LLC
Chambersburg PA
CBHW070728160426
43192CB00009B/1352